GOOD CAME OUT OF NAZARETH

HERBERT C. GABHART

ISBN:0-9645163-5-7

TABLE OF CONTENTS

As man alone, Jesus could not have saved us; as God alone, he would not; Incarnate, he could and did.

—Malcolm Muggeridge

DEDICATION

This book is dedicated to those Spirit-led, open minded persons who want to continue to search the Bible for truth, who know the Bible is not owned by any particular group, who acknowledge that God is no respecter of persons, who have the courage to love in the midst of hate and tension, and to all who want to honor that name which is above every name, Jesus Christ, the Nazarene, who came out of Nazareth, to redeem and restore mankind's broken relationship with God.

And so this God-man Jesus belongs to the whole world. He is the one who came out of Nazareth. He is still calling people from the mills, the farms, the office towers, the institutions of higher learning, the merchants in the malls and those in the halls of science. They come from the ranks of mediocrity, the plush suites of the Fifth Avenues of our metropolitan cities and the gutters of sin. He calls them with a tap of his hand on their shoulder. He changes them and makes them messenger-servants in his global Kingdom of God.

The author's wish and prayer is that the book will not be just about Jesus but that through the ministry of the Holy Spirit the reader will experience Jesus.

The personal opinions expressed in this book are those of the author unless otherwise noted.

All Scripture references and quotations are from the King James translation.

Very special gratitude and appreciation are warmly and generously extended to my wife, Norma, and to my part-time associate, Patricia Long.

CHRISTIAN PERFECTION

The holiest of men still need Christ as their Prophet, as "the light of the world." For he does not give them light but from moment to moment; the instant He withdraws, all is darkness. They still need Christ as their King, for God does not give them a stock of holiness. But unless they receive a supply every moment, nothing but unholiness would remain. They still need Christ as their Priest, to make atonement for their holy things. Even perfect holiness is acceptable to God only through Jesus Christ.

—**John Wesley**

PROLOGUE

Significant events during the earliest days of Jesus' ministry began to pop up and explode like pop corn, fast and frequent. The day after the deputation from Jerusalem, comprised of Scribes and Levites and sent by the Jews, started the chain of events. The group came asking John the Baptist who he was: "Elijah, a prophet, just tell us." John's response was, "I am just a voice crying in the wilderness." Then they pressed their case, "Why are you baptizing your followers?" He responded by saying that his water baptism would give way to one whose sandals he would not be worthy to untie.

The following day he saw Jesus coming and introduced him as "the Lamb of God who takes away the sin of the world." The next day John stood with two of his disciples and when seeing Jesus he again remarked, "Behold the Lamb of God." Jesus seeing them asked, "What seek ye?" Their response to his question, "Where are you staying?" He said, "Come and see." One who heard him speak was Andrew from Bethsaida, whose brother was Peter. Andrew excitedly invited Peter saying, "We have found the Messiah" Jesus looked at Peter and said to him, "You shall be called Cephas, a stone."

The next day Jesus desiring to go to Galilee found Philip from the same city as Andrew and Peter and extended the invitation to Philip to follow him. Without delay, with excitement increasing, Philip sought out Nathanael and said, "We have found him whom Moses in the law and the prophets wrote: 'Jesus of Nazareth, the son of Joseph.' In these quick moving episodes Jesus is called "the Lamb of God," "the Messiah," and "Jesus of Nazareth, the son of Joseph."

The last title given to Jesus as being from Nazareth as Joseph's son triggered a quick response from Nathanael of Bethsaida. Probably without giving much thought to his response, he blurted out what came to his mind, "Can any good thing come out of Nazareth?" "Out of Nazareth, you must be kidding. That place. You really must be kidding. Get serious. That town, there is nothing in it of any worth. All is no good."

One cannot keep from wondering what had given Nazareth such a reputation. Was there bad blood between the people of Bethsaida and Nazareth? Wasn't there a good carpenter shop in the city? Environment may have been bad, but heredity plays a vital part in society. Then, too, the potential and worth of individuals should nix the word "any" which covers all things, animate and inanimate. The slur covered the hillside village.

As George Herbert wrote: "And here in dust and dirt, Oh, here the lilies of his love appears." Lilies, lovely white ones, grow in slimy ponds. Oysters inhabit undesirable waters but are among many persons' delectable diet and even if irritated can produce lovely pearls. Some say that forest fires are beneficial in purging forests for better growths.

The writer has been to Nazareth and even until this day there seem to have been no city planners at work to improve its beauty but it seems happy nestled between two ridges. Tourists do not go there for its beauty but to walk where Jesus walked. The author is thus poised to refute Nathanael's statement about the home town of Jesus for the thesis of this book is GOOD CAME OUT OF NAZARETH.

> Had there been a lunatic asylum in the suburbs of Jerusalem, Jesus Christ would infallibly have been shut up in it at the outset of his public career. That interview with Satan on a pinnacle of the Temple would alone have damned him, and everything that happened after could but have confirmed the diagnosis.
>
> —Havelock Ellis

I couldn't help writing on Jesus. Since I first met him he has held my mind and heart. I grew up, you know, on the border of Poland and Russia, which was not exactly the finest place in the world for a Jew to sit down and write a life of Jesus Christ. Yet even through these years the hope of doing just that fascinated me. For Jesus Christ is to me the outstanding personality of all time, all history, both as Son of God and as Son of Man. Everything he ever said or did has value for us today and that is something you can say of no other man, dead or alive. There is no easy middle ground to stroll upon. You either accept Jesus or reject him. You can analyze Mohammed and . . . Buddha, but don't try it with him. You either accept or you reject. . . .

—**Sholem Asch**
Yiddis Author
1880-1957

CHAPTER I

SOURCE MATERIAL USED

THE AVAILABLE SOURCE MATERIAL—
TOO LITTLE, TOO MUCH

In trying to support the major thesis of this book that "Good Came Out of Nazareth," one is immediately faced with the question: What material is there available to substantiate the claim? There is an instant consciousness that there is a paucity of material: four gospels, Matthew, Mark, Luke and John, which together contain only 92 brief chapters. They touched on only 30-35 days of his active public ministry which is one-thirtieth of his public ministry. The thirty to thirty-five days touch only on three-hundredths part of his earthly career. The rest is hidden. What is recorded of his sayings could be read or recited in less than five hours.

So meager is the report given by the gospel writers that one could easily become discouraged. However, there is more to add to this situation, even though nothing is given of his physical appearance. No material evidence of his life such as a cross, a broken alabaster box, or his garment has been preserved. There is truly a paucity of material. The gospel writers were not writing biographies of the life of Jesus. They focused much on his life and deeds of love, mercy and grace. But the picture is not one of gloom and doom for there are gleams and glimpses which tease one's imagination and there are distant rays of light which beckon one onward.

Instead of a paucity of material there is an abundance, a prolific amount available to one who is willing to dig and delve into "them thar hills" as the old gold-rusher exclaimed years ago.

Each of the gospel writers wrote from a different perspective. Matthew wrote to connect Jesus with Abraham and David to show Jesus as the Messiah who fulfilled the promises of the

Old Testament. His genealogy of Jesus is traced back by listing fourteen generations from Abraham to David, fourteen from David to the carrying away to Babylon and fourteen to the birth of Christ.

Mark wrote to show the affinity of Jesus with the Gentile world. He had the Roman readers in mind. He began his writing at the ministry of Jesus Christ.

Luke wrote to show that Jesus is the Saviour for all persons and that there is no limit to God's love, all for rich and poor alike. He begins with John the Baptist as the forerunner to Jesus and details the birth of the Christ-child whose mother was the Virgin Mary.

John described Jesus as the eternal word, the Son of God. He began his gospel by saying, "In the beginning was the word and the word was God."

There is much good in reading these books because of their different approach and emphasis upon the life and ministry of Christ. In this respect the paucity of material takes on an enlarged value.

One is left to wonder just what is the full meaning and impact of John's gospel when he wrote: "But these are written, that ye might believe that Jesus is the Christ, the Son of God; and that believing ye might have life through his name" (John 20:31). Additionally, "There are also many other things which Jesus did, the which, if they should be written every one, I suppose that even the world itself could not contain the books that should be written" (John 21:25). The meaning and inferences of these passages provide enough roaming room for the outreach of the mind and the imagination.

The writer is a believer in the veracity of the Bible as being the word of God. Even though there is no original manuscript that has been preserved, for us it is a "lamp unto our feet and a light unto our pathway." Since it is the word of God there is no need to add adjectives to describe it. The application of the teachings are more important than just a mere affirmation of it.

THE CANON OF THE BIBLE

In the first Christian century there was a body of sacred litera-ture called the "Scriptures." They were generally described and limited to three groups: The Law, the Prophets and the Writings, totaling 39 books which comprised the Old Testament.

The New Testament Canon formation was desperately needed to preserve and consolidate the books of widely diverse origin. Several suggestions were made by men such as Clement of Rome, Ignatius, Papias Tatian, Iranaeus, and Tertullian to pro-duce such a work. The real landmark came in a document known as the Muratorian Fragment found in Milan in 1740. It gave the names of those thought worthy to be included in the Canon but it was rejected. Earlier Origen in the third century shared his thoughts on the subject. Two other outstanding Christian leaders dealt with the canon formation. They were Eusebius of Carthage and Athanasius, bishop of Alexandria. Their list consisted of 27 books. Several councils considered what books should be included and it was at the Council of Carthage meeting in 397 A.D. that approved the list which gave final authenticity to the grouping. This virtually settled the question of the canon of the New Testament.

There were quite a few books which had been written but were excluded from both the Old and New Testament Canons. These were called the "apocryphal books." (See Appendix 1 in the back of the book.)

Both the contents of the books of the New Testament canon and the number of 27 have stood the textual criticism that fre-quently comes with Bible study. It has not been easy to deter-mine the date of the writing of each of the books of the New Testament but the most acceptable dating list is found in Appendix 2.

I concur with the words of William Cowper:

God moves in a mysterious way
His wonders to perform
He plants his footsteps in the sea
And rides upon the storm.

Some seem to think that the Bible was specially wrapped, and divinely delivered to King James in 1611 A.D. after being edited by the scholars appointed by him. The king's motive in having the work done was to endorse the divine right of the kings.

It is interesting to consider how we got our Bible in the first place. How, why and by whom was it written? The Bible, especially the New Testament, has this to say: "All scripture is given by inspiration of God, and is profitable for doctrine, for reproof, for correction, for instruction in righteousness: That the man of God may be perfect, thoroughly furnished unto all good works" (II Timothy 3:16, 17). Did Paul think of himself as he wrote those words as writing something to be included in the Bible? Peter wrote in II Peter 1:21 these words: "For the prophecy came not in old time by the will of man: but holy men of God spake as they were moved by the Holy Ghost." Did he think while writing his words that they would be part of the Bible? I think not.

Since the Bible was written under the inspiration of the Holy Spirit just how did that transpire? There are four theories as to the inspiration of the Scripture. First, there is the Plenary Verbal theory. In this view, every word used was chosen by the Holy Spirit and given to the writer, thus leaving no room for human error. Second, the Naturalistic theory holds that all persons are inspired since God dwells in all persons. Third, the Mechanical theory holds that the writer is simply a machine doing God's direction without choice or responsibility. Fourth, the Dynamical one is that the Holy Spirit directed the writers through their natural and spiritual faculties. You, the reader, must accept which you feel comfortable with.

One must bear in mind that other books were written dealing with similar events but were not included in the Bible canon. These are called the "apocryphal books" and there are both New Testament and Old Testament apocryphal books.

Dr. W. O. Carver, longtime missions professor at the Southern Baptist Theological Seminary in Louisville, Kentucky during the first half of the twentieth century, gave five reasons why he felt the writers wrote the New Testament as they did:

- The Literature of an Extending Gospel
- The Literature of a Growing Church
- The Literature of a Developing Theology
- The Literature of a Controverted Faith
- The Literature of a Persecuted People

The bottom line about why and how the Bible was written is that the leadership of the Holy Spirit inspired the persons who wrote. This precious word of God has filtered through many different writers, many different languages, many different versions and translations but its place and power in the Christian faith has not wilted and died. The search for truth is a worthy and gratifying pursuit.

The shared stories of the life of Christ as recorded in the Gospels by the apostles and writers have a cohort who gave a strong testimony regarding the good which came out of Nazareth. Flavius Josephus was born in 37 A.D. in the city of Jerusalem and witnessed the seize and fall of Jerusalem in 70 A.D. He was related to the house of the Maccabees. His well known writings entitled *Jewish Antiquities* comprised 20 books and another work *The History of the Jewish War* was comprised of seven books. Both groups of books were historical as well as controversial but they assist one in understanding the world of the first Christian century which world impacted the life of Jesus and his ministry as the Messiah.

The following quote is from chapter III of his *Antiquities of the Jews* (p. 635).

> Now there was about this time Jesus, a wise man, if it be lawful to call him a man; for he was a doer of wonderful works, a teacher of such men as receive the truth with pleasure. He drew over to him both many of the Jews and many of the Gentiles. He was [the] Christ. And when Pilate, at the suggestion of the principal men amongst us, had condemned him to the cross, those that loved him at the first did not forsake him; for he appeared to them alive again the third day; as the divine prophets had foretold these and ten thousand other wonderful things concerning him. And the tribe of Christians, so named from him, are not extinct at this day.

It is quite a surprise to the students of the Bible when they come to the realization that there is not a single original manuscript of any of our New Testament books. All we have are copies of these first manuscripts. With that knowledge in mind the question of the authenticity of these books raises some doubt. That doubt is diminished with an awareness that God's Spirit was not asleep and there are a great many old manuscripts. Someone has estimated that there are close to 2,500 of these. The three oldest and most reliable are described briefly. They are called codices.

The Codex Sinaticus, so named because it was found in the monastery of St. Catherine on Mt. Sinai, is the only extant manuscript which contains the entire New Testament. It was found by a German scholar, Constantine Tischendorf, while visiting the monastery in 1844. It was found in a trash basket, waiting to be destroyed. It contained forty-four leaves dating back to the first half of the fourth century A.D. After a fifteen year search for the remainder of the leaves he was successful, coming up with a priceless 347 page manuscript. It now resides in the British Museum.

The Codex Vaticanus resides in the Vatican Library. It does not contain the entire New Testament but is the oldest and best of the Greek manuscripts. It is dated around 350 A.D. It contains part of the Old Testament and was placed in the library in 1481.

The Codex Alexandrinus is also in the British Museum. Its date is around 425 A.D. and includes most of the Old and New Testaments.

These countless other discoveries through the centuries add great support to the veracity of our Bible.

Jerome's Latin Vulgate was begun in 383 A.D. and completed in 404 A.D. It became the basis of the English Bible and the first English translation from the Latin Vulgate was made by John Wycliffe in 1383 A.D. Jerome was one of the earliest of the church fathers and contributed to the development of our Bible into different languages.

The earliest of the manuscripts did not have any chapter or verse divisions. The chapter divisions were made by Stephen Langton, an English archbishop of Canterbury in 1229 A.D. This division was first made in The Latin Vulgate but finally found its way into the Greek New Testament. The modern verse arrangement is meant to be sense clauses but that order often mars the sense of the clause more than helping it. They and the sentence punctuation were made by Robert Stephanus in 1551 A.D. on a journey from Lyons to Paris, France. There are some scholars who feel that perhaps the horse he was riding jarred the pen and put the marks in the wrong places.

The time from the original writings, the gaps in the periods of time through the canonization of the Bible to the present form as they appear in many versions and translations, could leave room for much uncertainty but the reverse is true. Time has strengthened the veracity and faith in our present day composition of the Bible. Man and God have worked together.

REVELATION OF GOD TO HIS PEOPLE

Not only were the writers of the Gospels inspired to write but God has been in the revelation business since the Garden of Eden. He has not forsaken mankind since expelling them from that Garden but has been constantly trying to make himself better known by them.

Dr. E.Y. Mullins gives three fundamental facts about God's revelation to man. First, the very conception of religion contains at its heart, the idea of revelation. Second, the general religious life of mankind, with scarcely any exception, exhibits belief in revelation as essential to religion. Third, the unique and unparalleled revelation which God has made in and through Jesus Christ.[1]

There are many expressions of God's revelation. Nature shows God. The poet Edna St. Vincent Millay said, "O God I can push the grass apart and lay my finger on thy heart." Meister Eckhart once said, "God is like a person who clears his throat while hiding and so gives himself away." Ralph Waldo Emerson put it this way, "There is a crack in everything God has made." This crack is enough for man to get a glimpse of what is on the inside.

The wind, the rain, and the heavens all reveal God. The seed, the plant and the fruit reveal God to man. Springtime does a marvelous thing in bringing life out of the earth and out of trees displaying the hidden leaves of the wintertime. The snow that falls from God's heavenly storehouse is a revelation of his beauty, no two designs alike (Job 38:32).

Through the presence of His Son who dwelt among us, God was revealing himself through Jesus' miracles and parables. Through the prophecies of his servant He has made himself known. He did this to Moses through the burning bush that was not consumed.

God's purpose was to reveal himself, not just something about himself. It was a spiritual transaction more than just a spark of illumination of the intellect. It was rooted in the life and needs of his people. A response to God was expected. God did not reveal to his people all that he wished to reveal to them all at one time. It is progressive.

When good came out of Nazareth it was to reveal God in a special way and in and through a special person.

ARCHAEOLOGICAL DISCOVERIES— THE EARTH YIELDS SOME TREASURES

It would be difficult to imagine what might be in the bosom of the earth and what could some day yield yet priceless findings to enhance our understanding of the Book of all Books and indirectly shed light on the One who came from Nazareth. Books have been written on Biblical archaeological discoveries, all too numerous to mention. Oliver Wendell Holmes said, "I believe in the spade. It has fed the tribes of mankind. It has furnished water, iron, coal and gold. And now it is giving them truth, historic truth, the mines of which have never been opened to our time." He said this in speaking of the great discoveries of archaeological efforts. Here are a few of the more important ones:

The archaeological discovery of the Oxyrhynchus papyri in 1897 by Grenful and Hunt in the Fayum Egypt area was a notable one. The workman had been finding nothing but sacred crocodiles. And of what value are crocodiles when one is hoping to find valuable papyri? Finally on January 16 one of the workmen was so overcome with stupid anger that he threw down one of the sacred crocodiles because he had hoped to find jewels of some princess and it broke open. Lo and behold it was stuffed with papyri. The papyri contained the *Sayings of Jesus* and some documents regarding the Roman census. Some of the sayings of Jesus occur in the New Testament while others do not. The sayings are too numerous to be dealt with here, but here is one. Jesus saith, "Wherever there are two, they are not without God, and wherever there is one alone, I say, I am with him" (See Matt. 18:20). The aarcheologist would say, "Raise the stone and thou shalt find me, cleave the wood and there I am."

Another discovery of great significance was that one in 1947 found in a cave on the northwest shore of the Dead Sea at Masada. The Dead Sea Scrolls was an exciting discovery of New Testament times. It contained the earliest known fragment of the New Testament, a part of the eighteenth chapter of John's gospel. These were found by a shepherd lad in 1947. He did not know what he had and sold them for a pittance. The scrolls belonged to a religious commune, known as the Essenes. The scrolls were a part of their library and had been hidden in the caves when the Roman army advanced against the rebel Jews in 68 A.D. Some think that at one time John the Baptist had some association with the Essenes.

The most recent find, which has received much attention, was the finding of a box which carries the earliest reference to Jesus. It is a limestone box going back to 63 A.D. which is believed to have once contained the bones of James, the brother of Jesus. There is an inscription on the box reading "James, the son of Joseph, brother of Jesus." The extensive story first appeared in the November-December 2002 issue of the *Biblical Archaeology Review.* It was purchased about 15 years ago by a private collector who was told it had been unearthed near the Mount of Olives. Its authenticity is yet to be determined which will decide its value.

Two items which from time to time have drawn again interest to them as having an image of Christ upon them are: The Shroud of Turin and The Veil of Veronica. The Shroud of Turin has been venerated as the burial cloth of Jesus. It came to light around the middle of the fourteenth century. The picture on the shroud is that of a man, supposedly imprinted on the cloth by a fire that accompanied the disappearance of Christ's body from the tomb. Many have tried to identify the person and authenticate the claims but there are still those who count it worthy.

The veil of Veronica is another sacred object and the image on the veil resembles that on the Shroud of Turin. These images alleged to Jesus indicate how the Roman church reveres such relics.

FURTHER SOURCE MATERIAL

The serious student of the Bible will probably blush at the abundance of available material which could be called "aids to Bible study." There are numerous versions and translations of the New Testament. A comparative study of the wording in these should shed much light on the meaning and infer at times proper application to give in compliance with the meanings.

There are commentaries and Bible encyclopedias which are great for understanding the life and times of the people of the Bible. No person is an island and needs to participate in the social life and political life of the society of the day.

It is well to understand the historical setting of the verse or verses under consideration. It is difficult to understand the Bible fully until one sees it in the light of history.

Attention given to a consideration of the harmony of the Gospels is very rewarding. If one writer should give a different slant to the meaning of a verse that is good, for no one is ever able to wring all the possible good out of biblical topics or the meaning of the intent and truth of the writer.

Every student should have a Bible concordance to aid in finding Scripture words. This becomes a time-saving aid for all words of the Bible are listed alphabetically.

The author has found a good practice is to have a book written by different authors on each book of the Bible.

One should not approach a study of the Bible with pre-conceived ideas of what he/she thinks the meaning is and seek only to find some proof text. That is reverse study because it seeks to dictate truths and meanings in order to support a pre-conceived thought or meaning.

Tradition's imagination has suggested that the way Abraham came to a belief in monotheism is not an impossible deduction. The story goes that one night Abraham, while pondering his father's work of making and selling idols to people, believed that certain of the idols had special power. He went then into his father's storehouse and mutilated one of the higher-powered idols. The next morning his father, Terah, saw what had happened and questioned his son about the situation. Abraham said to Terah, "Father, last evening the bigger idol in that corner got mad at another idol and attacked it." "But, son, those idols have no physical power of strength and mobility and could not have done it." "Well," said Abraham, "then why do we worship them? There is but one God who revealed himself to Adam and Eve and who created the world." The story is rather far-fetched, but there is a bit of truth in the tradition and a slight suggestion that the God of Abraham, Isaac and Jacob is the only true God.

It was very difficult for the Hebrews to wean themselves from devotion to and worship of other gods. The pagan world had a bevy of gods worshipped by them and their neighbors. There were sun-gods, fertility gods, goddesses of love; too many to make a roll call of the Greek pantheon.

Rachel, wife of Jacob, worshipped images of gods. "And Laban went to shear his sheep: and Rachel had stolen the images that were her fathers" (Genesis 31:19). "Now Rachel had taken the images and put them in the camel's furniture, and sat upon them. And Laban searched all the tent, but found them not" (v. 34). Rachel was determined to have her gods. This is a reflection of how great a problem it was for God's people to come to worship the One True God. Moving from polytheism to monotheism was a difficult thing for magnificent temples had been erected to some of the more popular gods. Moses in giving the 10 Commandments gave as the second commandment: "Thou shalt not make unto thee any graven images, or any likeness of any thing that is in heaven above, or that is in the earth beneath, or that is in the water under the earth" (Exodus 20:4). God is a jealous God.

Another story comes from *The Aquarian Gospel of Jesus the Christ* by Levi Dowling. "The richest gift that you can give to me on my seventh birthday is your permission to go out and find these needy ones and bring them here that they may feast with us. Joachim said, 'Tis well; go out and find the needy boys and girls and bring them here; we will prepare enough for all. And Jesus did not wait; he ran; he entered every dingy hut and cabin of the town; he did not waste his words; he told his mission everywhere. And in a little time one hundred and three-score of happy, ragged boys and girls were following him up Marmion Way. The guests made way; the banquet hall was filled with Jesus' guests, and Jesus and his mother helped to serve. And there was food enough for all, and all were glad; and so the birthday gift of Jesus was a crown of righteousness."[2]

I could wish that my Bible, the inspired, revealed word of God, could have had a similar story. The thought of Jesus at that age wanting to provide a good meal for boys and girls is great. He did say similar words during his ministry in telling a parable to his disciples: "For I was an hungred, and ye gave me meat: I was thirsty, and ye gave me drink, I was a stranger, and ye took me in" (Matt. 25:35). "And the King shall answer and say unto them, Verily I say unto you, Inasmuch as ye have done it unto one of the least of these my brethren, ye have done it unto me" (Matt. 25:40).

In this chapter dealing with the source materials in order to deal with the primary thesis, "Good Came Out of Nazareth," one is not left in a dry land. If one keeps an open mind, an active imagination and sees biblical characters as persons with likes and dislikes comparable to self, one will find there is someone in the Bible just like you and me. It will produce chill bumps. "Study to show thyself approved unto God, a workman that needeth not to be ashamed, rightly dividing the word of truth" (II Timothy 2:15).

THE PRE-EXISTENCE OF CHRIST AND THE TRINITY

The Jewish people were familiar with the thought of actual pre-existence as is evidenced by the writings of John and Paul. John wrote at the beginning of his gospel "In the beginning was the Word, and the Word was with God, and the Word was God" (John 1:1). Paul in his epistle to the Galatians put it thusly, "But when the fullness of time was come, God sent forth his Son, made of a woman, made under the law" (Gal. 4:4). Philo speculated on a similar pre-existent state of Christ. This evidence for deity and pre-existence of Christ seem also to confirm the Trinitarian doctrine—a tough one to handle adequately and clearly.

The Trinity is a revealed doctrine implied in the Old Testament and proclaimed in the New Testament. The word "trinity" is not in the Bible but the truth of it is far more important than just exact words. The conception of God and the Trinity is far better than a consideration of him as a monad, an inexplicable unit, an abstract monad.

Was an idea of a Trinity latent in the early chapters of Genesis? In 1:1: "In the beginning God" (*Elohim*, a plural form of the word *El*) indicative of plurality? If so, then who other than God participated in the creation? Later in Genesis 1:26a: "and God said, Let us make man in our image, after our likeness." Here again the word "us" appears coupled with the word "our" Again the question: who were the "us" and the "our?" In 1:2b: "And the Spirit of God moved upon the face of the waters." Is the third person in the Trinity, the Holy Spirit, synonymous with the spirit thus mentioned? No one can clearly state just how involved were Jesus and the Holy Spirit in the creative acts of God.

The Father, the Son and the Holy Spirit work together and stand over against each other as I and Thou and He. The best identification of the Trinity functioning together came in the words of the Great Commission given by Jesus to his disciples in Matthew 28:19: "Go ye therefore, and teach all nations, baptizing them in the name of the Father, and the Son, and of the Holy Ghost (Spirit)."

It helps to explain distinctives in the Godhead but a God without such distinctives would be far less useful and become a God of absoluteness which would cloud understanding of Him and negate the possibility of some relationship with him. The doctrine of the Trinity, the Father, Son and the Holy Spirit, three in one and equal yet one, pushes the finite mind in describing the infinite. A belief in the Trinity does not make it easy to explain and more difficult to explain away. Illustrations are inadequate but sometimes helpful in seeing things more clearly. I, the writer, am three persons in one. I am the chancellor of Belmont University, I am a husband and I am a father, all in one, functioning at times as all three. There is water, H2O, and at times ice and at other times steam but it is still water. My finite mind cannot comprehend the infinite.

It could well be a labor of frustration, but the attempt would be of some help, in trying to define and describe the function and role of each: God, Christ and the Holy Spirit. The frustration would stem from the limitations of finiteness dealing with the infinite.

God

God is not a "Who" or a "What" or an "It" or a "The". God is God. An article before his name or any adjective, adverb, or noun all are inadequate and feeble. God is intelligence, energy and love. God is not in the world, the world is in God, even though Habakkuk wrote in 3:3: "God came from Teman (the name of a district and town in the land of Edom) and the Holy One from Mount Paran."

God has been theologically described as being Omnipotent, all powerful; Omnipresent, equally present at the same time; Omniscient, having all knowledge. These three terms give a good and helpful light on some of the characteristics of God.

Additionally, "God is love" (I John 4:8). We are to love also for the first part of the verse says "He that loveth not, knoweth not God." Love has been labeled by some as the greatest thing in the world. The apostle Paul wrote a love chapter in I Corinthians 13 in which he concluded the chapter after saying in beautiful language the characteristics of love in these words, verse 13: "And now abideth faith, hope, love, these three; but the greatest of these is love."

God is intelligence for only God "can make a tree." Only an intelligent God could take nothing and make something out of it. Only a God could create a starry sky and a sunset. He made man from the dust of the earth but when he made Adam a helpmate he had some material, for he took a rib from Adam's side and "built" woman. (Now if a person says of a woman, "she is beautifully built., he is scripturally correct.)

God is eternal, timeless, before time. He is infinite. He is at the starting gate of all things. God's energy is inexhaustible. He is still moving in perfect rhythm across the pages of history.

When God called Moses to lead the children of Israel out of Egypt, Moses tried excuse-making, a natural human tendency. He asked God, "Behold, when I come unto the children of Israel, and shall say unto them, The God of your fathers hath sent me unto you; and they shall say to me, What is his name? what shall I say unto them? And God said unto Moses, I AM THAT I AM: and he said, Thus shalt thou say unto the children of Israel, I AM hath sent me unto you" (Exodus 3:13-14). In other words, God said, "I am Jehovah. I am the great I am. I was, and I will be."

So God is dependable, powerful, helpful and lovable. God is always available. John in 4:24 recorded that Jesus said to the woman at the well when she inquired of Jesus where one should worship God, "God is a Spirit: and they that worship him must worship him in spirit and in truth."

Christ

The Trinity places the Deity of Christ as a full and participating member. Jesus defined his own deity qualities as recorded in the Gospels by giving his I Ams to his followers.

28

"Believest thou not that I am in the Father, and the Father in me? the words that I speak unto you I speak not of myself: but the Father that dwelleth in me, he doeth the works. Believe me that I am in the Father, and the Father in me: or else believe me for the very works sake" (John 14:10-11). "I and my Father are one" (John 10:30). (A list of the I AMs of Jesus is in Appendix 3.)

Holy Spirit

The Holy Spirit, is the third member of the Trinity. "And I will pray the Father, and he shall give you another Comforter, that he may abide with you for ever; Even the Spirit of truth; whom the world cannot receive, because it seeth him not, neither knoweth him: but ye know him; for he dwelleth with you, and shall be in you" (John 14:16-17). What good is it to send the Spirit if the world cannot receive him? The word "receive" should be translated "arrest" which is more nearly in keeping with the Greek meaning. The truth is that Jesus was arrested, falsely accused and condemned to death, but such an ignoble thing would not come to the Spirit. The Spirit would be called "the paraclete, the comforter as one called alongside to help."

The Holy Spirit has multiple functions to perform. (A list of the work of the Holy Spirit is in Appendix 4.)

Following Jesus' life on earth, Christians have found the presence and work of the Spirit most valuable. Grateful are they that the invisible Spirit cannot be compressed into a limited area.

In an attempt to place limitations on the thoughts, interpretations and expression of the word of God, creeds and confessionals have been as troublesome as the congealing of the canon of the Bible and the proper relationship of the Trinity. The search for truth never ends. Creeds and confessionals are mere guidelines. Original thoughts of God come not from these. The author has tried to stress that the knowledge of God, Christ and the Holy Spirit have come from Christ's life on earth, the records of the New Testament and personal experience of God through the work of the Holy Spirit.

The Apostles Creed is the oldest and is the basis of most of the others. The old Roman form, adopted in 341 A.D. came out of the baptismal formula confession: "In the name of the Father, the Son and the Holy Spirit." There is a tendency to project guidelines into creeds and use the acceptance of a creed to support a congregation, a group of a denomination's self proclaimed protectors of orthodoxy. One thing is for certain, the one who came out of Nazareth did not spend his time formulating creeds and confessionals. He dealt with weightier matters.

Man's ultimate destiny depends not on whether he can learn new lessons or make new discoveries and conquests, but on his acceptance of the lessons taught him close upon two thousand years ago.

—Inscription at the Eastern Entrance of Rockefeller Center, in New York City

CHAPTER II

AN UNUSUAL BIRTH

PROPHECIES, TAXES AND A CHILD IS BORN

The time had come for Joseph and Mary to pay their taxes. A decree had gone out from Caesar Augustus that all the world should be taxed. This decree was made when Cyrenius was governor of Syria. Everyone had to go to his own city and that meant Joseph had to go from Nazareth to the city of David called Bethlehem, because he was of the house and lineage of David. But this was not the best time for Mary for she was pregnant with child, for the birth time was close upon her.

Prior to these days unusual things had happened to them. The time also had Herod as King of Judaea who ruled in an atmosphere of fear, created by him. There was also a certain priest named Zacharias whose wife was Elisabeth. They were good people but had not been able to have children because Elisabeth was barren. They both were well along in life. An angel appeared to Zacharias and informed him that his wife would have a child, a son and that he should be called "John." Good words were spoken of what this child would do and become. This startled the aged priest and he asked of the angel to give him some confirmation of this marvelous message. He was told that he would not be able to speak until the promise was fulfilled.

Gabriel, the angel who had spoken the message to Zacharias, visited the city of Nazareth and spoke to a virgin named Mary, who was espoused to Joseph. The news shared with her was that she would conceive and bear a son and they should call him Jesus, "God saves" (Immanuel).

Neither Zacharias and Elisabeth or Joseph and Mary were aware that God's plan of the ages was working itself out through them. They did not realize that they were soon to become the principal persons in bringing 2,000 years of prophecy to fruition. Being righteous persons they probably knew that a Messiah was coming and may have known of some of the prophecies, but were in the dark as to when and how this would transpire.

Dr. John R. Sampey, eminent Old Testament scholar and one-time president of the Southern Baptist Theological Seminary in Louisville, Kentucky during the first half of the twentieth century, authored a book entitled, *Syllabus For Old Testament Study*[1] in which he related at least 62 prophecies concerning Christ and his coming.

Sampey began his list with Genesis 3:15: "And I will put enmity between thee and the woman, and between thy seed and her seed; it shall bruise thy head, and thou shalt bruise his heel." He concluded his prophecy listing with Malachi 4:6: "And he shall turn the heart of the fathers to the children, and the heart of the children to their fathers, lest I come and smite the earth with a curse," which is the last verse in the Old Testament. Sampey concluded with these words:

> The trickly stream of promise, which took its rise in Eden on the day when sin first broke the harmony between God and man, gradually grew in depth and volume with the passing of the centuries until it became a river of mighty blessing, a glorious gospel of hope that cheered the faithful in earlier ages. To us the same great truths are made clearer and surer by the advent of the Messiah and His perfect life, His sublime death, and His glorious resurrection. Many kings and righteous men longed to see the wonders of His reign, and died in hope. We, too, are "prisoners of hope"—He will come again.[2]

The prophecies were abundantly given, quite adequate and accurate and greatly appreciated by scholars who have seen in these the hands of God at work. One of the most familiar of prophecies is in Isaiah chapter 53.

The story of the birth of Jesus is again in focus. The virgin Mary likewise asked of the angel "How shall this be, seeing I know not a man?" (Luke 1:34). She was told that the Holy Ghost would make this possible and that the son should be called "the Son of God." These unusual happenings were discussed by Mary and Elisabeth, who was a cousin of Mary, with Elisabeth exclaiming "Blessed art thou among women, and blessed is the fruit of thy womb" (Luke 1:42). With an obvious exalted feeling Mary broke forth into singing The Magnificat in which she praised God who had so blessed her. She stayed three months with Elisabeth and then returned to Nazareth. Her condition gave Joseph grave concern. Should he proceed with their plans now that Mary was facing motherhood? He was indeed perplexed. He approached Mary with divided doubt. He was willing to give her a private "bill of divorcement" to avoid scandal. Joseph's fears were put to rest by divine assurance that he too was a part of God's plan.

The time had come for Joseph and Mary to begin their trek to Bethlehem from Nazareth, approximately 75 miles away, in Mary's uncomfortable condition. No doubt Bethlehem would be crowded with countless others who had come to pay their taxes. The Nazareth town had no way of calling ahead to make some sort of overnight reservations. They had to take their chance of finding something. The long hard trip would be exhausting and tedious and not very pleasant for a woman riding a donkey in Mary's condition. It called for patience from each; husband and wife.

Upon arrival in Bethlehem they found the city very, very overrun with others who had come to pay their taxes. The best lodging they could find was in an innkeeper's stable. There had been no baby shower given for Mary's anticipated child. Little luggage accompanied them, but God's plan was not to be thwarted, "And Mary brought forth her first born child and wrapped him in swaddling cloth." There was no baby bed, just manger straw for a bed. Obviously there was no mid-wife.

Mary was alone with Joseph when the child was born, but not alone in the plan of God. Strange things began to happen.

Shepherds were tending their flocks by night and heard an angelic voice which said to them in their trembling state, "Fear not: for, behold, I bring you good tidings of great joy, which shall be to all people. For unto you is born this day in the city of David a Saviour, which is Christ the Lord" (Luke 2:10-11). All of a sudden an angelic host began praising God and saying "Glory to God in the highest, and on earth peace, good will toward men" (v. 14).

With consternation amid the conversation of the shepherds they decided to hasten to Bethlehem to see what had happened. They were shocked at finding this exciting birth of a boy, but they made haste to share the news, naturally causing much wonder among those who heard them.

A calm mother kept all the excitement, attention given her and the joy she had and pondered them in her heart. As usual a mother knows more than she chooses to share. It was a night she would never forget. It was a night, like the nights when sons are born to parents that would change their lives and in this case would change the world.

That Night

That night when on the Judean hills
A mystic star dispensed its light
A blind man moved in sleep
And dreamed that he had sight.

That night when listening shepherds heard, as
The song of the angelic choir rang clear
A deaf man stirred in slumber
And dreamed that he could hear.

That night when in the cattle stall
Slept child and mother, cheek by jowl

A cripple turned his twisted limbs
And dreamed that he was whole.

That night when o'er the newborn babe
The gentle Mary rose to lean
A loathsome leper smiled in sleep
And dreamed that he was clean.

That night when to the Mother's breast
The little King was held secure,
A harlot slept a happy sleep
And dreamed that she was pure.

That night when in the manger lay
The Saviour who came to save
A man moved in the sleep of death
And dreamed there was no grave.

—Anonymous

After the birth of the first born child a mother's work always increases. The male child must be circumcised on the eighth day, according to the Jewish law. Mary and Joseph needed to move out of the manger and went from Bethlehem to Jerusalem, only about five miles distance. It is believed that they sought temporary residence in the home of friends in Jerusalem. On the fortieth day the Holy Family went to the temple to dedicate their son to the Lord and for the rite of purification to be observed by Mary. The sacrifice of a lamb was required by those who could afford it. In this case, the family being poor paid the acceptable price of a pair of young pigeons.

While at the temple aged Simeon, a priest beheld the Christ and holding him in his frail arms sang his song:

Now lettest thou thy servant depart, Lord
According to thy word, in peace
For mine eyes have seen thy salvation,
Which thou has prepared before the face of all peoples

A light for revelation to the Gentiles
And the glory of thy people Israel.
(Known as Nunc Dimittis)

Temple worship has been an example for the godly in all ages to follow.

The child was now forty days of age. In the meantime unusual things had been happening. Magi from the east had been following a new star in the sky. As astrologers they believed that this star was leading them to a fulfillment of prophecy of a coming King.

They began to inquire "Where is he that is born King of the Jews? for we have seen his star in the east, and are come to worship him" (Matthew 2:2). Herod heard of these happenings and had found out that the place was Bethlehem in the land of Judah. He told the wise men to go there and search diligently for the child and when you have found him come and tell me so I can come and worship him. Herod was playing a trick on them. They found the child and presented unto him their gifts of gold, symbolic of royalty, frankincense to be used in worship and myrrh, used at burials. Was the gold what sustained Joseph, Mary and the child later on while in Egypt? Possibly so.

Being warned of God in a dream, the wise men did not return to Herod but made their way home by another route. Mary did not have a camera to take baby pictures of the Christ-child. The world has nothing to show that would give some insight as to how the child looked, not even how he looked as a man. So there were no pictures of Jesus in Joseph's billfold for him to show his customers. We think often that we are poorer because of having nothing to show and tell of his youth but we are probably blessed because there would be a tendency to ascribe too much significance to the relics and divert that attention and love we should give to him and share with others.

Not only was the Holy Family barren of such items and personal information as to how Jesus looked as a baby but the three groups of non-family members never uttered a word in that direction. As a baby he was seen by Simeon and Anna in the temple, the happy shepherds and the Magi. Did he leave them all speechless? Did the heavenly host of angels "get a peek a boo" of him? Centuries later writers of poetry and prose have written of his birth. Here is a poem by G. K. Chesterton which illustrates the glory of that night when Jesus was born.

A Christmas Carol

The Christ-child lay on Mary's lap,
    His hair was like a light.
(O weary, weary were the world,
    But here is all aright.)

The Christ-child lay on Mary's breast,
    His hair was like a star.
(O stern and cunning are the kings,
    But here the true hearts are.)

The Christ-child lay on Mary's heart,
    His hair was like a fire.
(O weary, weary is the world,
    But here the world's desire.)

The Christ-child stood at Mary's knee,
    His hair was like a crown,
And all the flowers looked up at Him,
    And all the stars looked down.

Henry Van Dyke was so impressed with the visit of the wise men that he wrote a magnificent account describing *The Other Wise Man* whose name he gave as Artaban. The story recorded the sacrifices made, the dangers encountered and the time consumed in trying to overtake his three brothers, all in search of the birth of the king revealed in the stars. These astrologers, three of them, were the ones who came bearing their gifts of gold, frankincense and myrrh. Artaban found him years later as he had spent all in the search with his last deed that service to a young woman about to be sold for a debt incurred by her father. As he was dying from a heavy tile shaken from the roof of the Praetorium, he had spent all, his quest was over.

Feebly his lips began to move: "When saw I thee in hungered and fed thee? Or thirsty, and gave thee drink?......and when saw I thee sick or in prison and came unto thee? Three and thirty years have I looked for thee, but I have never seen thy face, nor ministered to thee, my King."

Faintly he heard these words "Verily I say unto thee, Inasmuch as thou hast done it unto one of the least of these my brethren, thou hast done it unto me." A calm radiance of wonder lighted his face. The Other Wise Man had found the King.

Picking up the story again of the birth of Christ and its imprint upon the world, the author is very much indebted to Harry Emerson Fosdick, author and minister of the twentieth century, who wrote a book entitled, *Living Under Tension*, in which there is a chapter dealing with the decisive babies of the world. (Would to God that somehow King Herod could have read or heard this sermon.)

> The year 1809, for example, was one of the most discouraging in Europe's history. Napoleon was dominant, as Hitler is now. His battles and victories were the absorbing news, and, evil as our times are, I suspect that to those who lived then, 1809 seemed as bad or worse. But think of what was going on in 1809 that was not in the news at all. In that year Charles Darwin was born. In that year Lincoln was born. In that year Gladstone was born, and Tennyson, and Edgar Allan Poe, and Oliver Wendell Holmes, and Cyrus McCormick, the inventor of the harvester, and Mendelssohn. At the very least, one must say that the world was not as hopeless as it looked.

Indeed, how transient for the most part are the effects of the decisive battles, and how permanent, often, are the effects of the decisive babies! Concerning the wars of 1809, history in the main writes, "futility," but concerning the babies of 1809, history will be thinking seriously for ages yet. [3]

All through the centuries since that memorable night in Bethlehem's manger various ones have speculated in their hearts what the shepherds and what wise men might have said when beholding the Babe. W.H. Auden wrote a Christmas Oratorio, *For The Time Being*, and it has the three wise men saying, "O here and now our endless journey stops." The idea being that they have found the Incarnate Babe they were seeking. They could return home. Auden, however, with keen insight has the shepherds, three in number, saying, "O here and now our endless journey starts." The inference being here they have found The Good Shepherd, the master shepherd, and they must share the good news to the lost sheep of the house of Israel.

So unusual was the birth of Christ that the author feels additional comments should be made regarding the unusual star, unusual appearance of angels, unusual dreams, unusual songs, unusual names given the babe, unusual effect upon a cruel king, unusual effect on the calendar of the world and the unusual effect that birth had and has had upon the world.

THE APPEARANCE OF THE
UNUSUAL STAR IN THE EAST

The Magi were students of the skies, known as astrologers, and were very familiar with the starry heavens. It was not unusual for men to be guided by certain known stars. Seamen and airmen have done that. But to the long-ago star students there appeared what to them was a supernatural phenomenon. It moved. They had become convinced that a special star among the millions in the heaven would lead them to the birthplace of the King of the Jews. They were from the East and they followed it to Jerusalem where they inquired: "Where is he that is

41

born King of the Jews?" It is most unusual that they should have
known of Jesus' birth. Even more so that they called him "King
of the Jews" and what was that to them, and more so still that
they had come to worship him.

This phenomenal star, when the Magi learned that the place
was Bethlehem and not Jerusalem, moved until it got over
Bethlehem and more specifically, the place, even after Joseph,
Mary and the child had moved from the manger possibly into a
house of friends.

Through the years there has been much discussion about the
star. Was it a conjunction of two planets? Was it a comet? Why
does it matter? Isn't one theory as good as another for whatever case one chooses the timing is the important thing? Certainly
God did not leave this matter dangling. His plan of the ages was
well planned.

The first stanzas of the following hymns throw extra light
on the importance of the star in the story of Christ's birth.

William C. Dix hymn: *As with Gladness Men of Old,* says:

> As with gladness men of old,
> Didst the guiding star behold
> As with joy they hailed its light,
> Leading onward beaming bright,
> So most gracious Lord, may we
> Evermore be led of Thee.

John H. Hopkins wrote the much used hymn, *We Three
Kings of Orient Are.*

> We three kings of Orient are,
> Bearing gifts we traverse afar
> Field and fountain, moor and mountain,
> Following yonder star.

> O star of wonder, star of night
> Star with royal beauty bright,
> Westward leading, still proceeding
> Guide us to Thy perfect light.

The Unusual Appearance of Angels

One cannot refrain from wondering if the heavenly host of angels who sang that night o'er the plains of Bethlehem as shepherds were tending their sheep was comprised of the seven mentioned in canonical and non-canonical writings. Gabriel and Michael are most frequently in the spotlight while the other five are Uriel, Raphael, Raguel, Sariel and Jerahameel are seldom mentioned. These seven have seven angelic virtues: faith, wisdom, patience, judgment, mercy, peace and goodness.

Angels are an order of supernatural or heavenly beings who serve God as sovereign messengers. They are submissive to God's will. Usually they appear as men, without wings, except in Revelation 14:6: "And I saw another angel fly in the midst of heaven, having the everlasting gospel to preach unto them that dwell on the earth, and to every nation, and kindred, and tongue, and people."

Jesus in his latter life believed in the existence and reality of angels. He seemed to accept the Old Testament about angels. They ministered unto him during the temptations (Matthew 4:11) and during the agony in the Garden of Gethsemane (Luke 22:43). Paul likewise spoke of them I Corinthians 6:3 as did Peter in I Peter 3:22.

At the birth of Christ they were quite busy. Three times they appeared to Joseph in a dream, as did Gabriel speaking to Zacharias and Mary. They sang to the shepherds at his birth.

Could it have been possible that with the coming of the Holy Spirit the work of angels ceased? Some have purported the theory that some persons claim to have special guardian angels looking over them. The Bible does warrant such a theory which eliminates, if they did exist, how they were appointed by God or chosen by the recipient. It does appear; however, that angels may still join in praise and adoration of God. An interesting sidelight is the story in the Old Testament of an angel wrestling with Jacob (Genesis 32:24f).

The Bible does not say specifically, but it is assumed, that the angels did sing to the shepherds at the birth of Christ. Luke put it this way: "And suddenly there was with the angel a multitude of the heavenly host praising God, and saying, Glory to God in the highest, and on earth peace, good will toward men." (Luke 2:13-14).

Art and music seem to be the source of angels with wings. One popular song speaks of being borne on angel wings.

James Montgomery's hymn, *Angels, from the Realms of Glory*, envisioned angels with wings.

> Angels from the realms of glory
> Wing your flight o'er all the earth
> Ye who sang creation's story.
> Now proclaim Messiah's birth.
> Come and worship, come and worship,
> Worship Christ, the new born King.

THE UNUSUAL USE OF
DREAMS IN MATTHEW'S GOSPEL

From among the gospel writers Matthew is the one who speaks of dreams as a method of divine communication. The Jews attached great importance to dreams.

Dreams are interesting, baffling to interpret and uncertain as to origin, meaning and influence. They can be of positive use as well as negative. The author once heard of a night watchman being fired from his job because he was reported as saying, "I dreamed last night." For night watchmen are not supposed to sleep on the job.

Dreams are somewhat enshrouded with mystery and are curious and speculative. There is not as yet a satisfactory explanation of dreams. Ideas and suggestions may birth them. Over eating plays its part. But we all dream and forget most of the facts associated with the dream before we awaken.

Dreams have played an important role in religion and at

times provide an explanation of otherwise inexplicable act of providence. Such was true in Old Testament literature.

Matthew was writing to the Jews to show them that Christ had come as the Messiah from the lineage of David. Five times he used the term "dream" in speaking of events associated with the birth of Jesus and immediate events following:

- Matthew 1:20—"the angel of the Lord appeared unto him (Joseph) in a dream."
- Matthew 2:12—"And being warned of God in a dream that they (the Magi) should not return to Herod, they departed into their own country another way."
- Matthew 2:13—"And when they were departed, behold, the angel of the Lord appeareth to Joseph in a dream, saying, Arise, and take the young child and his mother, and flee into Egypt, and be thou there until I bring word: for Herod will seek the young child to destroy him."
- Matthew 2:19—"But when Herod was dead, behold, an angel of the Lord appeareth in a dream to Joseph in Egypt."
- Matthew 2:22—"notwithstanding, being warned of God in a dream, he turned aside into the parts of Galilee."

Dreams have been and still seem valuable in shaping persons thoughts and careers as well as playing a role in social and moral life. Dreams have had a vital role in providing inspiration and goals for individuals. Indirectly those dreams are a provider of energy in a person stretching forth muscle and nerve in accomplishing them. Another aspect of a dream, sometimes called "building castles in the air," is easier than building castles on the ground.

THE UNUSUAL MUSIC THEN AND NOW

It would be hard to think of the birth of Christ without thinking of the songs of praise, exaltation and shouts of joy that have been preserved for us. It was a happy time then and it is a most happy time for his followers as they celebrate his birthday, called "Christmas."

There were five special songs recorded in Luke's gospel. They are:

- The Song of Elisabeth, sometimes called the "Adormaus."—Luke 1:42-45
- The Magnificat of Mary—Luke 1:46-55
- The Benedictus of Zacharias—Luke 1:67-79
- The Song of aged Simeon called the "Nunc Dimittis."—Luke 2:25-35
- The Song of the Angel, called "Gloria in Excelsis."—Luke 2:14

Songs, singing, is part of worship in most religions. The Psalms of the Old Testament were mostly sung. One of the greatest testimonies ever given to Christ has come from Handel's *Messiah*. It is said that when it was sung at first that when the Hallelujah Chorus was given the audience was greatly moved.

Think of the beautiful Christmas songs we sing in our worship services. These are hymns of praise and adoration to Christ. Here are a few of them:

> *Silent Night, Holy Night*
> *O Come All Ye Faithful*
> *Hark, The Herald Angels Sing*
> *Away in a Manger*
> *I Heard the Bells on Christmas Day*
> *O Little Town of Bethlehem*

Today the average Protestant hymnal is comprised of about 550 songs of many varieties. There are hymns of adoration, aspiration, assurance. There are hymns relating to God, Christ and the Holy Spirit. There are hymns about the church,

Christian citizenship and dedication. Among the two most favorite would be:

Amazing Grace

Amazing grace! How sweet the sound
That saved a wretch like me!
I once was lost, but now am found,
Was blind, but now I see.
—Written by John Newton

The Old Rugged Cross

On a hill far away, stood an old rugged cross
The emblem of suffering and shame;
And I love that old cross where the
dearest and best
For a world of loss sinners was slain.
—Written by George Bennard

Music has been spoken of as medicine to the soul. There is plenty of heavenly music to those who are tuned in. Two hundred and seventy years ago William Congreve wrote. "Music hath charms to soothe a savage beast, to soften rocks, or bend a knotted oak." I think of God as a singing God, happy and content when his children hear and heed his voice.

The sweetest music of Christmas is that which glorifies Christ instead of magnifying the sound of the cash registers. Music can still the restless pulse of care.

Adelaide Anne Procter, author of *A Lost Chord*, has thrilled many a soul with her words:

Seated one day at the organ
I was weary and ill at ease,
And my finger wandered idly
Over the noisy keys.
But I struck one chord of music
Like the sound of a great amen.

If we would have the songs of Christmas in our hearts we must have faith in him for whom Christmas is named. We, too, should live pure and godly lives in order to hear the music of that first Christmas.

AN UNUSUALLY GOOD NAME

"And his name shall be called 'Immanuel'" (Isaiah 7:14). This was given to Jesus as recorded in the Bible in three passages: Isaiah 7:14, 8:8 and Matthew 1:23. It means "God with us." It was a sign that God gave to King Ahaz at a time when the house of David was beset by enemies. It was to shore up faith.

As the hymn writer called for a 1,000 tongues to sing praises to Jesus, 1,000 names would not be too many for him to be called by. The author wrote a book entitled *The Name Above Every Name*, in which he gave 366 names of Jesus. These names revealed his character and mission.

A name, a title, a family identification says much and signifies more. Most Christians refer to Our Saviour as Jesus Christ. "Jesus" is the Greek equivalent of the Hebrew "Joshua,". meaning Jehovah is Salvation. The name "Christ" is the Greek equivalent of the Hebrew for "Messiah," the Anointed One. Jesus Christ wears both of the names with royalty and love. No one name is adequate to describe him.

He could be called a "chef" for in John's gospel we read of him serving in that capacity. Seven of his disciples had fished all night and caught nothing. As they rowed toward the shore they heard Jesus extend a breakfast invitation, "Come and dine" (John 21:12). Breakfast is an important meal for fishermen who have fished all night. This invitation was extra special because it was the last extended by Jesus while on earth. And of all things the disciples saw fish being cooked over a fire of coals. Who had caught them?

It would seem highly appropriate that Jesus' present-day followers would do well to reciprocate the invitation by asking

Jesus to be the unseen guest at their table. Would his presence affect the conversation? Would it call for manners frequently overlooked? Jesus can fit into any role assigned to him. He understands each one and in loving humility would respond graciously. Just call on him for he, too, may have moments of loneliness.

Charles Wesley wrote a hymn, *Blessed Be the Name*, the second stanza speaks to the theme under consideration.

> Jesus the name that calms my fears
> Blessed be the name of the Lord!
> 'Tis music in the sinner's ears
> Blessed be the name of the Lord!

Christians should revere the name or names of Jesus. Each name represents the birth of the good that came out of Nazareth.

AN UNUSUAL TIME—THE FULLNESS OF TIME

God's clock and calendars are always on time, the right time, never too early, never too late. Prophecies had indicated "But when the fullness of the time was come, God sent forth his Son, made of a woman, made under the law, to redeem them that were under the law, that we might receive the adoption of sons" (Galatians 4:4-5).

It took time to bring about the fullness of time. Many component parts went into the making. Rome contributed much in bringing peace on earth, great roads and one language, the Greek language. East had met west and the philosophy of Greece and the religious consciousness of the Hebrews was pointing toward a new revelation. It was at a time of great crisis in the history of mankind. All national faiths had collapsed and religious precepts were lifeless. Property was insecure and there was undisciplined individualism.

The world was ripe and ready, waiting and longing, for a new concept, to be infused into the lifeless precepts. Morally, religiously, economically and socially the world was bankrupt. It had no way to go, for it had hit rock bottom. The old gods of Greece were dead or dying. There was the pursuit that might makes right. The middle class, the last stronghold of a nation's virtue, had, too, disappeared. There were excessive, grinding taxation and a feeding of its sons into the military.

Christianity offered the world a light in darkness and a dynamic personality, Christ Jesus, who lived above the rabble of the world. The incarnation of the desire of all nations answered the age old question, where is He to be found whom we have been seeking for centuries? The answer is "He came out of Nazareth by way of Bethlehem."

As Mahaffy, an Irish scholar of the nineteenth century wrote, "the fullness of time for the gospel came when Greek conquered Jew and Jew conquered Greek; and the world inherited the legacy of their struggle through Roman hands."

And that fullness of time caused the calendars of the world to be changed from B.C. (before Christ) to A.D. (Anno Domini) In the Year of our Lord.

A POWERFUL KING BECAME UNUSUALLY UPSET

Herod the great upon learning of the birth of Jesus became terribly upset. What caused him to fear, "shake in his boots," over the birth of a baby boy? So upset was King Herod that Joseph was warned in a dream to take the child and his mother and flee into Egypt, totally removed from the king's jurisdiction. So severe was the king's reaction that Joseph was told "be thou there until I bring thee word: for Herod will seek the young child to destroy him" (Matthew 2:13…….. "and was there until the death of Herod" (v. 15).

Having been out foxed, Herod issued a decree that all male babies two years of age and under should be put to death. This was known as the massacre of the infants and when carried out about thirty were slaughtered. The king seemed to have known no other way to deal with problems other than through killings.

He put to death two of his sons in 7 B.C. Augustus Caesar said of Herod, "I had rather be his hog than his son." Under his rule the royal court was a hotbed of mutual recriminations, intrigues and catastrophes. He was "hell bent" in exterminating all who might challenge or provide any competition of his power. Herod's jealousy guarded his throne.

If Herod had been a smart politician he would have organized those young lads into The King's Club for as the old saying goes, "if you can't lick them, join them." The more he became frustrated, agitated and fluttered he became hotter and his blood boiled with his actions following suit. Why would a king in his right mind want to get rid of male babies? Wouldn't they eventually become potential soldiers in his army? Reason vanishes when one is distraught and infuriated. So evil was this man that he followed his initial reaction "I'll kill all the young male babies and that will put a stop to my worries." Had he never learned that they that take the sword shall perish by the sword? The answer to that question is "No," Herod had not learned that lesson and twenty centuries later the answer is still unlearned.

"Herod, you had your chance but you blew it, and the legacy of your life is not good, for the blood of those slain infants has written a sad closing chapter to your life. You cannot stand against God and bring the prophecies of the Old Testament to naught."

The great meltdown came in Herod's life and the Holy Family, still intact, returned. "But when Herod was dead, behold, an angel of the Lord appeareth in a dream to Joseph in Egypt, saying, Arise, and take the young child and his mother, and go into the land of Israel: for they are dead which sought the young child's life" (Matthew 2:19-20).

They borrowed a bed to lay His head
When Christ the Lord came down;
They borrowed an ass in the mountain pass
For Him to ride to town
But the crown He wore and the cross He bore
Were His own
The cross was His own.

—Anonymous

CHAPTER III

AT HOME IN NAZARETH

RETURNING HOME TO GROW UP

Matthew's gospel is very helpful in cuing his readers in on the return of Joseph, Mary and Jesus to Nazareth. "And he came and dwelt in a city called Nazareth: that it might be fulfilled which was spoken by the prophets, 'He shall be called a Nazarene'" (Matthew 2:23). (See Appendix 5.) The title "Nazarene" was not a very complimentary one, more of a slur than a sign of honor. It seemed to carry a stigma along with the slur. The city was not well planned nor too well inhabited. According to Acts 24:5 there was a sect of Nazarenes: "For we have found this man a pestilent fellow, and a mover of sedition among all the Jews throughout the world, and a ringleader of the sect of the Nazarenes." This reference was to the Apostle Paul as he was accused by Tertullus before the governor, Felix. There were, however, 22 references in the New Testament to the city of Nazareth. Physical environment is important in the life and development of those persons who live therein. Nazareth was certain to have made an impact on the growth and development of Jesus. It was the place chosen by God to become a human being while the human being was becoming God, the Incarnate One. Those days in Nazareth constituted thirty years of his thirty-three years on earth. They were definitely formative years.

The amazing thing about those years of his life was that the gospels gave only twelve verses that throw any light upon his activities. It is unrealistic, unbelievable that there should be so much silence as to what happened. The record of those years are in Luke 2:39-40 and Luke 2:41-51.

Luke 2:39-40:

> "And when they had performed all things according to the law of the Lord, they returned into Galilee, to their own city Nazareth. And the child grew, and waxed strong in spirit, filled with wisdom: and the grace of God was upon him."

Luke 2:41-52:

> "Now his parents went to Jerusalem every year at the feast of the Passover. And when he was twelve years old, they went up to Jerusalem after the custom of the feast. And when they had fulfilled the days, as they returned,the child Jesus tarried behind in Jerusalem; and Joseph and his mother knew not of it. But they, supposing him to have been in the company, went a day's journey; and they sought him among their kinsfolk and acquaintance. And when they found him not, they turned back again to Jerusalem, seeking him. And it came to pass, that after three days they found him in the temple, sitting in the midst of the doctors, both hearing them, and asking them questions. And all that heard him were astonished at his understanding and answers. And when they saw him, they were amazed: and his mother said unto him, Son, why hast thou thus dealt with us? behold, thy father and I have sought thee sorrowing. And he said unto them, How is it that ye sought me? wist ye not that I must be about my Father's business? And they understood not the saying which he spake unto them. And he went down with them, and came to Nazareth, and was subject unto them: but his mother kept all these sayings in her heart. And Jesus increased in wisdom and stature, and in favour with God and man."

Notice that verses 40 and 52 are quite similar. These silent years say so little that one must factor into them truths such as: "he was tempted in all points like as we are and yet without sin" (Hebrews 4:15). Was he not a physical person capable of experiencing the many things experienced by his peers? Isn't it quite unrealistic to think he appeared and leaped over those years uninvolved?

The two periods of silence are ages one through twelve and twelve to thirty. Since he grew in wisdom and stature and in favor with God and man, some things just had to happen and the author is going to use his imagination, rooted in peer experiences. He will also apply the same approach to both periods. This may be disagreeable with some persons but it makes good reason to think of him other than just being in a plastic coop during those years, protected by God.

The author furthermore begs to differ with Edgar J. Goodspeed, noted biblical scholar, who wrote: "Our ancient records leave the biographer of Jesus with a gap of twenty years (eighteen to be exact) of which they say nothing. This has led some imaginative people to fill in the period with fanciful journeys and studies, of little real service to the task of understanding Jesus and his message."[1] He is probably right in referring to "fanciful journeys and studies." but those silent years speak much about what he did, how he thought and how he felt. Then, too, if he grew in wisdom and stature and in favor with God and man, when did this occur? He formed opinions and developed character traits as he worked in the carpenter shop, growing tired and weary.

GROWING IN WISDOM AND IN FAVOR WITH GOD AND MAN

What is there to learn from the information given in Luke 2:20 and Luke 2:52 where the words are quite similar: "and he grew in wisdom and in stature and in favor with God and man and the grace of God was upon him." The average height of a Jewish man in those days was five feet two inches. Today one thinks of an outstanding person as being tall, dark and handsome. Did Jesus ever think of growing taller? Did he not say on one occasion: "which of you by worrying can add one cubit to his stature?" (Matthew 6:27). So he wasn't a physical runt, he was an average height person, but he was not born full grown. Physical growth is determined by parental genes and comes almost naturally with just eating and sleeping. Good health habits are important but by the time one is sixteen to eighteen the full measure of the person has reached its climax. Then if one lives to a ripe old age one will find a shrinking process has begun to take effect.

He "waxed strong." meant that he was developing into a healthy person but it does not eliminate the possibilities that Jesus was subject to accidents and maladies. He was not totally immune to the sicknesses common to growing up, often referred to as having growing pains. He no doubt ran and played, fell down and got up to keep on. He experienced those ups and downs which at time could have given him a fever, a cold and other childhood illnesses.

Growing in wisdom and in favor with God and man is an endless process and more tedious when the grace of God is upon one. Since persons are not born physically full-grown neither has anyone ever been born, endowed at birth with all knowledge. Learning can be a life-long process. Parents are usually much involved in the initial learning period. The ideal learning process is one of cross-pollination of teacher and pupil. No doubt as Mary pondered all these things in her heart, she became aware of the responsibility that was coming to her. It is easy to think of Jesus crawling up in Mary's lap and asking her to read some Bible stories to him: such as, Jonah and the Whale, the strong feats of Samson and the life of the shepherd boy David. There were schools associated with the synagogues and the family frequented the synagogues. There were rabbis who taught and had pupils to sit at their feet.

AT THE FEAST OF THE PASSOVER

When Jesus arrived at age twelve it was time for him to go to Jerusalem to observe the Feast of the Passover instituted by the Jews in commemoration of their being spared the death of a son which was the tenth plague they endured before leaving Egypt. It was connected with the Feast of Unleaven Bread. It had to be observed in Jerusalem on the fourteenth day of the Month of Nisan. It lasted for seven days. Joseph and Mary left the city enroute back to Nazareth thinking Jesus was coming along. But he had tarried in Jerusalem to listen and to ask questions of some of the renowned rabbi in the temple. They returned to find him and gave him a gentle rebuke. He responded by saying "How is it that ye sought me? wist ye not that I must be about my Father's business?" (Luke 2:49). At the age of twelve Jewish boys became "sons of the law" and began to assume responsibilities and participate in other activities of full-grown men. It was hard for his parents to understand that statement but he went down with them to Nazareth and was subject to them. Again it was recorded that he continued to grow in wisdom and stature and in favor with God and man. Period. The eighteen Silent Years begin and nothing more has been written as to his life, deeds and development.

That silence is a mystery but it was not without an importance in his life which he was fashioning. Twelve years of age until thirty years of age is a long time for silence to occur. That silence must be broken into in order to ferret out some realistic speculations of what might and could have happened. Such speculation is not harmful but such probing of the imagination will provide fertile soil.

Here are some questions which must be pondered:

- Did he not keep on growing? In what ways?
- Did he not, during those years, become aware of his Messiahship?
- He became a good student of the Old Testament, did he not?
- He, being the oldest of Mary and Joseph's children, did he not assume some family duties?
- Was he not a co-worker with Joseph in the Carpenter shop?

- Did he not frequent the synagogue?
- If he was subject to his parents, was that a good relationship?

And the questions seem to never end. (See Appendix 6.)

One of the greatest sacrifices Jesus ever made is when he left his place with his heavenly Father to come to earth through a virgin's womb and be subjected to "growing in wisdom and in stature and in favor with God and man." Was he an early student of the Old Testament? Possibly so, because he referred to many passages from that book. I don't think of him as a "book worm." He was an apt pupil and very sensitive to becoming filled with the wisdom of his relationship to God for himself and others. Did he pray to God for wisdom as we sometimes do? His brother James suggested this: "If any of you lack wisdom, let him ask of God, that giveth to all men liberally, and upbraideth not; and it shall be given him" (James 1:5). Perhaps James and Jesus studied together at times.

Whatever procedure Jesus and his parents followed in their part of the learning process obviously met with God's approval for at the baptism of Jesus by John in the Jordan River "And Jesus, when he was baptized, went up straightway out of the water: and, lo, the heavens were opened unto him, and he saw the Spirit of God descending like a dove, and lighting upon him: And lo a voice from heaven, saying, This is my beloved Son, in whom I am well pleased" (Matthew 3:16-17). What approbation, what an endorsement upon his life up to that time. God was keeping an eye upon him as most fathers do.

Jesus learned well at Mary's feet. He was a good pupil, possibly very inquisitive which at times would stump his Mother and she would reply, "Son, I cannot supply an answer but it will be revealed to you as you continue to grow in wisdom and knowledge." The author feels that Jesus had acquired the intellectual itch and was constantly striving to learn more. That would help explain his growing in wisdom which brought favor from his Father which is just another way of saying and "the grace of God was upon him."

THOSE SILENT YEARS: 12-30 YEARS

The most amazing thing about the eighteen silent years is how silent they were. Something worthwhile had to happen as Jesus grew in wisdom and stature and favor with God and man. And much did happen. It is left up to the writer to apply imagination which has the possibility of uncovering some very realistic events in Jesus' life. It is interesting to note that the only recorded words we have that Jesus spoke during that time are these: "Why is it that you sought me? Did you not know that I must be about my Father's business" (Luke 2:49).

In the total darkness of those eighteen years, how can one begin to penetrate the darkness. There is such a thing as one's imagination flashlight. In so doing these eight things must be kept in mind at all times:

- His only words—"must be about my Father's business."
- His family relationships and responsibilities—He was subject unto them
- How he continued to grow in wisdom and stature and in favor with God and man
- His work in the carpenter's shop
- His growing in Messianic consciousness
- How he handled, "He was tempted in all points yet with out sin"
- His normal religious studies and practices
- His peer relationships

We are not quite sure just how many members there were in Mary and Joseph's family. Matthew has tried to shed some light on this subject: "Is not this the carpenter's son? is not his mother called Mary? and his brethren, James, and Joses, and Simon, and Judas? And his sisters, are they not all with us?" (Matthew 13:55-56). Since Jesus was born of the Virgin Mary he was the oldest in the family and that position placed unusual spiritual and physical responsibilities on him. We do not know what age he was when he became an apprentice in the carpenter shop with Joseph.

There is a legend that over the door of the carpenter shop in Nazareth was a sign, "My yokes are easy." The assumption is that Jesus put the sign there for we read "Take my yoke upon you, and learn of me: for I am meek and lowly in heart: and ye shall find rest unto your souls. For my yoke is easy, and my burden is light" (Matthew 11:29-30). Someone once remarked that "those made in that shop were lined with love."

A carpenter shop is a place where one would get hot and sweaty and dirty. There would be some frustration associated with cutting, mitering, planning and hammering.

George Blair summed up Jesus' carpenter's experience so emotionally and beautifully in his poem *The Carpenter of Nazareth.*

The Carpenter of Nazareth

In Nazareth, the narrow road,
　　That tires the feet and steals the breath,
Passes the place where once abode
　　The Carpenter of Nazareth.
And up and down the dusty way
　　The village folk would often wend;
And on the bench, beside Him, lay
　　Their broken things for Him to mend.

The maiden with the doll she broke,
　　The woman with the broken chair,
The man with broken plough, or yoke,
　　Said, "Can you mend it, Carpenter?"

And each received the thing he sought,
    In yoke, or plough, or chair, or doll;
The broken thing which each had brought
    Returned again a perfect whole.

So, up the hill the long years through,
    With heavy step and wistful eye,
The burdened souls their way pursue,
    Uttering each the plaintive cry:

"O Carpenter of Nazareth,
    This heart, that's broken past repair,
This life, that's shattered nigh to death,
    Oh, can You mend them, Carpenter?"

And by His kind and ready hand,
    His own sweet life is woven through
Our broken lives, until they stand
    A New Creation—"all things new."

"The shattered idols of my heart,
    Desire, ambition, hope, and faith,
Mould Thou into the perfect part,
    O Carpenter of Nazareth!"

FROM BOYHOOD TO MANHOOD

In trying to see behind the veil of those silent years, one question leaps from one's imagination: did Jesus experience the impulses, motives, and thoughts of the average teenager? Were his actions those of a normal teenager?

Teenagers have been described as wanting independence, freedom from discipline. They are restless, reckless, and goalless. They have exalted opinions of their knowledge, succumb easily to peer pressure, and have a craving for love and security.

I think he was like other boys who played and played for

mastery and with skill. He loved to romp and run, always joyful and glad. He went to school with homework for the
evenings. No doubt he joked and laughed with lads his age and
found in them a fellowship of eagerness and joy. Boys will be
boys and he was no exception in that he strove for perfection,
without sin. He strove to be bravely true and did no wrong to
anyone. He was welcomed in the youthful crowd and took his
part as just one of them.

Jesus' earthly father Joseph seemed to have vanished from
the family scene, dying during Jesus' teen years when he was
near eighteen. He is not mentioned again in the gospels so Jesus
did not have much help and companionship from Joseph either
in the home or the carpenter shop. In other words, "Jesus had to
go it alone" other than the loving care of Mary, his mother. No
doubt, being human he was subjected to peer pressure. Jesus
didn't skip over those turbulent years. He, however, weathered
the storm.

He continued to grow in wisdom and stature and in favor
with God and man. He knew the Shema, the Jewish creed,
"Hear, O Israel: The Lord our God is one Lord."

The complete creed is found in Deuteronomy 6:4-9. He
observed the proper feast days; he attended the synagogue on the
Sabbath. He knew the Jewish laws and the Old Testament. He
obviously was familiar with the words of the Benediction quoted by priests: "The Lord bless you and keep you, The Lord
make his face to shine upon you, and be gracious unto you: The
Lord lift up his countenance upon you, and give you peace"
(Numbers 6:24-26).

The only recorded words, eleven in all, that we have which
he spoke during his thirty years before beginning his active ministry were: "Know you not that I must be about my Father's
business?" They kept resounding in his mind, heart and soul.
He was conscious of the work that he had to do and time was an

important factor then as it is today in Christian discipleship. It was imperative with him that he be about his Father's business.

Being the first-born of Mary's children and with Joseph dying during his youth, Jesus had to assume the running of the carpenter shop. He would be described in today's language as "the principal bread earner." Here is a hypothetical event fashioned in the author's imagination. Sepphoris, a city about four miles from Nazareth was destroyed by the Romans and rebuilt around 24 A.D. Was it not possible that Jesus, in case the work in the carpenter shop declined, sought work in Sepphoris? Some ready cash would be helpful. The Jewish carpenter was clever and industrious, willing to work and explore new venues. The family of Mary and Joseph was large which called for profitable labor to be the order of the day. Jesus was a diligent worker. He may have been the greatest bi-vocational worker the world has ever known. He had the work of his Father and he had to work as earthly father to provide for the family of his widowed mother. "for the works which the Father hath given me to finish, the same works that I do, bear witness of Me, that the Father hath sent me" (John 5:36). "I must work the works of him that sent me, while it is day: the night cometh, when no man can work" (John 9:4).

Two other poems speak well of his solitary work in the carpenter shop after Joseph's death. One is by John Oxenham, *His Youth*, a bit too long to share here in full so just excerpts are given.

> But all too soon the much loved father died
> And on his youth full early fell,
> Of her whose life was all bound up in him.........
> No labour was too great, no toil too long.
> His trade was humble,.but won fame beyond his borders,
> And men from far to buy his ploughs........So easy,
> So well fitting, that they made all burdens light........
> All that he did was always of his best,

To meet perfection he would meet the dawn,
And toil till daylight faded in the West........
And ever as he worked his mind ran deep,
Of life and death, and all that lies beyond........

As he grew,
There burned with him such a pure white flame
Of love and truth twixt man and man.......
But to all evil—a devouring fire........
The face was winning in its gladness,
The children crowded round him as he toiled,
Begging for stories........

And, as he sat, the birds and little beast,
Would creep up close and sit and watch him there,........
For they in him found sweet companionship,
And he found good and God in everything.

The other poem is by G.A. Studdert-Kennedy entitled, *The Carpenter.*

I wonder what he charged for chairs in Nazareth.
And did men try to beat him down
And boast about it in the town—
I bought it cheap for half-a-crown
From that mad Carpenter?
And did they promise and did not pay.
Put it off to another day,
O, did they break his heart that way,
My Lord, the Carpenter.

I wonder did he have bad debts,
And did He know my fear and frets
The gospel writer here forgets
To tell about the carpenter.

> But that's just what I want to know.
> Ah! Christ in glory, here below
> Men cheat and lie to one another so;
> It is hard to be a Carpenter.

A good carpenter did live and work in Nazareth.

Jesus also worked on learning the Scripture from the Hebrew translation of them for it had not been put in Aramaic. He was a good listener and could learn by listening to the weekly reading of them in the synagogue and their immediate translation into Aramaic. He, while working in the carpenter shop, did a great deal of thinking and in the evenings probably read the Psalms and the Prophets.

It would be very interesting to learn of how Jesus and his brother James fared with each other in the discussion of religious matters. James stressed faith and works while Jesus stressed the love of God which calls for faith in action. Did they discuss the Pharisees and the Sadducees? That would have been an apt subject.

THE RELIGIOUS GUESSING GAME —SEVERAL GOOD QUESTIONS

In trying further to fathom what might have occurred during those eighteen silent years, one yields to playing the religious guessing game which generated numerous questions which might penetrate the silence. Following this procedure calls for cooperation and fertilization of the imagination, understanding and purposive will.

Did Jesus develop a love for little children who perhaps played around the carpenter shop, gathering up the wood shavings? In Matthew 19:13-15 it is written: "Then were there brought unto him little children, that he should put his hands on them, and pray: and the disciples rebuked them. But Jesus said, Suffer little children, and forbid them not, to come unto me: for of such is the kingdom of heaven. And he laid his hands on them, and departed thence."

Did Jesus have goals in life? Yes, he did. "Jesus saith unto them, My meat is to do the will of him that sent me, and to finish his work. Say not ye, There are yet four months, and then cometh harvest? behold, I say unto you, Lift up your eyes, and look on the fields; for they are white already to harvest" (John 4:34-35).

Did Jesus ever do any traveling, away from home? Possibly so. He surely felt free to take a Sabbath day's journey which distance came from rabbinical usage to indicate the distance a Jew might travel on the Sabbath without transgressing the law. The limit set by the rabbis was 2,000 cubits from one's home which was about 3,000 feet or two-fifths of a mile, all by human locomotion for I surmise that he had no donkey of his own.

Did he prepare during those silent years for his public ministry? It is reasonable to think that he was storing up knowledge of the Old Testament and stretching the imagination a little further. He may have also given some thought to the sermon which he delivered on the mountain. He may have collected parables for use later on. If not, did he do everything impromptu without any preparation?

Was he a mystic, a dreamer, a pragmatist, an optimist, a pessimist? He was a realist, very pragmatic and saw things in their proper light.

Did he discuss his Messianic mission with anyone? Perhaps, but perhaps not. It could well have been a secret in his heart awaiting the time to be revealed. He was no braggadocio or chauvinist. He was meek and lowly in heart, a genuine humble person who did not "toot his own horn." The nature of his mission and the Messianic mantle which he wore would be difficult to explain and more difficult for the average person to accept even though there was continuous expectation of a coming Messiah.

Did he mix and mingle with the hoi polloi, the masses, or was he somewhat of a recluse? Did he enjoy being with others at social events? I think so. He walked quite a distance to attend a wedding feast in Cana and added to the life of the reception by turning the water into wine. No doubt he cherished moments when he could be alone and ponder what "being about my Father's business" entailed. John wrote that later in his life Jesus said, "I am come that they might have life, and that they might have it more abundantly" (John 10:10b). One is certain; he was not a kill-joy.

How was he subject to his earthly parent? During these silent years, since Joseph died when Jesus was eighteen, most of his relationship would have been with Mary, his mother. Mary appeared to be a sensitive person, not a mother who would be over-bearing, stern and domineering. No doubt Jesus respected and appreciated his mother. The eyes of imagination can see mother and son sitting together in the evening in mutual admiration and mutually rewarding conversation. He did not rebuke his mother nor did the mother rebuke her son.

How long did "and he grew in wisdom and stature with God and man" last? If he followed the normal physical maturity rate he would have reached maturity between eighteen and twenty years of age. Did he not continue to grow mentally and spiritually? Had the full messianic consciousness dawned fully upon him? Being a human being also, did he ever feel like wanting to sidestep such obligations and responsibility? In life it is possible to keep growing until overtaken by the grim reaper of death.

Did he turn his head when and if a pretty girl walked by the carpenter shop? Did he have sexual urges? He was tempted in all points like as we are tempted. "For we have not an high priest which cannot be touched with the feeling of our infirmities; but was in all points tempted like as we are, yet without sin" (Hebrews 4:15). Did he ever consider marriage and becoming an earthly father? How could he have the temptations and desires that we have without having such thoughts? The beautiful thing about Jesus is that he could master his passion, control his desires and replace such thoughts and desires with noble and pure thoughts.

How did he overcome temptations? The temptations in the wilderness show him as one who defeated the devil's allurements by quoting scripture.

- "It is written, Man shall not live by bread alone, but by every word that proceedeth out of the mouth of God" (Matthew 4:4).
- "It is written again, Thou shalt not tempt the Lord thy God" (Matthew 4:7).
- "Get thee hence, Satan: for it is written, 'Thou shalt worship the Lord thy God, and him only shalt thou serve'" (Matthew 4:10).

A little girl was asked on one occasion how she avoided yielding to temptation. This was her response, "when the devil knocks at the door of my heart I just say, 'Come Jesus, go with me to the door.'" When the devil sees me and Jesus holding hands he says, "Excuse me, I must be at the wrong place." Jesus kept his mind filled with high and holy thoughts.

What influence did his mother have upon him? Mary knew no doubt, the Scripture, "Train up a child in the way he should go: and when he is old, he will not depart from it" (Proverbs 22:6). She probably knew that "the hand that rocks the cradle rules the world." She had not forgotten the message of the angel before Jesus' birth that caused her to utter The Magnificat in which she thanked God for choosing her for a great task. Her heart was ever alert to the responsibility and honor that she bore. This caused her to deal delicately, lovingly and efficiently with Jesus. Jesus no doubt responded with obedience and respect to such tender loving care. His love and respect for his mother may have influenced him in his elevation of womanhood and motherhood.

Did nature and human nature affect his life? Certainly so. He spoke of the birds of the air, the foxes of the fields, yoke of oxen, the vine and the branches and the barren fig tree. He loved nature, the handiwork of God. He was affected by the actions of others: The widow putting in her mites, the ones who cast their pearls before swine, and the erring, prodigal son. Hypocrisy stirred his soul, using the temple as a marketplace raised his ire, false prophets were an anathema, and he had nothing good to say about the self-righteous.

Was he troubled by living in a troubled world? Certainly so. Nazareth could not escape the turmoil in the world. Taxes were high, the Romans were demanding. The rulers were self-ish and short on long-suffering. There were no daily newspapers or daily mail-deliveries but news got around through merchants following trade routes. There was a certain amount of fear in the air. He could have faced the possibility of being drafted into the service. He had worries to deal with. Times then, too, were uncertain. He had to determine right from wrong. He dealt with learning moral and ethical values. He had choices to make, decisions to consider.

He had a religious routine to follow. There were the Sabbath laws to obey, the synagogue to attend on the Sabbath. The Ten Commandments were to be applied. He probably was a reader in worship at the synagogue.

Those silent years in Nazareth were not listless and lifeless but active ones. We wish we knew more about them but they still remain silent, probed only by the imagination and the knowledge that they were important years in molding his character, future plans as he continued to grow in wisdom and stature and in favor with God and man. We must leave our considera-tion of what could have happened and proceed with defending the thesis that Good Came Out of Nazareth which will be forti-fied by a careful study of the records of his life and deeds dur-ing his three years of active ministry. His activities during his active ministry far overshadow any inactivity that might have occurred during the silent years.

Brief attention will be given to trying to understand what brought him the consciousness of His Messiahship.

Fortunately two good sources have come to light. John Erskine, educator and author of the twentieth century, is less dogmatic and approached it as gradual and progressive. Both Edersheim and Erskine have rendered a real service in sharing their scholarly belief. It is not purely a case that one is right and the other is wrong. Two theories are better than one. Erskine penned his thoughts in a book, *The Human Life of Jesus.* He saw several events which contributed to Jesus' consciousness of his Messiahship. These are summarized and succinctly listed as follows.

> The realization of his own nature and of the work which he was in the world to do, came to the human Jesus gradually. Step by step he saw what his teaching must be, and how his powers of healing must be integrated with the doctrine, and later how both his acts and his words could have their effect only if he made a supreme sacrifice of himself; and last of all he knew that his inability to give his allegiance to any but eternal values came from the fact that he belonged to eternity, that his nature was not only human but divine.

> The revelation spoke first, we may believe, in the constant reminder he had from his mother that he must be a great man to illustrate and restore the ancient glory of his people.
> Some critical self-examination must have preceded the acceptance of public baptism at the hands of John the Baptist.

> No doubt Jesus learned something of his mission from all the incidents which challenged him to a decision and so brought out the qualities of his nature. The repeated challenge together with the repeated admission that his doctrine was sound, led inevitably to his conviction that his doctrine came direct from God rather than from an earthly source.

> The progressive awareness of his own greatness and of his

mission on earth came to a climax in the episode called in the Gospel the Transfiguration.

It was while he was praying that the fashion of his countenance was altered.

The great final stages of the progressive revelation taught Jesus that he must illustrate his expanded doctrine of love by living it out. Instead of protecting himself from Judas he must forgive him. Instead of placating his enemies he must go where they could get at him, and he must preach to their face the doctrines which he had taught in safety when they were not present.

He saw it was not the Jews who would kill him, still less the Roman soldiery, but he would be slain by qualities in human nature, by self-interest and ambition, and narrow-mindedness, and by ambition and fear, and those qualities would be illustrated quite as often by his followers as by the Jewish people. Between him and other men, between his followers and other men, if he might have his way, there would be nothing but charity. The warfare in which he could be militant was a conflict not of persons but of ideas." [2]

Alfred Edersheim, scholar and lecturer at Oxford University, published in 1936 through the W.B. Erdman Company his two volumes on *The Life and Times of Jesus the Messiah*. Edersheim presented his belief in clear, concise and somewhat dogmatic words. His belief was that at the age of twelve, when Jesus was conversing and reasoning with the rabbis, it was at that time where he was fully conscious of his permanent role. The lengthy quotation which follows describe Edersheim's stance, a rather convincing one.

But most surprising—truly wonderful it must have seemed to Joseph, and even to the Mother of Jesus, that the meek, quiet Child should have been found in such company, and so engaged. The reply of Jesus to the half-reproachful, half-relieved expostulation of them who had sought Him 'sorrowing' these three days, sets clearly these three things before us. He had been so entirely absorbed by the awakening thought of His Being and Mission, however kindled, as to be not only neglectful, but forgetful of all around. Nay, it even seemed to Him impossible to understand how they could have sought Him, and not known where He had lingered. Secondly: we may venture to say, that He now realized that this was emphatically His Father's House. And, thirdly: so far as we can judge, it was then and there that, for the first time, He felt the strong and irresistible impulse—that Divine necessity of His Being-to be 'about His Father's business.'

That forgetfulness of His Child-life was a sacrifice-a sacrifice of self; that entire absorption in His Father's business, without a thought of self, either in the gratification of curiosity, the acquisition of knowledge, or personal ambition—a consecration of Himself unto God. It was the first manifestation of His passive and active obedience to the Will of God. Even at this stage, it was the forth-bursting of the inmost meaning of His Life: 'My meat is to do the Will of Him that sent Me, and to finish His work.' And yet this awakening of the Christ-consciousness on His first visit to the Temple, partial, and perhaps even temporary, as it may have been, seems itself like the morning-dawn, which from the pinnacle of the Temple the Priest watched, ere he summoned his waiting brethren beneath to offer the early sacrifice.

It was self-denial, self-sacrifice, self-consecration to His Mission, with all that it implied. It was not self-examinanition but self-submission, all the more glorious in proportion to the greatness of that Self. [3]

In the best sense of the word, Jesus was a radical. . . . His religion has been so long identified with conservatism—often with conservatism of the obstinate and unyielding sort—that it is almost startling for us sometimes to remember that all of the conservatism of his own times was against him; that it was the young, free, restless, sanguine, progressive part of the people who flocked to him.

—**Phillips Brooks**

CHAPTER IV

BEGINNING OF
ACTIVE MINISTRY

LEAVING NAZARETH AND
THE CARPENTER SHOP TO SERVE AS MESSIAH

The time had come at the age of thirty for Jesus to leave Nazareth, his earthly family and the carpenter shop, to preach, teach and heal and to proclaim the Kingdom of God. The Silent Years had ended. His life was now in the open.

Nothing else is said about his leaving Nazareth except the words given by Mark in his gospel: "And it came to pass in those days, that Jesus came from Nazareth of Galilee, and was baptized of John in Jordan. And straightway coming up out of the water, he saw the heavens opened and the Spirit like a dove descending upon him: And there came a voice from heaven, saying, Thou art my beloved Son, in whom I am well pleased" (Mark 1:9-11).

One cannot but wonder when in his departure if he brought a tool kit from the carpenter shop. Was there an occasion in honor of his departure? Did he carry a suitcase with some extra clothes and sandals and other personal articles? (Many university students today when they arrive on campus come with their car and a U-Haul affixed.) His leaving his family and work seemed to be of little consequence to his Nazareth friends.

After his baptism by John in the Jordan River he was led by the Spirit into the wilderness where he fasted forty days and forty nights and then was tempted by Satan; and he was with wild beasts. Those temptations were discussed earlier. No doubt those days in the wilderness were days of contemplation and cogitation regarding the next step of his ministry. Upon his return to Bethany beyond the Jordan, John seeth Jesus coming and said, "This is he of whom I said, After me cometh a man which is preferred before me: for he was before me. And I knew him not: but that he should be made manifest to Israel, therefore as I come baptizing with water." (John 1:30-31).

With the introduction of Jesus by John over, there was work for Jesus to begin, the choosing of the twelve disciples.

THE CHOOSING OF THE TWELVE

The author is of the opinion that Jesus gave much thought about this even though the record in the Scripture is very casual and incomplete.

The selection of the twelve came about without Jesus using any consultant, except possible his heavenly Father. He did not advertise that he needed twelve. He discussed nothing with them about salary, sabbaticals, vacations, retirement support or an expense account. His call was quite simple: "Follow me" and "I will make you fishers of men." Their response was quite simple also, "and they forsook all and followed him." In the selection at first only four were named: Peter, Andrew, John and his brother James. Matthew was called a little later. As to the remaining seven, we must assume that they became members of the twelve during the first year of Jesus' ministry. None of the twelve were from Nazareth. Peter seemed to have been the only married one. They were all sincere, energetic men of Galilee. They were not too proud to be disciples of the Nazarene.

This is the composition of the twelve as A.B. Bruce listed them in his book, *The Training of the Twelve.* Bruce was professor of Apologetics and New Testament Exegesis, Free Church College of Glasgow, Scotland. [1]

First Group

Simon Peter	The man of rock
Andrew	Peter's brother
James	Son of Zebedee and son of thunder
John	Son of Zebedee and son of thunder

Second Group

Philip .The earnest inquirer
Bartholomew,
 or Nathanael . . . . .The guileless Israelite
Thomas . . . . .The melancholy
Matthew . . . . .The publican
                             (so called by himself)

Third Group

James (the son) of Alphaeus . . .(James the Less?)
Lebbaeus,Thaddaeus,
Judas of. James . . . . .The three-named disciple
Simon .The Zealot
Judas, the man of Kerioth . . . . .The Traitor

Such were the men whom Jesus chose to be with Him while He was on this earth, and to carry on His work after He left it.

These men were all of different personalities but all were loyal and faithful, even with some weaknesses, even unto death.

Judas, who betrayed Jesus, returned the silver he was paid and went out and hanged himself.

John Fox, fellow of Magdalen College in England in the sixteenth century wrote a book, *Martyrology*, which became *Fox's Book of Martyrs*, listed how the twelve disciples of Jesus met their death.

- James the Great, beheaded in 44 A.D.
- Philip placed in prison, later crucified, 54 A.D.
- Matthew slain with a halberd, 60 A.D.
- James the Less, age of 90, beaten and stoned by Jews with fuller's club, date unknown
- Matthias, one who replaced Judas, stoned and beheaded, date unknown
- Andrew, crucified on a cross, date unknown
- Peter, crucified, head downward, 67 A.D.
- Jude, crucified in Edessa, 72 A.D.

- Bartholomew, beaten, then crucified, date unknown
- Thomas, thrust through with spear, date unknown
- Simon Zelotes, crucified, 74 A.D.
- John, only one to escape violent death [2]

Jesus did not promise them a bed of roses. He asked only that they be faithful unto death. They had to be willing to deny themselves and endure the shame.

These twelve men Jesus chose as his disciples were raw recruits. They were placed on the job without any job training. There was no school for training disciples; they got their training from being with Jesus. They were simply believers in him who were committed to following him. They found themselves insufficient for the task at times and made two requests of Jesus: "Lord teach us to pray as John also taught his disciples" (Luke 11:1), and "Lord, increase our faith" (Luke 17:5). They early saw the importance of developing a prayer life and that service in the Kingdom of God called for faith. Two were impetuous and were called "the sons of thunder" (Mark 3:17) and on one occasion there arose a dispute among them as to which of them would be the greatest. To resolve that dispute Jesus took a little child and placed in their midst and said: "Whosoever shall receive this child in my name receiveth me: and whosoever shall receive me receiveth him that sent me: for he that is least among you all, the same shall be great" (Luke 9:48). One, Peter, denied his Lord on three consecutive occasions and another was called doubting Thomas. Peter repented of his denials and later Thomas became the only one of the twelve to acclaim Christ as "My Lord and my God" (John 20:28). They were a somewhat "motley crew" but following Jesus changed their landscape.

Jesus had to teach them also lessons on humility and love for all. Their horizon was somewhat narrow but here again the Master Teacher extended their vision and world outlook. All disciples and followers of Christ find it imperative to sit at the feet of Jesus and learn from him. They all became itinerant workers with Jesus: learning, giving, loving and serving.

It will be interesting as the ministry of Christ unfolds to see how well they worked together as well as separately.

JESUS BEGINS HIS ACTIVE
MINISTRY WITH HIS DISCIPLES

After Jesus had chosen his disciples, he performed his first miracle by turning the water into wine at the wedding in Cana. (My Greek professor said that he turned the water in the well into wine and they drew therefrom.) He then made his first sojourn in Capernaum and following that he performed the first cleansing of the temple at the Passover (John 2:13-22).

Next Jesus had his first interview and it was with Nicodemus, a ruler of the Jews, and a Pharisee who came to him at night. In the discussion Jesus responded to Nicodemus by pointing him to salvation in Christ by being born again, giving to him the very familiar saying: "For God so loved the world, that he gave his only begotten Son, that whosoever believeth in him should not perish, but have everlasting life" (John 3:16).

This ministry was in Perea but Jesus had stirred up enough dissention that he had to leave that part of the country. "When therefore the Lord knew how the Pharisees had heard that Jesus made and baptized more disciples than John, (Though Jesus himself baptized not, but his disciples,) He left Judaea, and departed again into Galilee. And he must needs go through Samaria" (John 4:1-4). Herod the Tetrarch was causing a bit of trouble.

As Jesus went through Samaria he came to Jacob's well in Sychar and engaged a Samaritan woman in a conversation in which the masterful teaching ability of Jesus was evident. This is fully recorded in John 4:5-42. The discussion was over a drink of water from the well and the Living Water. It unfolded further in a discussion as to where was the proper place to worship, "this mountain" or as Jesus said, "Jerusalem." Jesus firmly said that worship was not affixed to a particular place but that

"God is a Spirit: and they that worship him must worship him in spirit and in truth" (John 4:24). Do not many today become more on line with their church rather than worshipping God? Here Jesus identified himself as the Messiah. As this incident became known many Samaritans believed on Him by the words of the woman and the Samaritans asked him to abide with them which he did for two days. Many more believed because they heard him and accepted him as the Saviour of the world. Jesus did not have the disciples with him on this occasion. In fact, many of His first acts were done alone.

The evidence is becoming quite heavy and believable that Good Did Come Out of Nazareth.

JESUS THE MASTER-TEACHER OR THE MASTER PREACHER-TEACHER

Aren't they inseparable? Yet both have some distinctive qualities. It is not like big brother versus little brother. Preaching usually takes place before an audience, while teaching can transpire in a one-on-one situation. The aim of preaching is to inform, inspire and evoke commitment while teaching is the dissemination of knowledge, producing questions and answers or further discussion with assignments made for the next period. Jesus was a master of the teaching craft and as a preacher he knew no peer. In our religious environment there are those who are great preachers and those who are great teachers.

The teachings of Jesus have been more abundantly recorded than his sermons. Three definite sermons have been given in the gospels. The Sermon on the Mount is recorded in chapters 5-7 of Matthew's gospel. The scathing sermon which he delivered about the Scribes, hypocrites and Pharisees is found in the 23rd chapter of Matthew. The third one was to his home-folks in Nazareth (Luke 4:16-31) which was rejected by the hearers.

In preaching there are two types: Expository and Evangelical. In teaching there are at least two distinct types: the purely lecture method or the Socratic Method which is the asking of questions to bring out answers which are implicitly known. Jesus was also a master of this method. The Bible seemed to place Jesus, therefore, in both categories as preacher in Mark 1:14: "Now after that John was put in prison, Jesus came into Galilee, preaching the gospel of the kingdom of God" then as a teacher in Mark 1:22: "And they were astonished at his doctrine: for he taught them as one that had authority, and not as the scribes."

Everything in Christ astonishes me. His spirit overawes me, and his will confounds me. Between him and whoever else in the world, there is no possible term of comparison. He is truly a being by himself. I know Man, and I tell you that Jesus is not a man. Alexander, Caesar, Charlemagne and myself founded empires; but upon what did we rest the creations of our genius? Upon force. *Jesus Christ alone founded his empire upon love; and at this hour millions of men would die for him.*

—**Napoleon**

CHAPTER V

HIS THREE SERMONS

THE SERMON ON THE MOUNT

The Sermon on the Mount was delivered by Jesus during the Great Galilean Ministry. It is not clear whether he preached it to a great multitude or to his disciples who no doubt were closest to him. It was a masterpiece and dealt with Christ's standard of righteousness as opposed to that of the Scribes and Pharisees, for real piety, true righteousness was so unlike the ostentatious hypocrisy of Pharisees as to almsgiving, prayer and fasting. (See Appendix 7.) Included in this ostentatiousness were matters relating to worldly aims, judging others, etc. but he also gave the Golden Rule—Matthew 7:12: "Therefore all things whatsoever ye would that men should do to you, do ye even so to them: for this is the law and the prophets."

The Sermon is recorded in Matthew chapters 5-7. Even though it is called a "sermon" the writer in verse 2 says "And he opened his mouth, and taught them, saying." Jesus did not seem to take the Old Testament wording as sacred for he six times in the Sermon says "Ye have heard it said, but I say unto you." (See Appendix 8.) He began with stating the special privileges coming to his followers called the Beatitudes, there being nine in all. Some have called them the Happy Attitudes. (See Appendix 9.) There are eight "do nots" also in the Sermon. (See Appendix 10.)

The Sermon has been highly praised by statesmen, scholars and religionists. It has been said that Gandhi once remarked to Lord Irwin, returning from a peace conference, "If the teaching of Matthew 5-7 were put into practice, peace would come on earth."

THE DISCOURSE (SERMON) IN THE TEMPLE

This sermon was delivered three days before the crucifixion. Jesus spoke very plainly, strongly and harshly to the Scribes and the Pharisees, denouncing upon them a series of mournful woes. After this he spoke no more in public but left the temple and gave his final discourse to his disciples on the Mount of Olives. This diatribe against the Scribes and Pharisees was terrible words to come from his lips into which grace was poured and bold words to those who held his life in their hands.

Gratefully Matthew recorded these harsh words in the twenty-third chapter. It is well to remember that the mills of God's justice grind very slowly, very surely and exceedingly small. Dissecting the entire chapter of thirty nine verses, one is not at a loss to imagine the emotion with which Christ spoke. His harsh words matched the severity of the sins described. For a full wording of the eight woes denounced, see Appendix 11.

Here follows the analysis of the sermon. Jesus told the Scribes and the Pharisees:

- They love to sit in Moses' seat (v. 2)
- They say and do not do (v. 3)
- They lay heavy burdens on others which they do not bear (v. 4)
- They dress up to be seen while working (v. 5)
- They love the best seats at meals and worship (v. 6)
- They loved to be called in the marketplace "rabbi" (v. 7)
- They don't realize only Christ deserves that appellation (v. 8)
- Do not call anyone on earth your Father, He resides in heaven (v. 9)
- Only Christ is Teacher. Do not call anyone else that (v.10)
- The greatest among you, let him be servant of all (v. 11)
- Don't exalt yourself, to be exalted, humble yourself (v.12)

- Do not shut up the kingdom (v. 13)
- Quit devouring widow's houses (v. 14)
- Quit going far and near to make a proselyte (v. 15)
- You are swearing blind guides (vs. 16-22)
- Keep paying the tithe but remember justice, mercy and faith (v. 23)
- Quit straining at a gnat and swallowing a camel (v. 24)
- Wash out of the cup extortion and self-indulgence (v. 25)
- Cleanse both sides of the cup (v. 26)
- Whitewash the tombs but get rid of uncleanness (v. 27)
- Be righteous and rid yourself of hypocrisy and lawlessness (v. 28)
- Quit building tombs of the prophets when you take their lives (vs. 29-30)
- You are witnesses against yourself; you murdered the prophets (v. 31)
- Accept some of the guilt of your fathers (v. 32)
- You are serpents, brood of vipers; you can't escape condemnation (v. 33)
- Quit mistreating prophets and wise men (v. 34)
- Remember what was done to Zechariah (v. 35)
- All of these things will come upon this generation (v. 36)
- And Jesus wept over Jerusalem (v. 37)
- Your house is left to you desolate (v. 38)
- You will see me no more until you say, "Blessed is he who cometh in the name of the Lord" (v. 39)

And thus he ended this unusual utterance against the Scribes and Pharisees. This entire message came from the center of the spiritual gravity of our Lord and would become that for Christianity just like in the Mosaic faith. The truth in both was that the ethical is far more important than the ceremonial. False religion is very apt to make the pupil far worse than the teacher. Rochefoucauld said: "hypocrisy is a sort of homage that vice pays to virtue."

If one is blind, who would want a blind guide for the blind cannot lead the blind. Jesus is the light of the world and is most capable to lead us through barren or fertile land. What opportunities the Pharisees and the Scribes spurned and closed their eyes to the rich horizons which were out before them.

The Chivalry

That dares the right disregards
alike
The yea and nay of the world.
—Robert Browning

SERMON AT NAZARETH

Luke 4:16-31

"And he came to Nazareth, where he had been brought up: and, as his custom was, he went into the synagogue on the Sabbath day, and stood up for to read. And there was delivered unto him the book of the prophet Esaias. And when he had opened the book, he found the place where it was written, The Spirit of the Lord is upon me, because he hath anointed me to preach the gospel to the poor; he hath sent me to heal the brokenhearted, to preach deliverance to the captives, and recovering of sight to the blind, to set at liberty them that are bruised, To preach the acceptable year of the Lord. And he closed the book, and he gave it again to the minister, and sat down. And the eyes of all them that were in the synagogue were fastened on him. And he began to say unto them, This day is this scripture fulfilled in your ears. And all bare him witness, and wondered at the gracious words which proceeded out of his mouth. And they said, Is not this Joseph's son? And he said unto them, Ye will surely say unto me this proverb, Physician, heal thyself: whatsoever, we have heard done in Capernaum, do also here in thy country. And he said, Verily I say unto you,

No prophet is accepted in his own country. But I tell you of a truth, many widows were in Israel in the days of Elias, when the heaven was shut up three years and six months, when great famine was throughout all the land; But unto none of them was Elias sent, save unto Sarepta, a city of Sidon, unto a woman that was a widow. And many lepers were in Israel in the time of Eliseus the prophet; and none of them was cleansed, saving Naaman the Syrian.And all they in the synagogue, when they heard these things, were filled with wrath, And rose up, and thrust him out of the city, and led him unto the brow of the hill whereon their city was built, that they might cast him down headlong. But he passing through the midst of them went his way, And came down to Capernaum, a city of Galilee, and taught them on the Sabbath days."

The Master Preacher-Teacher was run out of his home town of Nazareth. He returned home after having spent much time after having an extended ministry in and around Jerusalem. It was probably wise that he did not begin his ministry in Nazareth for "a prophet is not without honor save in his home town." However, the time had come that Jesus felt he should go back home and acquaint his town's folk of his messiahship and mission. So as was his custom he went into the synagogue on the Sabbath where he felt much at home and among those whom he presumed were his friends. But he was in for a rude awakening. After prayer it was time for the reading of the scripture, so he stood up, probably without being asked, which was not impolite, for he had done such before, and began to read from the book of Isaiah the prophet which followed the reading from the book of the Law. He took the scroll and read: "The Spirit of the Lord God is upon me; because the Lord hath anointed me to preach good tidings unto the meek; he hath sent me to bind up the brokenhearted, to proclaim liberty to the captives, and the opening of the prison to them that are bound; To proclaim the acceptable year of the Lord, and the day of vengeance of our God; to comfort all that mourn" (Isaiah 61:1-2). Then he handed the scroll to the attendant. All was alright to this point, but then he added, "Today the Scripture is fulfilled in your hearing." For a moment nothing happened until one asked "Is not this Joseph's son?" That did it. A carpenter's son and a carpenter once himself making such claims. Further remarks (verses 24-27) by Jesus only worsened the situation. They had drawn their conclusion that nothing good like that could come out of a carpenter shop in Nazareth.

Something had to be done to this hometown egotist. What he had said sounded to them much like blasphemy in the synagogue. They felt obligated to take action. He had asserted himself beyond the limit. They didn't think he could deliver on what he stated. The four symbols he had employed: the poor, the captives, the blind, the bruised all resulted from sin and who was he to make such claims. Sin impoverishes and imprisons and in the case of Samson of old sin caused him to be blinded, bound and he was forced to grind grain. It still does!

Then, too, he did not detail the means by which he would bring about the year of Jubilee, the acceptable year of the Lord. The Nazarenes listened but that did not quiet the carping critics and gave no satisfactory answer to their cold questions. Enough is enough and they had heard enough and they were filled with anger. "And all they in the synagogue, when they heard these things, were filled with wrath, And rose up, and thrust him out of the city, and led him unto the brow of the hill whereon their city was built, that they might cast him down headlong. But he passing through the midst of them went his way" (Luke 4:28-30). Case closed, opportunities overlooked, the blinders on their eyes had treated the home town lad badly and narrow-gauged deductions caused nothing less than a fiasco for mob reaction is usually reckless. One has to wonder were any members of Jesus family present, if so what was there stance in this?

The good had to come out of Nazareth for they wanted Him

not. What a travesty, a falsification of the facts. What could have been a brotherly welcome turned out to be a bitter religious abortion. Never again, as far as we know, did Jesus return to his home town. Why should He? He had claimed not only to be the Messiah but to bestow the blessings of which he spoke. They wondered at his words, but their hearts were turned aside into the desert of disbelief. Their hearts were frozen and the flow of faith had stopped, all to their detriment.

APOLOGY FOR THE CHRISTIAN FAITH

The Christians do not commit adultery. They do not bear false witness. They do not covet their neighbor's goods. They honor father and mother. They love their neighbors. They judge justly. They avoid doing to others what they do not wish done to them. They do good to their enemies. They are kind.

—St. Aristides

CHAPTER VI

THE HEART OF HIS MINISTRY

TEACHING BY PARABLES

Jesus did most of his teaching using parables. "And with many such parables spake he the word unto them, as they were able to hear it. But without a parable spake he not unto them: and when they were alone, he expounded all things to his disciples" (Mark 4:33-34). Dr. A.T. Robertson in *A Harmony of the Gospels* gave a list of 52 parables. H. Wayne House in *Charts of the New Testament* placed the number at 32.

The word parable comes from two Greek words meaning "to throw alongside" The Master Teacher knew how to use a parable masterfully. Sometimes they were used to either conceal or reveal. But most of the time the parables made contact with a prevalent truth, an eternal verity, and the application to daily living was the important goal in the use of them. One should not go to the extreme in interpreting a parable or in fact in any interpretation of scripture. There is great danger in matching biblical words with current happenings which is frequently done. In February of 2003 a television minister quoted Isaiah 30:12-14 "Wherefore thus saith the Holy One of Israel, Because ye despise this word, and trust in oppression and perverseness, and stay thereon: Therefore this iniquity shall be to you as a breach ready to fall, swelling out in a high wall, whose breaking cometh suddenly at an instant. And he shall break it as the breaking of the potters' vessel that is broken in pieces; he shall not spare: so that there shall not be found in the bursting of it a shard to take fire from the hearth, or to take water withal out of the pit" The minister called "bulge in high wall" a tower and put his mental finger on the 9-11-2001 Trade Tower destruction. Such handling of God's word is ridiculous. He even went further to say that God had known for 3000 years that the towers would be hit by airplanes. This style of "fixing interpretation" is "like dancing through the raindrops."

Parables have also been called metaphors or extended metaphors. Christ is the only one to use parables in the New Testament. There are forty-four of them listed by George A. Buttrick, eminent scholar and preacher of the past century, in his book, *The Parables of Jesus*[1]. His list of parables is listed in Appendix 12. It is difficult to group the parables but Buttrick does so dividing them into three groups as follows:

- The Good News of the Kingdom of God—14 parables
- The Children of the Kingdom of God—20 parables
- The Kingdom of God as Judgment—10 parables

It is interesting to note that 20 of the parables relate to the children of the Kingdom. The children of the Kingdom does not describe those who are young but it speaks to his followers. Since they are babes in Christ their mission is to grow and develop as tried and proven followers.

Parables cannot and should not be used for doctrinal argument but for illustrative enlightenment. To try to deal with all 44 of them would be like trying to siphon a good sized lake with a soda straw. Here are a few of the more familiar ones:

- The Rich Fool—Luke 12:13-21
- The Prodigal Son—Luke 15:11-24
- The Two Debtors—Luke 7:40-49
- Talents—Matthew 25:14-30
- The Good Samaritan—Luke 10:25-37

A study of these 44 parables would provide the average minister a year of focused teaching-preaching.

There are various listings and numbers of the parables made by various scholars. See Appendix 13 which also includes nine Old Testament parables.

SEVENTY SENT ON A MISSION

Jesus appointed seventy to go on a special mission different from that of the twelve. The twelve were sent primarily to the Jews while the seventy to the half-Gentiles on the east of the Jordan. Today this effort would be designated as a great mission tour of love.

Some have said there were seventy-two but that is not significant. They were sent out two-by-two. They were to cover the area like the dew covers Dixie, going into every village, house and farm. They were to make a clean sweep of the territory. It was fertile territory, the fields were white unto harvest. That would mean an abundant harvest. It would be a dangerous mission, as lambs among wolves. They were not to take extra clothes or money and were not to pay deference to any one. They were to go in peace and be willing to accept amenities from those who would offer it. This freedom from dependence added to their journey of faith. They were promised that an unusual thing would happen and unusual results would come to pass.

They were to shake the dust off their feet if a village or city did not receive them. They were "to accent the positive and eliminate the negative and have nothing to do with Mr. In Between."

Thirty five teams of two each did cover much in a day's time. It is not known how long the seventy were on this mission. Long enough however to cause many things to happen, strange and unique things.

When the seventy returned they made glowing reports. They had seen miracles and they were filled with joy. God does not choose followers to do a certain work without giving them power to accomplish the mission. The good out-weighs the bad. New experiences can either be joyful or sad, mostly refreshingly joyful.

The contrast between the twelve is that they were for permanent work while the seventy were sent on a transitory mission. There was not time for time to weigh heavily on the seventy. They had to be motivated by the Spirit of God and greet each morn with expectancy and optimism. Why not have such a spirit when Christ told them they were to heal the sick and do diverse things. There was no drabness in this mission. No doubt everything that occurred was new and unexpected. They had no prior experience or training. They were neophytes, but were rarin' to go. To them the sky was the limit. There was an overpowering impulse which over-rode any laziness.

The world today is full of opportunities. The fields are still white unto harvest. There is more to be done than there are doers. Jesus stands at the starting gate and will be at the finish line, rejoicing with those who rejoice. Service is the emblem to be worn by Christ's followers.

There are fields white unto harvest in front yards, backyards and next door for those who will heed the call. Christ used helpers.

Jesus Christ—and We

Christ has no hands but our hands,
    To do His work today;
He has no feet but our feet
    To lead men in His way;
He has no tongue but our tongues
    To tell men how He died;
He has no help but our help
    To bring them to His side.

We are the only Bible
    The careless world will read;
We are the sinner's gospel,
    We are the scoffer's creed;
We are the Lord's last message
    Given in deed and word—
What if the line is crooked?
    What if the type is blurred?

What if our hands are busy
　　With other work than His?
What if our feet are walking
　　Where sin's allurement is?
What if our tongues are speaking
　　Of things His lips would spurn?
How can we hope to help Him
　　Unless from Him we learn?
　　　　　　—Annie Johnson Flint

GROUPS JESUS HAD TO DEAL WITH

Pharisees:

Probably the Pharisees were the most prominent sect of Jews during the life of Christ. Josephus mentioned them frequently. They came out of a group known as the "Hasmoneans" under Judas Maccabaeus and changed the name to Pharisees and were known as "Separatists" instead of saints. They were strong in the Sanhedrin and tended to ascribe all things to hands of God. They thought every soul immortal. They believed in angels and spirits. They were not mentioned in the Old Testament but in the Gospels and Acts are mentioned about 24 times. They added traditional beliefs to the Law. They harbored a Messianic hope and had a reputation with the people for piety but showed arrogance toward the Jews. They were scrupulous toward obedience to the Law. All righteousness with them was external. They thought of themselves as "watchdogs" of Jesus' teaching. There were seven classes of them.

Sadducees:

They were a party of wealth and of priestly descent. They are not mentioned in the Old Testament but eleven times in the New Testament. Their ministry was primarily in and around Jerusalem. Jesus spent most of his time in Galilee and thus had minimal association with them. They put much stress on the ceremonial of sacrifice. They denied presence of angels. They were buddies of the Pharisees but of a priestly oligarchy. They did not believe in the resurrection. Little was heard of them until Christ claimed to be the Messiah which caused excitement among the people. They were allies of the Herodians and Jesus never denounced them alone always in cahoots with another party. They probably thought of Jesus as a harmless fanatic.

Scribes:

They are mentioned in the Old Testament in connection with Ezra. They copied the written Law and helped to formulate details of the Law. They had a voice in the rules of the oral laws. They could be called professional students of the Law. Much attention was given by them to paganistic culture, to the neglect of the Law. In the New Testament they were called "students of the scriptures" (See Matthew 22:35). Luke referred to them as doctors of the law: "And it came to pass on a certain day, as he was teaching, that there were Pharisees and doctors of the law sitting by" (Luke 5:17).

Hypocrites:

A hypocrite was thought to be a person of profaneness, a godless person. They sought to cover up their actions by at times appearing to be good, but were deceitful. They acted a part they were not. They are mentioned three times in the New Testament: Matthew 7:5; Luke 6:42 and 13:15. In the plural they are mentioned seventeen times with eight times in conjunction with the Pharisees.

Greeks (Grecians):

They were people who promoted the Hellenistic culture. "Hellas" means that they were Hellenes who flourished during days of Alexander the Great. It is said that after Alexander conquered the Persians in three quick battles (Arbela, Issus and Granicus) he sat down and wept because there were no more worlds to conquer. Jesus looked over the city of Jerusalem and wept (Matthew 23:37-39) because it had spurned him. Jesus however said, "I am the way, the truth and the life" and that truth is today the way Jesus will conquer peoples' hearts! The Greek language became a world language and Greece had some golden years (around 400-33 B.C.). It was one of the three languages placed over the cross.

Jesus and Alexander the Great

Jesus and Alexander died at thirty-three,
One lived and died for self; one died for you and me.
The Greek died on a throne; the Jew died on a cross;
One's life a triumph seemed; the other but a loss.
One led vast armies forth; the other walked alone;
One shed a whole world's blood; the other gave His own,
One won the world in life and lost it all in death;
The other lost His life to win the whole world's faith.

Jesus and Alexander died at thirty-three,
One died in Babylon; and one on Calvary,
One gained all for self; and one Himself He gave,
One conquered every throne; the other every grave.
The one made himself God; the God made Himself less;
The one lived but to blast; the other but to bless.
When died the Greek, forever fell his throne of swords;
But Jesus died to live forever Lord of Lords.

Jesus and Alexander died at thirty-three,
The Greek made all men slaves; the Jew made all men
    free.
One built a throne on blood; the other built on love,
The one was born of earth; the other from above;
One won all this earth, to lose all earth and heaven;
The other gave up all, that all to Him be given.
The Greek forever died; the Jew forever lives,
He loses all who gets, and wins all things who gives.

                        —Author Unknown

Romans:

There was a saying: "See Rome and die" as if there was nothing left to see. The Romans were a proud people whose eternal city, Rome, cast long shadows over the world. It was a city built on seven hills. They had many gods, a polytheistic society with the home of the gods, the Pantheon. The Romans were the protectors of Greek culture. The land of our Lord was under Roman procurators and governors. The Jews who had Roman citizenship felt somewhat blessed. There were three classes of citizens: senatorial, equistrien (persons who owned property) and plebian, the common folk. Rome gave the world a good system of law. Julius Caesar was probably the most outstanding Roman who ever lived. He is remembered for having said after one of his campaigns, "I came, I saw and I conquered—veni, vidi and vici" Their history goes back to 753 B.C. Rome was known as the Mistress of the World. To be a Roman citizen was one of the greatest honors the world could afford. For back of every citizen stood the vast power of the Empire. It was during the reign of the emperor Tiberius, a very unscrupulous person, that Jesus was crucified. They were also famous for their system of roads. In 476 A.D. the ruler of Rome was a boy named Romulus, the same name as the founder of the city, and its glory came tumbling down.

Pilate was the official representative of the Roman government during the trials of Jesus. He gave the impression that he could release or crucify Jesus. He was in for a surprise, especially since time puts things in a different light. Read Appendix 14 and you will realize that what Fairbairn wrote was a beautiful testimony of future events. Fairbairn's words fall right in line with the words of Charles Swinburne: "Thou hast conquered O Pale Galilean." Pilate lives in the memories of the centuries in infamy while Jesus the Christ lives in glory.

Jews:

"He came unto his own, and his own received him not"

(John 1:11). Jesus was a good Jew biologically but a bad one spiritually. The Jews were called "Israelites" as well as "Hebrews," but it is of interest to see how these names began to be used interchangeably.

The Jew got that name originally as inhabitants of Judah, two tribes of the Southern Kingdom. The first mention of them is found in II Kings 16:6. "At that time Rezin king of Syria recovered Elath to Syria, and drove the Jews from Elath: and the Syrians came to Elath, and dwelt there unto this day."

The Israelites name came from Jacob (see Genesis 32:28). "And he said, Thy name shall be called no more Jacob, but Israel: for as a prince hast thou power with God and with men, and hast prevailed." They are Semites descendants of Shem, son of Noah.

The Hebrews are mentioned in Genesis 14:13. "And there came one that had escaped, and told Abram the Hebrew; for he dwelt in the plain of Mamre the Amorite, brother of Eshcol, and brother of Aner: and these were confederate with Abram." Originally the term meant "one is from across the river." The Jews, Israelites and Hebrews were special people chosen of God to play a vital role in eventually ushering in the Messiah.

Gentiles:

The Gentiles were the "ethos," the people. In the New Testament they are dealt with as a people with extreme aversion, scorn and hatred. Many of them were regarded as unclean. It was unlawful for Jews to have friendly relations with them. The knowledge of God had been denied Gentiles unless they had become proselytes. Jews were even forbidden to counsel with them.

Zealots:

They were a group headed by Judas of Galilee who opposed taxation at the census of Quirinius. They have been by some identified as having a close relationship with Christ. Others have identified them as followers of Nathanael, the leader of the group.

Sinners:

Devoted to sin, erring ones: "When Simon Peter saw it, he fell down at Jesus' knees, saying, Depart from me; for I am a sinful man, O Lord" (Luke 5:8). This was a lack of faith.

Publicans and sinners, Luke 13:2; Heathen; Matthew 26:45; Woman taken in adultery, Luke 7:37.

Sin is transgression of the law, breaking the 10 Commandments; it is willfully blind to the truth, it is missing the mark; innate evil and moral blindness.

We are all sinners or just sinners saved by grace.

Herodians:

The term is thrice mentioned in the Gospels: Matthew 26:16; Mark 3:6; Mark 12:13. This was not a religious sect but merely supporters of Herod. They were those who tried to strengthen themselves by joining the most powerful party. Jesus spoke of the "leaven of Herod" (Mark 8:15) and the leaven could refer to this group.

The opposition against Jesus by these parties kept building and if there was no outright opposition their very presence was a factor of negativism while in their presence.

MIRACULOUS POWER

ACCOMPANIED THE NAZARENE

Jesus was a miracle worker. Miracles are a vital part, and always have been, of the Judao-Christian faith. A miracle is the interference and reaction of nature by a supernatural power.

The Old Testament and the New Testament are full of records of miracles. There are in the Old Testament forty-nine miracles described, mostly performed by God alone. However, in some cases God works with and through others. Eleven times he was associated with Elisha and five times with Elijah. Even those that were done by God alone were done that His will might be accomplished.

In the New Testament thirty-five were done by Christ and nineteen by his disciples. (See Appendix 15 where these are listed.)

Miracles are done to bless others not to "show off" the power of the miracle worker. A miracle is done to restore health, to bless others, to increase faith, to promote the work of His kingdom and to bring about what seems impossible into the realm of possible, or at least probable. Miracles usually come to pass when an individual or individuals exert faith and express that faith in prayer. All asking should be done in faith which is essential to prayer and prayer enhances faith.

The miracles which Jesus performed were usually done after much faith and prayer. The greatest one of them all was when God descended from heaven in the person of His son, only to have His son re-ascend at a later time. Jesus had work to be done while on earth and the performance of miracles was included in that work.

His disciples were so impressed with Jesus as they saw what faith and prayer he put into performing miracles that the two requests of him were: "Lord, teach us to pray and Lord, increase our faith" (Luke 11:1 and Luke 17:5).

The Christian religion is interwoven with miracles. The nineteen miracles performed by his disciples were accomplished with faith and prayer and the support of the Holy Spirit.

Healing power has not been declared null and void. It is still on the table as one of the great blessings available to his servants. Jesus never performed his miracles for show or for material gain. He never had to redo one that he performed. They were complete and permanent.

It is very regrettable that today many try to use healing power as an attraction and allurement to gain a crowd and to enhance their coffers. There seem to be "quacks" in every calling. Perhaps the title "false prophets" is a better one. Some healing attention has been focused on healing waters, shrines and idols. These are questionable. The marvelous things that are done today by medical science are almost in the category of miracles. Most assuredly the author feels that God has given knowledge and skills to aid in providing for better health and the cure of certain diseases which once were thought incurable. Personal experiences in the family have strengthened that belief.

The touch system was used frequently by Jesus in healing those who had faith in him and either came to him or were brought to him to be healed. He had no elixir; he did not practice exorcism; he did not have a mantra nor did he chant some magic words like abracadabra or hocus-pocus. The simple touch was either by him to another or another touching him. The results came from the touch, from faith and from a need. Many passages in the Gospel attest to this fact.

Matthew 8:1-3

"When he was come down from the mountain, great multitudes followed him. And, behold, there came a leper and worshipped him, saying, Lord, if thou wilt, thou canst make me clean. And Jesus put forth his hand, and touched him, saying, I will; be thou clean. And immediately his leprosy was cleansed."

Matthew 8:14-15

"And when Jesus was come into Peter's house, he saw his wife's mother laid, and sick of a fever. And he touched her hand, and the fever left her: and she arose, and ministered unto them."

Matthew 14:34-36

"And when they were gone over, they came into the land of Gennesaret. And when the men of that place had knowledge of him, they sent out into all that country round about, and brought unto him all that were diseased; And besought him that they might only touch the hem of his garment: and as many as touched were made perfectly whole."

As a reader you will not want to miss the wonderful story recorded by Mark in 5:21-43. This story is quite unusual in that in proceeding to grant a request from one of the rulers of the synagogue, Jairus, whose twelve year old daughter was at the point of death, a woman reached out and touched his garment. She had been the victim of an issue of blood for twelve years. She had been to many physicians and spent most of her money but to no avail. Her faith caused her to reach out and touch Jesus and straightway the blood flow dried up and her body was healed. Jesus graciously told her to go in peace because her faith had made her whole.

People in the literary world have written about the power in a human touch. Tennyson in his poem, *Break, Break, Break,* penned these words:

> But O, for the touch of a vanished hand
> And the sound of a voice that is still.

In another of his poems, his immortal tribute to Arthur Hallam, his friend, he wrote these words in the poem, *In Memoriam*, "God's finger touch'd him, and he slept."

Further illustrations from both poetry and music adorn with splendor the power of the touch.

The Touch of the Master's Hand

'Twas battered and scarred, and the auctioneer
Thought it scarcely worth his while
To waste much time on the old violin,
But held it up with a smile:
"What am I bidden, good folks," he cried,
"Who'll start the bidding for me?

A dollar, a dollar"; then, "Two!" "Only two?
Two dollars, and who'll make it three?
Three dollars, once; three dollars, twice;
Going for three—" But no,
From the room, far back, a gray-haired man
Came forward and picked up the bow;
Then, wiping the dust from the old violin,
And tightening the loose strings,
He played a melody pure and sweet
As a caroling angel sings.

The music ceased, and the auctioneer,
With a voice that was quiet and low,
Said: "What am I bid for the old violin?"
And he held it up with the bow.

"A thousand dollars, and who'll make it two?
Two thousand! And who'll make it three?
Three thousand, once; three thousand, twice;
And going, and gone," said he.
The people cheered, but some of them cried,
"We do not quite understand
What changed its worth" Swift came the reply:
"The touch of a master's hand."

And many a man with life out of tune,
And battered and scarred with sin,
Is auctioned cheap to the thoughtless crowd,
Much like the old violin.
A "mess of pottage," a glass of wine;
A game—and he travels on.
He is "going" once, and "going" twice,
He's "going" and almost "gone."
But the Master comes, and the foolish crowd
Never can quite understand
The worth of a soul and the change that's wrought

By the touch of the Master's hand.

—Myra Brooks Welch

Since prayer and faith are so essential in faith-healing and miraculous healing extra attention will be given to prayer and faith.

PRAYER

Jesus was a man of prayer. The Gospels record twenty-two times that he prayed. (See Appendix 16.) He taught his disciples how to pray. He gave the Model Prayer in response to a request as to how to pray. In those seventy-two words in Matthew 6:9-13 there is a model which challenges not only to pray but how to word one that would be pleasing to God. The prayer is addressed to God who gave us the privilege of communicating with him. It is meant to glorify his name as well as to make requests of him. He wants to hear from us.

There are seven petitions in this prayer:

- Hallowed be thy name
- Thy kingdom come
- Thy will be done on earth as in heaven
- Give us our daily bread
- Forgive us our trespasses, as we forgive
- Lead us not into temptation
- Deliver us from evil.

Prayer is a powerful privilege which when used properly may cause wonderful things to happen. Alfred Lord Tennyson wrote: "More things are wrought by prayer than this world dreams—wherefore let thy voice rise like a fountain for me day and night."

It has been said that there are no atheists in fox holes because there is no one to talk to. It is amazing how little such a wonderful opportunity is left unused. Dare man stand at the judgment bar of God with an awareness that prayer has had such little usefulness in his life.

There are 667 recorded prayers in the Bible with 454 recorded answers. If one prays in faith that one cannot live in doubt neither can one pray properly if the heart is filled with hatred.

It is a privilege to talk with God through prayer. He puts no limit on what we might ask of him. He wants to hear from us. He wants to bless us. One writer said that he would receive whatever he might ask in prayer if the prayer met three conditions: if it was a soul's sincere desire, if the one praying would leave the answer fully with God and if after receiving the request from God would be willing to give the fruits of the response back in God's service.

Kneeling keeps one in good standing with God. Praying removes much doubt. There are seven essentials helpful in praying. They are:

- Listening to God who takes the initiative
- Feeling free to call him "Abba, Father, Daddy" (Romans 8:15)
- Entering boldly into the throne of Grace (Hebrews 4:14)
- Drawing Jesus into our hearts
- Lying in the sunshine of God's grace
- Claiming the fruits of faith by continuously asking (Matthew 21:21)
- Being sure to thank him for his gracious mercy

One of the most fruitful studies one can make is a careful study of *The Lord's Prayer* which is recorded in the seventeenth chapter of John. Most persons interpret the prayer as having three requests: He prays for himself. He prays for others. He prays for all who will become his followers. Those three are certainly in that prayer. There is; however, another approach one can take. It falls in what has been called The Farewell Discourse which Jesus made enroute for the last time to

Jerusalem. It could well be a report of his stewardship of his earthly ministry in which he acknowledged what the Father had given him, what he did with what was given to him and what was left still undone.

In the prayer he addressed his Father as:

- Father—verse 1
- O Father—verse 5
- Holy Father—verse 11
- O Righteous Father—verse 25

Alexander Maclaren wrote years ago that "the prayer that begins with trustfulness, and passes on into waiting will always end in thankfulness, triumph, and praise."

Philip Brooks said: "A prayer in its simplest definition is merely a wish turned God-ward."

Prayer then is like two buckets in a well, as one comes up the other goes down.

One prayer we can all pray with good results: "O Lord, fill my mouth with worthwhile stuff and nudge me when I have said enough." The soul then without prayer is like lungs without air. It is necessary for a healthy Christian life.

Because prayer is so necessary for a full life in Christ, Christ gave implicit instructions that we should feel free to ask anything of Him. Anything is not limited. It is an open door at all times in the heart of Christ. When Jesus says "anything" he meant anything. The anything is synonymous with "whatsoever." "And whatsoever ye shall ask in my name, that will I do, that the Father may be glorified in the Son" (John 14:13). Jesus was so strong in underscoring that truth that he repeated it. "And in that day ye shall ask me nothing. Verily, verily, I say unto you, Whatsoever ye shall ask the Father in my name, he will give it you" (John 16:23).

James, our Lord's brother, put prayer into a working category. "And the prayer of faith shall save the sick, and the Lord shall raise him up; and if he have committed sins, they shall be forgiven him. Confess your faults one to another, and pray one for another, that ye may be healed. The effectual fervent prayer of a righteous man availeth much" (James 5:15-16).

So important is prayer to the one praying and to God who hears that the Holy Spirit is making intercession with the Father on our behalf. "Likewise the Spirit also helpeth our infirmities: for we know not what we should pray for as we ought: but the Spirit itself maketh intercession for us with groanings which cannot be uttered" (Romans 8:26). "Wherefore he is able also to save them to the uttermost that come unto God by him, seeing he ever liveth to make intercession for them" (Hebrews 7:25).

It is well to remember that prayer is not "saying prayers." Prayers must be made in the name of Christ. They must be made in faith. If it is a petition the request may not be granted instantly and God wants us to not give up but keep the prayer line busy. There is an interesting incident in the life of the great preacher, Henry Ward Beecher, one of the most effective and powerful preachers of the mid-nineteenth century that the United States has produced. It is said that one day in the presence of a friend Beecher seemed to be nervous and somewhat irritable. "What is the matter, Beecher?" asked the friend. "Well, I am in a hurry and obviously God is not."

Prayer, at times, tries one's patience but patience will pay off. Patience is not always idleness but preparation for better things.

The more prayer is used, the better. But do not be so repetitious as to bother God. Prepare to talk with God. His time may be precious also. Keep thoughts flowing heavenward.

FAITH

What a word. What a noun that should be a verb. What a pregnant word. It is the workhorse in much of the activity that is generated in life. It is the glue that holds many things alive and in line. It is the supplier of much expended energy. It provides the light for life's pathway for as the Apostle Paul wrote to the Corinthians "For we walk by faith and not by sight" (II Corinthians 5:7). Faith has no physical dimensions such as weight, height or radius or circumference.

In our world we live daily in faith. When a light switch is flipped we expect to see the light bulb glow. We do not see the electrical current. There is scientific faith which works with the scientist as he plods along the uncertain pathway. He believes he is going the right way and that what he is in faith seeking will be helpful. There is religious faith which deserves much attention just here. "I had fainted, unless I had believed to see the goodness of the Lord in the land of the living. Wait on the Lord: be of good courage, and he shall strengthen thine heart: wait, I say, on the Lord" (Psalms 27:13-14).

Roger Hazelton says of faith:

It is particularly hard to say what faith means because the word itself is clothed with treasured memories and charged with intimate associations. It is like a coat of many colors whose meanings merge and alter as the light of truth plays ceaselessly upon it. Or it is like a complicated poem with many stresses and accents woven delicately together, so that the very inflection of a line or phrase often determines its significance. Clearly, faith is one of the words that belongs to the eager, dim, enormous language of the human heart. [2]

Dr. A.H. Compton, learned scientist of a previous generation said:

For myself, faith begins with the realization that a supreme intelligence brought the universe into being and created man. It is not difficult for me to have this faith, for it is incontrovertible that where there is a plan, there is intelligence, and the universe testifies to the truth of the most majestic statement ever uttered…. 'in the beginning God.'

Blaise Paschal, French philosopher and mathematician of the 17th century, put it this way:

> Faith is a gift from God; do not believe that we said it was a gift of reasoning. Other religions do not say this of their faith.

Emily Bronte in one of her writings, *Last Lines*, penned these words:

> No coward soul is mine,
> No trembler in the world's storm-troubled sphere:
> I see heaven's glory shine,
> And faith shines equal, arming me from fear.

Jesus lived a life of faith. He defined it by his example. The author of the book of Hebrews sought to define it. "Now faith is the substance of things hoped for, the evidence of things not seen. For by it the elders obtained a good report. Through faith we understand that the worlds were framed by the word of God, so that things which are seen were not made of things which do appear" (Hebrews 11:1-3). The word for substance is a Greek word "hupostasis" which means "title-deed" It is difficult to define the substance of a hope but people understand the meaning of a title deed for it is an official document of ownership which cannot be taken away. Faith then is an act of the individual to avail himself/herself of the gifts of God for Jesus is both the author and finisher of our faith (see Hebrews 12:2).

Faith is a gift from God served to us by his Son. It can work wonders when used properly. It can purify, justify, sanctify, unify and fortify. Most miracles are the results of faith coupled with prayer. "And it came to pass, that, when Jesus was returned, the people gladly received him: for they were all waiting for him. And, behold, there came a man named Jairus, and he was a ruler of the synagogue: and he fell down at Jesus' feet, and besought him that he would come into his house: For he had one only daughter, about twelve years of age, and she lay a dying. But as he went the people thronged him. And a woman having an issue of blood twelve years, which had spent all her living upon physicians, neither could be healed of any, Came behind him, and touched the border of his garment: and immediately her issue of blood stopped. And Jesus said, Who touched me? When all denied, Peter and they that were with him said, Master, the multitude throng thee and press thee, and sayest thou, Who touched me? And Jesus said, Somebody hath touched me: for I perceive that virtue is gone out of me. And when the woman saw that she was not hid, she came trembling, and falling down before him, she declared unto him before all the people for what cause she had touched him, and how she was healed immediately. And he said unto her, Daughter, be of good comfort: thy faith hath made thee whole; go in peace. While he yet spake, there cometh one from the ruler of the synagogue's house, saying to him, Thy daughter is dead; trouble not the Master. But when Jesus heard it, he answered him, saying, Fear not: believe only, and she shall be made whole" (Luke 8:40-50). The daughter was healed.

Faith worketh patience. Followers of Jesus brought a paralyzed man to Jesus but could not get near Him for the crowd so they went up on the housetop and let the man down through the roof, bed and all.

We as followers of Christ must have a faith for all seasons. Faith is not faith if it is just for fair weather and not for foul weather also. Faith must be able to know that there are seeds under the sepulcher of snow and that there are leaves of the springtime under the dead looking limbs of winter trees.

Faith then is like the diver who seeks out pearls from the bosom of the waters. There are says MacLaren, two points in the adventure of the diver.

One when, as a beggar, he prepares to take the plunge
One when, as a prince, he rises with the pearl.

Faith is at times irritated by troublesome doubts. Doubts are like a rocking chair, they will give you something to do but get you nowhere. Dr. R.G. Lee, longtime pastor of the Bellevue Baptist Church in Memphis, Tennessee during the middle of the twentieth century said: "Unless you believe your beliefs and doubt your doubts you will believe your doubts and doubt your beliefs." One must have faith in faith. One must have the bi-focals of faith that look back to the past and forward to the future with gratitude and excitement.

We live today in an age that if a person doesn't like the way the face looks one can get a face lift. This is a familiar saying "color the hair, cut the lids, look in the mirror and see what the surgeon did." The more important question here is: How can one get a faith-lift? One must go to the Great Physician for his work is better than that of the cosmetic surgeon. The faith-victories that come through faith-prayers will go a great distance in removing the wrinkles in the face from the cares of the world.

William Booth, the founder of the Salvation Army, lived a life lifted by faith. It was said of him:

> Booth died blind and still by faith he trod,
> Eyes still dazzled by the ways of God.

To those who daily ride the subway in New York City they are able to hold one hand to a strap and read the daily paper, well-balanced. There are many faithstraps in the Bible for steadfastness and security. But here are three:

Philippians 4:13
"I can do all things through Christ which strengtheneth me."

Philippians 4:19
"But my God shall supply all your need according to his

riches in glory by Christ Jesus."

Philippians 4:6-7

"Be careful for nothing; but in every thing by prayer and supplication with thanksgiving let your requests be made known unto God. And the peace of God, which passeth all understanding, shall keep your hearts and minds through Christ Jesus."

Many features and gifts of the individual are inherited or determined by genes. Faith may be transmitted by genes but more is vitalized through learning and practice. Ponder these words of St. Paul to his son in the ministry, Timothy. "When I call to remembrance the unfeigned faith that is in thee, which dwelt first in thy grandmother Lois, and thy mother Eunice; and I am persuaded that in thee also. Wherefore I put thee in remembrance that thou stir up the gift of God, which is in thee by the putting on of my hands. For God hath not given us the spirit of fear; but of power, and of love, and of a sound mind" (II Timothy 1:5-7). Faith is so vital, so visionary, so helpful that at times it is easy to think that it might be like the mythological Argus who had 1,000 eyes. Elements and activities of faith may be working from ten different angles, along with ten other energy activities on ten occasions and 10 x 10 x 10 equals 1,000.

Christopher Columbus was a man of great faith and vision. The vision would have been of little value were it not for his faith. In 1492 Columbus sailed the ocean blue not knowing exactly where he was going and not knowing where he had been when he returned. But faith drove him onward. The poem *Columbus* by Cincinnatus Miller gives a beautiful word picture of his faith in operation.

Columbus

They sailed. They sailed. Then spake the mate:
"This mad sea shows his teeth to-night;

He curls his lips, he lies in wait,
 With lifted teeth, as if to bite:
Brave Adm'r'l, say but one good word;
 What shall we do when hope is gone?"
The words leapt like a leaping sword:
 "Sail on! sail on! sail on! and on!"

Then pale and worn, he kept his deck,
 And peered through darkness. Ah, that night
Of all dark nights! And then a speck-
 A light! a light! a light! a light!
It grew, a starlit flag unfurled!
 It grew to be Time's burst of dawn.
He gained a world; he gave that world
 Its grandest lesson: "On! sail on!"

One of the greatest poems ever written by Tennyson was a poet's plea for faith, entitled *In Memoriam A.H.H.* In addition to the prologue and epilogue there are 131 four-line stanzas. The first stanza of the prologue:

> Strong son of God, immortal love,
> Whom we who have seen thy face
> By faith, and faith alone, embrace,
> Believing where we cannot prove.

and the last stanza of the epilogue:

> That God which ever lives and loves,
> One God, one law, one element
> And one far-off divine event,
> To which the whole creation moves.

My, O my, what wonderful faith-theology is in that poem as well as an uplift for the soul. Faith is wonderful, more wonderful when it is actively working. It never, however, becomes a cocoon of comfort. It acts, however, as a protective cocoon from a harsh and unfriendly environment. The disciples seemed to want Jesus to bring such a cocoon on board by asking him "When they therefore were come together, they asked of him, saying, Lord, wilt thou at this time restore again the kingdom to Israel? And he said unto them, It is not for you to know the times or the seasons, which the Father hath put in his own power. But ye shall receive power, after that the Holy Ghost is come upon you: and ye shall be witnesses unto me both in Jerusalem, and in all Judaea, and in Samaria, and unto the uttermost part of the earth" (Acts 1:6-8).

The author and finisher of our faith who came out of Nazareth gave the world a faith that there is something worth standing for, a solid foundation to stand on and most of all someone to stand along with the person who has faith.

Two great stalwarts of faith: Emil Brunner and Studdert Kennedy have given strong expressions of the place of faith in their thoughts and lives. Kennedy in his poem *Faith* wrote:

> I bet my life on Christ—Christ crucified.....
> For God is love, such is my faith
> And such my reason for it, and I find them strong,
> Enough. and you? You want to argue? Well
> I can't. It is a choice. I choose the Christ. [3]

Brunner wondered if faith made a person lazy and came out firmly on the other side. Here are his words:

Ask a Luther, a Zwingli, a Calvin whether this "God alone" faith made them lazy! Examine the lives of others who have really received this "God alone" faith in all of its depth and magnificence, and inquire whether it has made them morally indifferent or lazy. It is the great mystery of God that men do not become strong until they know their weakness, and expect all things from the power of God. The strong, the real "doers" in Christendom have been those who relied solely on the work of God, and not those who trusted much in human activity. For God's power is made perfect in weakness, and only when a man knows how weak he is can God become mighty in him. It is precisely the truly good that is done 'by faith alone.' [4]

Faith and reason do not fight each other nor does faith restrict one's freedom. To show more clearly the relationship between faith and reason along with the difficulty in making clear the role of each in relationship to each other, I want to record three quotations. The first two were uttered by Martin Luther and appear to be somewhat in juxtaposition of each other.

Reason is the greatest enemy that faith has: it never comes to the aid of spiritual things, but-more frequently than not-struggles against the divine Word, treating with contempt all that emanates from God.

The second statement from Luther is more mellow and contemplative.

Prior to faith and a knowledge of God, reason is darkness, but in believers it's an excellent instrument. Just as all gifts and instruments of nature are evil in godless men, so they are good in believers. Faith is now furthered by reason, speech, and eloquence, whereas these were only impediments prior to faith. Enlightened reason, taken captive by faith, receives life from faith, for it is slain and given life again.

The third quotation is from Cardinal John Henry Newman of the Catholic faith of the 19th Century.

Reason....is subservient to faith, as handling, examining, explaining, recording, cataloguing, defending the truths which faith, not reason, has gained for us, as providing an intellectual expression of supernatural facts, eliciting what is implicit, comparing, measuring, connecting each with each, and forming one and all into a theological system.

In Matthew's gospel we have the story of Jesus stilling the waves of the sea. That is a story that doesn't fit the actions of a reasonable person for that person would seek shelter from the storm. To Jesus such action called for faith so he spoke to the waves. Jesus spoke to the disciples rebuking them: "And he saith unto them, Why are ye fearful, O ye of little faith? Then he arose, and rebuked the winds and the sea; and there was a great calm" (Matthew 8:26). Another illustration of faith and reason is found in Matthew 14:21-36 and recounts Jesus walking on water, a very unreasonable expectation of anyone. Reason gave way to faith but reason called faith into action. At this storm at sea Jesus said to his disciples, "Be of good cheer: It is I: be not afraid." Faith and reason could be called "buddies" mutually holding each in respect. Reason does not take away faith, for faith is at times based on reason.

John Donne, an English divine and poet of the sixteenth and seventeenth centuries gave these succinct thoughts: "Reason is our soul's left hand, faith her right, by these we reach divinity."

Thomas Acquinas, an Italian theologian of the thirteenth century, gave reason a clearer definition when he wrote:

> The discourse of reason always begins from an understanding and ends at an understanding, because we reason by proceeding from certain understood principles, and the discourse of reason is perfected when we come to understand what we did not know before. Hence the act of reasoning proceeds from something previously understood.

Faith seldom stands alone. It needs to be attached to something, an association with someone and somehow do its job for somebody. Some persons are willing to let God do it all. Their faith seems inactive for it is more adoration then activity.

Browning in *Andrea del Sarto* gave faith a challenge in the words: "Ah, but a man's reach should exceed his grasp or what's a heaven for." It will be great to be led into the future by faith. Faith's eyes will be scouting out the future, looking for challenges and service opportunities.

A Faith To Live By

Give me the faith of adventure, Lord,
The courage to try the new,
The will to press on in spite of the dark,
Knowing I walk with You.

Give me the faith of desire and hope,
The inward urge to achieve.
All things are possible with You.
O Lord, let me believe!

Give me the faith of awareness
Of beauty everywhere,
Eyes to see, and ears to hear-
An open heart to care.

Give me a faith to live by,
Joyous and unafraid,
A glorious faith to match the dawn
Of this day you have made!
—Helen Lowrie Marshall

The more the author ponders faith in all of its ramifications, the more he longs to use it as a verb: faith, faithed, faithing. This has been my feeling for years and I was glad to read the following from former president Jimmy Carter's book, *Living Faith*. "Throughout these three score and ten years, my faith as a Christian has provided the necessary stability in my life. Come to think of it, stability is not exactly the right word, because to have faith in something is an inducement not to dormancy but to action. To me faith is not just a noun but also a verb."

118

Faith then is both excitement and enthusiasm but also a magnificent work habit. It is the fashioning of the grand drama of life. What faith Jesus manifested when at the tomb of Lazarus who had been dead four days he spoke these words: "Lazarus come forth" (John 11:43). That faith was rewarded for Lazarus came forth.

In bringing this discussion of faith to a close, it is not possible to do so without giving the statement of Jesus to his disciples in Matthew 17:20. "And Jesus said unto them, Because of your unbelief: for verily I say unto you, If ye have faith as a grain of mustard seed, ye shall say unto this mountain, Remove hence to yonder place; and it shall remove; and nothing shall be impossible unto you." Mustard seed faith must be pure, unadulterated faith. If one would put a living faith, even small in Christ, the gospel and the Holy Spirit the problems of life would yield to such power.

Think on these paraphrased words:

> Without the way, there is no going
> Without the truth, there is no knowing
> Without the life, there is no living
> Without the faith, there is no doing.

O, for a faith that will not shrink or grow weary but that stays virile and vibrant. Man's faith coupled with God's power can do a lot to remove a mountain if man will use the right implements. A caution here might be worth a mite; fanatical faith can be toxic. If God promises faith then faith must go into action. There is nothing wrong with putting faith to the test. Use faith rightly, use it prayerfully. Use it not as a crutch but as a staff.

THE KINGDOM—GOD, CHRIST, HEAVEN

The kingdom of God, Christ and Heaven are one and the same. It is a spiritual kingdom and not a renewal or continuation of the kingdom of David. David and his kingdom had a special place in the providence of God but with the coming of the King in the new dispensation, Christ, a new kingdom was to be established. In Matthew 3:1-2, John the Baptist who was to prepare the way of the Lord, proclaimed, "Repent ye: for the kingdom of heaven is at hand."

There are three salient points about this kingdom. First, it was to be a spiritual kingdom. Christ would be the king. His subjects would be those who had come into the kingdom through salvation made possible in him. The gospel of the kingdom was the gospel of salvation. The king of the kingdom would establish a reign of righteousness, love and faith. "For I say unto you, That except your righteousness shall exceed the righteousness of the Scribes and Pharisees, ye shall in no case enter into the kingdom of heaven" (Matthew 5:20). There would be no palaces built for the King, no military establishment to heed his every beck and call. The King would levy no taxes for his personal support.

Second, the kingdom had come. It was present, established. It was not some far off event that would come in some glorious, magnificent manner. After Jesus began his Galilean ministry and had departed from Nazareth, "From that time Jesus began to preach, and to say, Repent: for the kingdom of heaven is at hand" (Matthew 4:17). If it had not come, how could Jesus have said to Peter? "And I will give unto thee the keys of the kingdom of heaven: and whatsoever thou shalt bind on earth shall be bound in heaven: and whatsoever thou shalt loose on earth shall be loosed in heaven" (Matthew 16:19). Jesus gave a group of parables to a multitude who stood on the shore as he spoke to them from a boat. He explained the nature and work that would be done within the kingdom confines.

Jesus was so adept in the use of parables that he gave to a great group seven parables with the hope that these parables would somewhat enlighten them more as to the kingdom. These have been recorded in the thirteenth chapter of Matthew. Mark added an eighth parable about the kingdom in Mark 4:26-29.

PARABLE 1

This is called "The Sower and the Seed" (Matthew 13:3-23). There seems to have been nothing wrong with the seed which were cast out. Some fell by the wayside and were picked up and eaten by birds while others fell on stony places where there was not much soil for rootage and were parched by the sun. Others fell among thorns and were choked out but some of the seed fell on good ground and produced a good harvest. Such is the gospel which is preached. Not all have ears to hear it, others hear but "in one ear and out the other ear," while others receive the message and bear much fruit. Of such is the kingdom of God.

PARABLE 2

This is called the Parable of the Tares, verse 24. Tares are bearded darnel, degenerated wheat which has little value. At harvest it is weeded out and fed to fowl and animals. This could represent the infiltration of evil into the ranks of the subjects in the kingdom.

PARABLE 3

It is the Parable of the Mustard Seed, verse 31. Mustard seeds are very small but in the seed is the potential of a large plant. The mystery of this parable is that Christianity has had great, expansive growth in some areas. The fields are white unto a good harvest if only the laborers will sow the seed, cultivate the plants and then harvest the grain. The gospel has great power.

PARABLE 4

The Parable of the Leaven dealt with how leaven, yeast,

will quietly permeate bread dough and cause it to rise, expand, verse 33. In most cases in the Bible leaven refers to evil but in this case it is a positive element. Yeast also adds flavor to bread.

PARABLE 5

The Parable of Hidden Treasure described a treasure which has been hidden in a field and later discovered. The finder hid it temporarily and went and sold all he had to buy the field and thus he would own the hidden treasure. When the gospel of salvation has been "discovered" the finder will rejoice and will be willing to sacrifice in order to have the joys and blessings of salvation, a gift from God.

PARABLE 6

The Parable of the Pearl of Great Price described a merchant who searched diligently for a beautiful pearl. It was something desired by the merchant, verse 45. One does not know whether the merchant wanted it for himself or to resell. Whatever the case might have been, the reign of the Messiah in the kingdom of God was a special, beautiful privilege of unusual joy to the finder and the beholder.

PARABLE 7

"Again, the kingdom of heaven is like unto a net, that was cast into the sea, and gathered of every kind: Which, when it was full, they drew to shore, and sat down, and gathered the good into vessels, but cast the bad away. So shall it be at the end of the world: the angels shall come forth, and sever the wicked from among the just" (Matthew 13:47-49). This was the Parable of the Dragnet.

PARABLE 8

There is an eighth parable, The Parable of the Growing Seed, recorded in the Gospel of Mark 4:26-29. "And he said, So is the kingdom of God, as if a man should cast seed into the ground; And should sleep, and rise night and day, and the seed should spring and grow up, he knoweth not how. For the earth bringeth forth fruit of herself; first the blade, then the ear, after that the full corn in the ear. But when the fruit is brought forth, immediately he putteth in the sickle, because the harvest is come."

Third, there would be a fulfillment, an end, of the earthly kingdom "When the Son of Man shall come in all his glory, and all the holy angels with him, then shall he sit upon the throne of his glory: And before him shall be gathered all nations: and he shall separate them one from another, as a shepherd divideth his sheep from the goats: And he shall set the sheep on his right hand, but the goats on the left" (Matthew 25:31-33).

Jesus in speaking of the kingdom spoke of the culmination that was to come. This would be the end of time. Jesus backed away from predicting when that would be because he admitted that he did not know and that only the Father knew. "But of that day and hour knoweth no man, no, not the angels of heaven, but my Father only" (Matthew 24:36). Some ministers have been more brazen and have offered their two-bits of wisdom by trying to make such a prediction.

In a spring 2001 issue of the *Nashville Tennessean* there appeared an article/advertisement under the caption: *8 Compelling Reasons Why: Christ Is Coming Very Soon*. One wonders immediately what time element is involved in "very soon?" The eight reasons are listed without comment on each one.

- Israel's rebirth
- Plummeting morality
- Famines, violence and wars
- Increase in earthquakes
- Explosion of travel and education
- Explosion of cults and the occult
- The New World order
- Increase in both apostasy and faith

The author of the article added two other items: The Escape Plan and How to Receive Him (Christ).

Much of what was written in the article is a true description of the world today. The oft referred to Gay Nineties were not lily white morally and theologically. But many of the things covered in the advertisement have been in the world for years. None of them is dated nor is there any way to tell when they all will come together and supposedly usher in the Lord's return.

In the meantime the harvest-time of the kingdom is at the end and the subjects in the Kingdom should remember that the kingdom will continue to grow as a grain of mustard seed. It will take time for this to be accomplished. Those within the kingdom must show faith, love and forgiveness and continue to grow in the knowledge of the King of the kingdom. There should be a feeling of community among all with no feeling of first or second class members. It is a situation of one for all and all for one. A mutuality of respect and spirituality should be working.

What a God and to Him be all the glory now and forever-more.

As Jesus was seated on the Mount of Olives, after having visited the temple, the disciples came to him privately and asked "What will be a sign of your coming?" After mentioning a reference to Daniel, he spoke in a clear, concise and confident voice. "But of that day and hour knoweth no man, no, not the angels of heaven, but my Father only. But as the days of Noah were, so shall also the coming of the Son of man be. For as in the days that were before the flood they were eating and drinking, marrying and giving in marriage, until the day that Noah entered into the ark, And knew not until the flood came, and took them all away; so shall also the coming of the Son of man be. Then shall two be in the field; the one shall be taken, and the other left. Two women shall be grinding at the mill; the one shall be taken, and the other left. Watch therefore: for ye know not what hour your Lord doth come. But know this, that if the good-man of the house had known in what watch the thief would come, he would have watched, and would not have suffered his house to be broken up. Therefore be ye also ready: for in such an hour as ye think not the Son of Man cometh" (Matthew 24:36-44). From this passage and other related ones, one can safely deduct that the following admonitions were given the disciples:

- Be prepared
- Be watchful
- Be ready
- Beware of false prophets
- Be busy
- Be expectant

The uncertainty of the time of Christ's return keep his followers ever active and standing on tiptoes for there is much to be done in the meantime and speculation is a practice in futility. If God had wanted us to know in advance he would have told us just as the coming of Christ was predicted but as to time not pinpointed. Those who spend so much time trying to predict his return are somewhat like the people of Milan, Italy about whom it was said that "they did not study opera, they just inhaled it."

THE CRYSTAL

But Thee, but Thee, O sovereign Seer of time,
But Thee, O poets' Poet, Wisdom's Tongue,
But Thee, O man's best Man, O love's best Love,
O perfect life in perfect labor writ,
O all men's Comrade, Servant, King, or Priest,-
Oh, what amiss may I forgive in Thee,
Jesus, good Paragon, thou Crystal Christ?
                                    —Sidney Lanier

CHAPTER VII

PROPHET AND PRIEST

PROPHETS, PROPHECIES AND THE TRUE PROPHET

Prophets have played a prominent, notable and vital role in the religions stemming from our Bible. In the Old Testament there were schools of the prophet since the time of Samuel. Even in recent centuries the Theological Seminary in Louisville, Kentucky, affiliated with the Southern Baptist denomination has been called "School of the Prophets." The Old Testament books are divided into three groups: the Law, the Prophets and the Writings. There were twenty-six books in the category of prophets: four designated as major prophets: Isaiah, Jeremiah, Ezekiel and Daniel. There were twelve designated as minor prophets, a title assigned by St. Augustine only because the books were smaller. These are: Obadiah, Joel, Jonah, Amos, Hosea, Micah, Zephaniah, Nahum, Habakkuk, Haggai, Zechariah and Malachi. These are in no way minor in the teachings they purport because they contain many major truths. Space does not permit a consideration of the books individually but a bit more is included in Appendix 17.

Basically, a prophet was considered a spokesperson and messenger of and for God. A prophet was a forth teller, an announcer of things to come. Some prophets were considered attackers of idolatry. Most of them had a keen sense of social justice. The language of the prophets was usually of gloom and doom, weal and woe yet most of them dealt in judgments and a hope for the future. Their advice and interpretation of events was sought by kings. They were king shakers, king makers and king breakers. Isaiah 6:1-6 will cast a bit of light on the role and life of a prophet.

Prophets had both a good and a tenuous life. Some were

treated quite well while others often felt the wrath of kings and priests. Prophets usually acted under tension of time and integrity. There was usually present in the life of the prophet a feeling of compulsion. His voice was that of personal consciousness. A prophet stood and still stands to be judged by that which he is prophesying. A prophet then reveals God to persons and persons to themselves.

Many false prophets through the centuries have come and gone and their prophecies have been buried with them. They have wilted and faded as flowers on a grave. Some false prophets have peddled cheap grace and sold it for a pittance while wrapped in easy merit. It is difficult for a false prophet to see his face which is behind a mask. Many of them spend too much time in the past rather than thinking of eternities. They want the world to think of the church as "their church" robed in garments of flowery rhetoric. They seem to "have a constipation of truth and a diarrhea of words." There is an insidiousness about their proclamations and they are rather weak-kneed doing obeisance to a flimsy self-righteousness.

Dwight E. Stevenson, in his book, *The False Prophet*, wrote these cutting words: "One of the most interesting—and most sinister—figure to appear within the story of the Bible is the false prophet. He moves across the pages of both Testaments. Sometimes he is a sulking figure darting through the shadows of back alleys, but more often he is comfortably lodged in a palace or temple, a well-known and fully accepted member of the religious establishment, dressed in the fine robes and faring sumptuously. He is detected with difficulty, if at all, and exposed infrequently."[1]

The false prophet is alive and well today. Many of them are more concerned with property, prosperity and public support than with being a true prophet with both tenderness and toughness. Some are so wrapped up within themselves as to be like a porcupine pricking themselves with their own needles. And the packages are quite small.

Jesus alerted his disciples to the danger of the "leaven of the Pharisees and Sadducees," "And when his disciples were come to the other side, they had forgotten to take bread. Then Jesus said unto them, Take heed and beware of the leaven of the Pharisees and of the Sadducees. And they reasoned among themselves, saying, It is because we have taken no bread. Which when Jesus perceived, he said unto them, O ye of little faith, why reason ye among yourselves, because ye have brought no bread? Do ye not yet understand, neither remember the five loaves of the five thousand, and how many baskets ye took up? Neither the seven loaves of the four thousand, and how many baskets ye took up? How is it that ye do not understand that I spake it not to you concerning bread, that ye should beware of the leaven of the Pharisees and of the Sadducees? Then understood they how that he bade them not beware of the leaven of bread, but of the doctrine of the Pharisees and of the Sadducees" (Matthew 16:5-12). Leaven was regarded in the law as symbolically impure. It is important to watch associations and affirmations. False prophets have a tendency to lull their listeners into a false sense of security because there is no solid foundation upon which the spiritual security would rest.

The present emphasis that is given to a false doctrine is that placed on "The Rapture."

In the last two decades of the 20th century there emerged a renewed interest in what has been called "the rapture." It seems that this interpretation of certain passages of the New Testament has come out of the theological mothballs and has been given an airing though books, videos and the movies. The books are more fictional than factual and the writing has a sensational flair born of imagination that causes the fiction to lean at times toward outright fabrication of scriptural passages.

The word "rapture" is not in the Bible. It comes from the Latin word "rapio" which means to snatch, to seize and carries at times an ecstasy of spirit which goes so far as to infer the removal from one place to another. There is a Greek word "harpazo" which carries the idea of being caught up. Philip was caught up by the Spirit after baptizing the eunuch and afterwards the eunuch went on his way rejoicing. Philip was then found later at Azotus and went on his way preaching until he came to Caesarea (Acts 8:39-40). Paul refers to being caught up into Paradise by the Spirit. He does not say whether it was a vision but he experienced ineffable things (see II Corinthians 12:2-5 and interpret it as you wish). Paul's language in his letter to the church in Thessalonica (I Thessalonians 4:17) requires a removal of the saints of the earth at the time of the Lord's return. These Scriptures do not suggest such actions as have been incorporated in books, videos and the movies in their portrayal of what they call the rapture.

In an issue of *The Nashville Banner*, about 15 years ago, which was then an evening newspaper now extinct, these words were in an advertisement paid "by born-again Christians."

> Yes, Jesus Christ might return very soon. If He does come September 11-13, 1988 for His Church, will you be able to return to heaven with Him or will you have to remain on earth and endure the Tribulation?

Well, Christ did not return on the date suggested so where are we now? Where is the Rapture?

A half-century or more ago Herbert Lockyer wrote a book, *The Rapture of the Saints*, in which he substituted the words "the Advent" instead of the rapture. He does not go into detail as to what will take place when Christ comes again. He speaks more as to the significance of His coming as the elements of hope consisting of desire, expectation and patience.

More recently two movies have been released detailing events which will occur when Christ comes again and "rapture his saints." In Margaret R. Miles' book, *Seeing and Believing*, she wrote: "Michael Tolkin, director of *The Rapture*, was a religion major at Middlebury College. He first conceived the film when he saw a bumper sticker that read: "Warning: in case of the rapture, this car will be unmanned." Subsequently he read of a woman killing her three children to send them to heaven. He made *The Rapture*, he said, to investigate the emotional state that might lead someone to such an act. Here, finally, is a film that presents religious belief and commitment as its explanatory thesis. Unfortunately, according to Tolkin, what religious commitment motivates is pathological compulsiveness and murder."[2]

These words may strike one as being a bit harsh and far-fetched but they seem to fit some of the modern writers fancy.

There came off the press in 1995 a book entitled, *Left Behind*, a novel of the earth's last days, written by Tim LaHaye and Jerry B. Jenkins, which has also been made into a movie. The book became immediately a best seller and the movie and videos have caught the attention of some church leaders. The press has been extravagant in praising the book and the movie. On the back of the book cover are these words regarding the rapture: "In one cataclysmic moment, millions around the globe disappear. Vehicles, suddenly unmanned, careen out of control. People are terror stricken as loved ones vanish before their eyes. In the midst of global chaos, airline captain Rayford Steele must search for his family for answers, for truth. As devastating as the disappearances have been, the darkest days may lie ahead."[3]

Only fictional imagination could have thought up such chaos. But whatever the case, the books have sold and the movie is popular even being shown in churches by paying a high fee to get the video.

One supposes that there might be an underlying motive of hoping to scare people into God's kingdom, but one cannot escape the belief that there was as much commercial motivation as religious motivation.

There are two passages in the New Testament which appear to provide a landing place for rapture devotees. They are the 24th chapter of Matthew and I Thessalonians 4:13-17.

Matthew chapter 24 is a pivotal passage in the rapture theory. The message given by Jesus occurred on Tuesday of Passover Week. His itinerary was leading him toward Jerusalem. In chapter 23 Jesus had harsh words for the Scribes, Pharisees and hypocrites. He accused them of killing the prophets and stoning those sent to the city. He wept over the city and predicted the destruction of the temple and the city. Most scholars believe his prediction came true in the destruction of the city in 70 A.D. by Titus. The seize lasted 134 days and the last days found utter destruction and the city in flames. Thousand were killed.

This prediction was made when Jesus was in the temple. From there he headed toward the Mount of Olives and in route his disciples asked him to show them the buildings of the temple: "Do you not see all these things? I tell you not one stone shall be left here upon another, that shall not be thrown down" (Matthew 24:2). As the disciples pressed Him to tell them when these occurrences would transpire, what would be the sign of his coming and the end of the age, he gave an interesting response. He cautioned them not to be deceived by false prophets claiming "I am the Christ" (v. 5). He stated that the gospel must be preached in all the world. He referred to the abomination of desolation which could be translated according to the Greek as "the abomination caused by the desolation" which apparently meant the destruction of Jerusalem. Next he touches on the coming of the Son of Man heralded by His angels and then gives the parable of the fig tree to illustrate his comments.

Jesus moved from the parable to speak to them in no uncertain terms that no one is certain of the time of His return save the Father and that they should beware of false leadership and stay watchful and busy. "Watch therefore, for you know neither the day or hour in which the Son of Man is coming" (Matthew 25:13). He skillfully dodged any reference to time, place and events that could be thought of as the rapture. The disciples thought he might give them a tip on this matter, but he did not. There were more important details to share with them. (Read

Matthew 25:31 to the end of the chapter.) His words in that connection were poignant, soul searching and provocative.

He did not satisfy their curiosity, nor does the Scripture satisfy man's present day curiosity about the future. They must, and we must, seek to avoid misconceptions and restrain our impatience and incur perpetual watchfulness and faithfulness.

He was not unkind to the disciples. He courteously responded to their inquiries and gave them many other things to think about and to do.

Every person in the world at His coming must be ready to give a self-accounting of both sins of omission and sins of commission.

His coming, therefore, will be sudden, unannounced, unpredictable and unrevealed. No greater concern is there than to be watchful and ready through faithful service to Him. Vain credulity is an enemy of true faith and true faith involves stern refusal to believe in falsehood.

Some writers claim that the rapture question is neglected by modern liberals. They also claim that it is the main area of dispute in conservative eschatology. If these statements are true then the rapture question seems to be on very shaky and uncertain ground. Yet there are those who claim that the passage in I Thessalonians 4:13-17 is enough ground to build a case on. They predict the church will be raptured, "caught up" to heaven when the Lord returns. If it could be established that such is true then it would become an important event for Christians to strongly and consistently pursue.

Most every one agrees that there are problems with detailing events related to the rapture. Since the word "rapture" does not appear in the Bible and more importantly, not in the New Testament, perhaps a close look at a sane interpretation of the Thessalonian passage would be helpful and very worthwhile.

Paul in that letter writes about the *parousia*, The Lord's return, in I Thessalonians 4:13 through 5:28. It is well to bear in mind that much of prophecy is symbolic. How, but we must try to distinguish between positive teachings of Christ's followers and their personal hopes, aspirations, and impressions coupled with their expectations. Paul seemed to say, "Let God's message which I have written to you always be that Jesus died and rose again and even so shall all the members of his body." Therefore, we should banish our fears and our sorrows for everyone living and dead will be taken care of according to God's plan of grace and redemption through Jesus Christ.

He was further trying to assure them that the tenants of the tomb would be in proper order of procedure and it would be done by the Lord himself.

To calm their concern and provide an inner tranquility for his friends, Paul wrote these clear, simple words: "Then we which are alive and remain shall be caught up together with them in the clouds, to meet the Lord in the air: and so shall we ever be with the Lord. Wherefore comfort one another with these words" (I Thessalonians 5:17-18). All will assemble together, the dead and the living.

Following that comforting statement Paul stated that no one knew the times or the seasons...it will "come as a thief in the night". So do not become so heavenly as to be of no earthly value for there is much that must be done. Next came a long list of things to be done by the members of the Thessalonian church. It is the longest list of duties recorded sequentially in the Bible. Here is the list (I Thessalonians 5:6-26).

- Watch and be sober (free from stupefying effects of self-indulgence and sin)
- Put on the breastplate of faith and love as a helmet of hope and salvation
- Comfort and edify one another
- Recognize those over you
- Be at peace among yourselves
- Warn the unruly: ones who leave their post of duty
- Comfort the feeble-minded, those despondent and weak in courage

- Support the weak
- Be patient toward all men
- See that none render evil for evil
- Follow that which is good, both among your selves, and to all men
- Rejoice evermore for that will eliminate fear
- Pray without ceasing
- In everything give thanks. This is the will of God.
- Quench not the Spirit
- Despise not prophesyings
- Prove all things
- Hold fast to that which is good
- Abstain from all appearance of evil
- May the God of peace sanctify you wholly
- Pray for us
- Greet one another with a holy kiss…

What a list!

The list is comprised of twenty-two different duties to be fulfilled in Christian service. How could there be any time left for trying to figure out the unknowns of Christ's return. There would be no time. An idle brain is the devil's workshop.

Isn't it a reasonable conjecture to conclude that Paul considered it more important to watch, pray and keep busy till Christ comes rather than trying to concoct a plan of events that would be associated with His return? (See Appendix 18.)

Augustine once said: "If nobody ask me about it, I know. If I want to explain it to somebody who asks me about it, I don't know."

Paschal put out a good thought: "One should be able to deny well, to doubt well and to believe well."

Eschatological certainty is hard to come by. Prophetic symbolism, fragmentation of unassailable facts and paucity of biblical clarity tend to nullify much of the sensationalism and commercialism associated with rapture books and movies.

People need to realize that their life in this world is going to end someday, either prior to Christ's return or at his return. If the return, being uncertain, is delayed for an extended period of time, those living today will grow old and die. Nothing then is more important than that a person give primary attention to his spiritual life and less attention to future earth destruction.

The fear created by imaginary occurrences at the Lord's return have a negative effect on the youth and weak Christians. Fear and faith have a hard time living together in a person's mind.

It is hard to become excited about a rapture that is obsessed with countless horrifying details that are terrifying to the reader and the viewer for little of substantive value is ever achieved.

Certainly the Lord will return. He said he would. Most assuredly He will come for his own. Judgment is inevitable. What gain is there in getting on a sidetrack or going off on a tangent theologically?

Christ's return is the goal of all believers. That is a part of our prayer: "Thy kingdom come, thy will be done." Even the Psalmist said: "My soul looketh for the Lord, more than watchmen look for the morning" (Psalm 130:6).

Jesus is the True Prophet, and interestingly enough he did not spend a large portion of his time dealing with future events. He tried to stretch the present horizons of his disciples and made them conscious of the fields already white unto harvest and of the many crying needs of society. He was an on-hands person.

One of the great evidences of the inspiration of the Bible is the way God moved good men to predict things to come and the remarkable way these predictions came true and were fulfilled. Many of the erroneous theories of today are based on what is claimed as unfulfilled prophecy. But as a matter of fact, have they not been fulfilled and man has failed to understand? Jesus affirmed "Think not that I am come to destroy the law, or the prophets: I am not come to destroy, but to fulfill" (Matthew

5:17). The serious question: Did He fail in His mission? The Christian cannot afford to say He did.

Matthew 11:13: "For all the prophets and the law prophesied until John." And Luke 16:16: "The law and the prophets were until John: since that time the kingdom of God is preached, and every man presseth into it." Jesus considered that in him the message of the prophets was fulfilled.

In Luke 18:31 He says: "Then he took unto him the twelve, and said unto them, Behold, we go up to Jerusalem, and all things that are written by the prophets concerning the Son of Man shall be accomplished." Following this statement in Luke 24:44 after His resurrection, He made a startling statement: "And he said unto them, These are the words which I spake unto you, while I was yet with you, that all things must be fulfilled, which were written in the law of Moses, and in the prophets, and in the psalms, concerning me." Verse 45: "Then opened he their understanding, that they might understand the Scriptures." In verses 46-47 we have the declaration of the death and the resurrection of Christ and that repentance and remission of sins should be preached to all nations.

Jesus as the true prophet tried to tell the world several new truths that would turn the world upside down to get it right side up. He indicated that grace means God has a "yes" face, and that salvation is taking a person from where that person did an about face to the old life in order to keep that one moving in the right direction. He created the epitome of what Elton Trueblood described in his book, *The Incendiary Fellowship.* Christ was a fire-bringer who came to start a fire in the lives of his followers which would shine brightly and lighten the world in darkness and sin. A single log doesn't give forth much heat or much light, thus the fellowship of others is a necessity. To quote Trueblood: "The actual incendiary result of Christ's death and resurrection as recorded in the New Testament is really very impressive. Whatever else we can say about the fellowship, it was certainly intense. Not only did it produce Pentecost with its 'tongues of fire,' it also led Christians that they accepted for a time, unlimited economic liability for one another."[4]

Matthew gave a very stirring account of the Triumphal Entry of Jesus into Jerusalem. The crowd was shouting, some putting their garments on the road while others cut branches and also put them on the street, as Jesus came riding a donkey. The city was stirred with many asking, "Who is this?" It is no surprise that the multitude responded, "This is Jesus, the prophet of Nazareth." Paradoxical as it may seem, time was very short before the temper and tone of the same crowd changed from excitement of his coming to Jerusalem to his death on the cruel cross. A mob of people can be very fickle as well as forthright. A good prophet had come out of Nazareth and he was finally getting his dues.

JESUS, OUR HIGH AND HOLY PRIEST

The ancient priesthood was a group authorized or ordained to perform special functions. They grew rapidly during the monarchy and were frequently found in great favor with the kings. They were never too buddy-buddy with the prophets, often lashing verbal swords. "Then Amaziah the priest of Bethel sent to Jeroboam king of Israel, saying, Amos hath conspired against thee in the midst of the house of Israel: the land is not able to bear all his words. For thus Amos saith, Jeroboam shall die by the sword, and Israel shall surely be led away captive out of their own land. Also Amaziah said unto Amos, O thou seer, go, flee thee away into the land of Judah, and there eat bread, and prophesy there" (Amos 7:10-12). In Israel the priests were set aside as "holy unto the Lord." There were levels of service and recognition among them. The great high priest was almost a sovereign. His duty of service to the people was symbolized on his breastplate on which was inscribed the names of the twelve tribes of Israel. Jesus as the Great High Priest never wore a garment with a breastplate with such an inscription for his wardrobe consisted of a meager robe.

Priests acted on behalf of the people as a mediator, intermediary, between man and God. They performed responsibilities at certain feasts and festivals. After the exile, they gained great prestige and power.

With the coming of Christ, who became our Great High Priest, the role of the priests diminished. The book of Hebrews gives a good description of the superior role of the priest as carried out by Jesus Christ. He is pictured as being superior to Angels, Moses, Joshua, Aaron and as one forever after the order of Melchisedec. "Who was faithful to him that appointed him, as also Moses was faithful in all his house" (Hebrews 2:3). "Seeing then that we have a great high priest, that is passed into the heavens, Jesus the Son of God, let us hold fast our profession" (Hebrews 4:14). "For every high priest taken from among men is ordained for men in things pertaining to God, that he may offer both gifts and sacrifices for sins" (Hebrews 5:1). "For the earth which drinketh in the rain that cometh oft upon it, and bringeth forth herbs meet for them by whom it is dressed, receiveth blessing from God" (Hebrews 5:7). "For this Melchisedec, king of Salem, priest of the most high God, who met Abraham returning from the slaughter of the kings, and blessed him" (Hebrews 7:1). "For he testifieth, Thou art a priest for ever after the order of Melchisedec" (Hebrews 7:17). "But this man, because he continueth ever, hath an unchangeable priesthood" (Hebrews 7:24). "Now of the things which we have spoken this is the sum: We have such an high priest, who is set on the right hand of the throne of the Majesty in the heavens" (Hebrews 8:1). "Now when these things were thus ordained, the priests went always into the first tabernacle, accomplishing the service of God" (Hebrews 8:6).

Jesus made the great sacrifice once and for all by the giving of himself. "It was therefore necessary that the patterns of things in the heavens should be purified with these; but the heavenly things themselves with better sacrifices than these" (Hebrews 9:23). "But this man, after he had offered one sacrifice for sins for ever, sat down on the right hand of God" (Hebrews 10:12). These eliminated further the offering of sacrifices. In this way he opened the door to the holiest place which had been restricted to the human great high priest. "But Christ being come an high priest of good things to come, by a greater and more perfect tabernacle, not made with hands, that is to say, not of this building" (Hebrews 9:11). "And for this cause he is the mediator of the new testament, that by means of death, for the redemption of the transgressions that were under the first testament, they which are called might receive the promise of eternal inheritance" (Hebrews 9:15). "For the law having a shadow of good things to come, and not the very image of the things, can never with those sacrifices which they offered year by year continually make the comers thereunto perfect" (Hebrews 10:1). We, as his redeemed followers, can enter the holiest place and "enter boldly into the throne of grace" (Hebrews 4:16).

We have the blessed privilege of offering up the sacrifice of praise: "By him therefore let us offer the sacrifice of praise to God continually, that is, the fruit of our lips giving thanks to his name" (Hebrews 14:15).

As a sure vindication of Jesus as the Great High Priest he made it possible for Christians to become priests. "Unto him that loved us, and washed us from our sins in his own blood, And hath made us kings and priests unto God and his Father; to him be glory and dominion for ever and ever" (Revelation 1:5b-6). As a result of all that Jesus as our High Priest did for us, we are to be bold, patient and steadfast putting our faith to work for him in his kingdom.

It must not be forgotten that Jesus was both prophet and priest and thus eliminated the tension between the two. There are still some religious groups who have priests functioning in special roles which are somewhat like "stacking the deck." The special privilege of going straight to Christ without any intermediary is an open door to the heart of God. Confession therefore can be made directly to the One who forgives sin. Every person who is a sinner saved by grace can become a saint and has no one to close the open door to the holy of holy and to hear the penitent's cry and praise.

TWO ORDINANCES: BAPTISM AND THE LORD'S SUPPER

There is nowhere any indication that Jesus was a "pack rat." He took very little with him on visits through the country-side and into the cities he visited: such as Bethlehem, Bethsaida, Caesarea, Cana, Capernaum, Chorazin, the Decapolis, Jericho, Sychar, etc. for he was a peripatetic, a walking preacher-teacher. There is no evidence of what things he might have had in a satchel. Nothing is said about any memorabilia or any auto-graphed notes or messages. Life and its belongings did not con-sume his intense desire to make known the primary things that constituted his mission. Did not any of the twelve have some treasured personal item? When asked about the importance of laws and commandments and which were the greatest, he men-tioned two: "And one of the scribes came, and having heard them reasoning together, and perceiving that he had answered them well, asked him, which is the first commandment of all? And Jesus answered him, the first of all the commandments is, Hear, O Israel; The Lord our God is one Lord: And thou shalt love the Lord thy God with all thy heart, and with all thy soul, and with all thy mind, and with all thy strength: this is the first commandment. And the second is like, namely this, Thou shalt love thy neighbour as thyself. There is none other command-ment greater than these" (Mark 12:28-31). No material reminders were ever mentioned by any of them. There are no sacred sights which he designated to be remembered by. The Garden Tomb in Jerusalem seems to be authentic but no cross or any part of it; no garments remain which were won by the sol-diers who gambled for them; no piece of furniture from the Nazareth carpenter shop. These things were not important to him. His mission was far larger than souvenir items. He was intent on leaving "footprints to glory in the sands of time."

He did set examples of two things which he desired of his followers: To share with him in the ordinance of baptism and the Lord's Supper. He identified his relationship with John's baptismal practice by submitting to him to be baptized in the Jordan River. This in itself was a symbolic act of significance. It did not follow any personal confession of faith or desire to join any group or church. Baptism today is an ordinance that redeemed persons voluntarily choose to participate in as an expression of salvation by grace through faith through a commitment as "Therefore we are buried with him by baptism into death: that like as Christ was raised up from the dead by the glory of the Father, even so we also should walk in newness of life" (Romans 6:4).

Jesus' submission to John in the act of baptism brought forth the descent of the heavenly Spirit of God, like a dove, and a voice from heaven saying, "This is my beloved Son, in whom I am well pleased" (Matthew 3:16-17).

Through the centuries since, and after the organization of the church(s) this ordinance has been observed. It is not a sacrament, only an ordinance. The word baptism comes from the Greek word, "baptizo" which means to immerse in water. The authority, which rests with the local church, is based on the practice and command of Jesus. The mode of baptism is by water immersion with the authority granted by a church. There is no Scripture which would substantiate the practice of infant baptism. That is, in part, why the baptism practiced by the church is called "believers baptism." Not all denominations follow the same belief and practice regarding baptism.

The Baptist denomination claims its rootage in John the Baptist and some adherents claim there has been an unbroken line of similar groups through the centuries. That cannot be proven since the groups were called at times "Separatists" and "Particular Baptists."

Today there are many varieties of Baptists; some say 57 varieties. They are organized into local associations, state conventions, southern and northern conventions and the Baptist World Alliance. They are committed to world mission efforts and are funded through a program called The Cooperative Program.

The basic beliefs of Baptists are these: salvation by grace through faith, believers' baptism, autonomy of the local church, every redeemed person is part of the priesthood of believers, separation of church and state with moral and ethical commitment to those values stemming from our Judeo-Christian faith with the Bible as the word of God. Various institutions, causes and programs are supported by their constituency. Some Baptists have a mind of their own and express it freely. They tend to be non-conformists, fighters for freedom to do their own thing. They have been known either to create a riot or a revolution. At times though an addlepated world has tried to corral them only to find that all the success they found was that they got their stamp on themselves. Baptists have given accolades to such men as James Madison, Patrick Henry, Thomas Jefferson and Roger Williams. Never take them lightly. Baptists have no creed but the Bible, yet there is a tendency today by some to insist that many of its servants, far and near, be forced to sign allegiance to what is called The Baptist Faith and Message. A goodly number of missionaries have returned from their God-called field of service because they have refused to sign such a statement. Because of this belief and demand the largest group of Baptists, The Southern Baptist Convention, is sharply divided into two camps, fundamentalists and moderates. Moderates see the fundamentalists as being in a power struggle, while the fundamentalists see the moderates as not believing the Bible as the inerrant, infallible word of God. It is a sad condition, one that shows a distorted, dispirited face to the world. Eventually they will see the error of their way and the two shall be one again.

The other ordinance, the Lord's Supper, was given to his disciples in an upper room "And he took the cup, and gave thanks, and said, Take this, and divide it among yourselves: For I say unto you, I will not drink of the fruit of the vine, until the kingdom of God shall come. And he took bread, and gave thanks, and brake it, and gave unto them, saying, This is my body which is given for you: this do in remembrance of me. Likewise also the cup after supper, saying, This cup is the new testament in my blood, which is shed for you" (Luke 22:17-20). This observance was to be repeated, "As oft as you do it." The elements used were bread, signifying his body, and wine, signifying his blood to be shed for the remission of sin. This reverent occasion has been called the "Eucharist," Communion, Breaking of Bread as well as The Lord's Supper. It is not an observance of the Jewish Passover meal, merely a remembrance occasion.

There are divergent theories regarding what and how to observe it. The first theory is called the "Transubstantiation." It is believed that when the priest blessed the elements they become the actual body and blood of Christ. This is a hard one to accept because the taste does not change nor the appearance either. The second theory is called "Consubstantiation." which carried the idea that bread and the wine have the actual presence of Christ within them, thus making the observance more realistic. This theory is difficult to support primarily because Jesus inferred nothing of that nature when he gave his command. It is questionable that Jesus ever intended or expected such heavy theories as these to enter the picture and thereby sidetrack the beautiful simplicity of his command. He said only "this do in remembrance of me," my sacrifice and your commitment to me in your taking of the bread and wine.

This was instituted by Christ on the evening before his death. That is significant. They were parting words. In essence he was saying "do not forget what I have done for you and for the world. As oft as you do it you will remind yourselves and others that I will come again."

Several ideas are conveyed in the repeating of the words,

"This do in remembrance of me." First, it was a ratification of the new covenant: I go but I will come again and I will not forsake you. Second, it is done as a memorial to him, precious because he instituted it and asked that we observe it to remember him. Third, actually before taking of the elements, the bread and wine, one should examine himself/herself. Self evaluation at such a reverent time is most worthwhile. Fourth, the elements are simple but they convey a serious sacrifice to be made: his death on the cross.

These three words comprise the symbolic ordinance: Remembrance, gratitude and recommitment. This is an ordinance to be observed by the church and it can be shared outside of the church by taking of the elements to a shut-in or those ill ones.

Someone once remarked that God gave us a memory so that we could have roses in December. Memories are the key tools in recalling the good things of the past and bringing back into the conscious mind those things which still have a freshness and relevancy. Kind deeds should be easier to remember than unhappy thoughts. Memories can be deceiving: Like remembering the Golden Rule but forgetting to put it into practice.

The beautiful symbolic act of the observance of the Lord's Supper should keep our hearts filled with gratitude and appreciation for the one remembered: The Prophet, High Priest and King from Nazareth.

Little things have oft thrown out the real significance in the observance of the supper. The use of the individual cup for the wine was a good replacement for the one cup. Before that transpired, some churches would wipe the cup from person to person. The author can recall a friend telling of being in a small, country church where several of the men chewed tobacco, which when emitted some of the juice would remain in their beards. Seeing the cup coming her way she pinched her less than a year old daughter to make her cry so she would have a legitimate reason to leave the sanctuary before the cup arrived. The individual cup affords the congregation the privilege of drinking the juice at the same time, making the observance more of a togetherness relationship.

The author likes very much to quote almost daily the following poem which serves as a remembrance of what God and his Son have done.

The Secret

I met God in the morning
     When my day was at its best,
And His presence came like sunrise,
     Like a glory in my breast.

All day long the Presence lingered,
     All day long He stayed with me,
And we sailed in perfect calmness
     O'er a very troubled sea.

Then I thought of other mornings,
     With a keen remorse of mind,
When I too had loosed the moorings,
     With the Presence left behind.

So I think I know the secret,
     Learned from many a troubled way:
You must seek Him in the morning
     If you want Him through the day!
          —Ralph Spaulding Cushman

THREE CROSSES

Three crosses stood on Calvary
Stark against the sky.
Roman soldiers laughed to see
Three ways a man may die.

Crosses still stand on Calvary
Stark against the sky,
And some still laugh to see
Men die . . . hear little children cry.

Who builds the cross on Calvary
Stark against the sky?
Who laughs at pain and want?
Can it be you—or I?
—Leila Avery Totherburger

CHAPTER VIII

FAREWELL DISCOURSE

THE ARREST AND TRIALS OF JESUS

In the Upper Room, just after the observance of The Supper, Jesus continued his Farewell Discourse which has been recorded in John's Gospel, chapters 14-17. Read chapter 14 which closes with the words, "Arise, let us go hence" (14:31). The discourse continued on the way to Gethsemane, which means "oil press." It closed with chapter 17 which is his Intercessory Prayer. Chapters 14-16 are designated as the heart of Christ. In them he speaks of himself as the way, the truth and the life as well as the vine. He told his disciples of the coming of the Comforter, the Holy Spirit, the Paraclete, who would be alongside of them.

His Intercessory Prayer was probably given on the street leading to the Garden of Gethsemane, located between the brook Kedron and the Mount of Olives. Upon entering the garden, it was late in the evening, he sat down a little way from his disciples (Peter, James and John) and asked them to watch and pray as he prayed three times: "Father, if it be possible let this cup pass from me" (Matthew 26:38-46). He found his disciples sleeping. In the early hours of the morning, as they were leaving the garden and while he yet addressed them "Lo, Judas, one of the twelve, came, and with him a great multitude with swords and staves, from the chief priests and elders of the people. Now he that betrayed him gave them a sign, saying, "Whomsoever I shall kiss, that same is he: hold him fast. And forthwith he came to Jesus, and said, Hail, master; and kissed him" (Matthew 26:47-49).

The kiss which Judas gave to Jesus was on the hand and not on the cheek, for if it had been on the cheek that would have been a sign of equality. Then, too, the pupil never kissed the teacher on the cheek. It was an act of betrayal of Judas' part for thirty pieces of silver. The other disciples seemed willing to fight for Jesus as shown by impetuous left-handed Peter as indicated by taking his sword and cutting off the right ear of Malchus, the servant of the high priest. Quickly Jesus told Peter to put up the sword for his kingdom was not one with a sword but one of love. Immediately Jesus was seized and bound and there followed six hasty trials all comprised of illegal conspiracies which were never meant to be fair, impartial or just. Of the six trials, three were ecclesiastical and three were civil trials. The Jews under the Roman rule could not condemn a person to death and could only have those cases of a religious nature. They could only give their assessment to a higher level of jurisdiction. Here are the disgraceful, illegal trials as to justice, truth and proper procedure.

The three ecclesiastical trials were as follows: The first trial was before Annas, an ex-high priest (John 18:12-14, 19, 23). Annas was the father-in-law of the then high priest, Caiaphas. This was a preliminary trial. Here nothing was accomplished. There was a bit of floundering and ineptness but enough feeling of freedom of action that Jesus was struck by the hand of an officer.

The second trial was hurriedly given by Caiaphas and the Sanhedrin at a very ungodly and illegal hour between a hastily gathered group around 3 to 4 A.M. It was on a Friday. All four of the Gospels gave an account of this trial but see Matthew 26:57-68. False witnesses, illegal in itself, were summoned to testify against Jesus. Even their testimonies did not agree one with the other. They spat on Jesus, nothing much worse than that of a person spitting on another. It was a vulgar religious meeting where they also mocked him and accused him of blasphemy. They claimed him to be worthy of death as the indignities, mockeries and insinuations multiplied by the minute.

It was between this trial and the next one that Peter on three occasions denied ever even knowing Jesus (Luke 22:56, 58-59). The crowing of the cock awakened his memory as it has awakened many memories through the centuries of those dwelling on a farm. So accurate was the sudden awareness of what Peter had done that he went out and wept bitterly. The tough old militant codger had had his heart pierced by the shrill crowing of the rooster.

The third ecclesiastical trial was before the Sanhedrin again, after dawn. One wonders just how efficient a sleepy Sanhedrin could handle such delicate matters for their weaknesses were obvious in their actions at this trial. With fuzzy minds they formally condemned Jesus. It was rather certain that two of the 70 were not present, Joseph of Arimathea and Nicodemus. Here Jesus was again subjected to mockery, abuse, anger and wrathful indignation. All of the actions, allegations and accusations were shot through with flagrant miscarriage of justice and fairness with truth absent.

"To understand what a farce this so-called trial before the Sanhedrin was we may note a few of the flagrant illegalities in it. (1) Jesus was arrested without a formal charge. (2) He was rushed to trial without an opportunity to defend his case. (3) They brought paid witnesses who bore false testimony. (4) They asked for no testimony in behalf of Jesus. (5) They put him on oath to condemn himself. (6) They allowed no discussion of the charge of blasphemy. (7) The time of meeting (before dawn) was illegal. (8) They had no authority to pronounce the sentence of death."[1]

The self-destruction of Judas had occurred. He could no longer live with himself and his act of betrayal and so he returned the thirty pieces of silver to the chief high priest and the elders (Matthew 27:3) and made a most remorseful statement to that group: "Then Judas, which had betrayed him, when he saw that he was condemned, repented himself, and brought again the thirty pieces of silver to the chief priests and elders, Saying, I have sinned in that I have betrayed the innocent blood. And they said, What is that to us? see thou to that. And he cast down the pieces of silver in the temple, and departed, and went and hanged himself. And the chief priests took the silver pieces, and said, It is not lawful for to put them into the treasury, because it is the price of blood. And they took counsel, and bought with them the potter's field, to bury strangers in. Wherefore that field was called, The field of blood, unto this day" (Matthew 27:3-8).

The three civil trials then took place. The first of the civil trials was before Pilate in Jerusalem. It was early Friday morning and three false claims were made before Pilate. He has perverted the nation. He has refused to pay taxes and he has set himself up as a king. These claims could touch a tender nerve in Pilate but he maintained his calm, having dealt many times with emotional Jews. Pilate said unto them "Take ye him, and judge him according to your law." They knew that they could not put him to death. It was not lawful. They were, however, very firm that Jesus should be put to death. Pilate called for Jesus to be brought to him and he asked Jesus, "Art thou the king of the Jews?" Jesus replied that his kingdom was not of this world. Pilate asked again if he was a king and Jesus answered that to this end was I born.

Since Pilate's primary interest was regarding the claimed kingship of Jesus, he thought it wise, since Jesus was from Galilee, to send him to King Herod Antipas. King Herod thought of Jesus as a quack, a showman, a stupid person unable to perform miracles and felt it not important enough for him to get embroiled in the matter so he sent Jesus back to Pilate. Jesus was mocked and robed in gorgeous apparel, itself an expression of humiliation and disrespect. From this time on Pilate and Herod became good friends: partners in a dastardly crime.

Since Herod did not want to have much to do with the Galilean he sent Jesus back to Pilate for the final trial. Now he was on Pilate's doorstep for disposal. The atmosphere was not good. There was a hell-bent mob waiting as a vulture to pounce upon a wounded carcass. Pilate was in no mood to argue with

the crowd for reason would be of little value. He began to look
for a loophole to shove Jesus through and get him off his hands.
It was customary to release a prisoner at the Feast of the
Passover so Pilate seized on this opportunity. Pilate trying to
salve his conscience took Jesus aside and sought some way to
release him but the raucous crowd was not disposed for anything
less than the elimination of the "trouble-maker" the Nazarene.
They even taunted Pilate by saying, "If thou let this man go,
thou art not Caesar's friend" (John 19:12). Pilate then offered
them a choice by asking which they would prefer that he release
Jesus or Joshua (Jesus) Barabbas, an insurrectionist, murderer
and a robber, a full-fledged criminal. The howling mob quickly
chose the release of Barabbas and so crucify Jesus. (See
Appendix 19.) What bad choices persons make under the influence of intoxication by the fervency of high-emotionalism. The
soldiers sensing the spirit of the crowd felt they had freedom to
whip Jesus with a whip of several thongs, putting stripes on his
back. But adding insult to injury and pain they pressed a purple
robe over his bleeding body and pressed a crown of thorns down
on his head. These actions were the epitome of an uncontrolled
crowd, bent on getting their pound of flesh. The die had been
cast for Jesus death, there was no further court of public appeal.
The civil trials were filled with multiple indignities just as were
the ecclesiastical trials.

These six trials brought to light many of the worst injustices, illegalities, and actions of man's inhumanity to man. The
trials pitted God's best in a struggle with man's worst. It brought
into clear focus the insatiable thirst of a mob for the blood of its
victim. It threw on the screen of the centuries (eternity) that
superior goodness founded on love is at times at the mercy of
inferior evil where the arena finds extreme action the order of
the day. Furthermore, in the final analysis through the resurrection of love, it was found "that truth crushed to the earth shall
rise again for the eternal years of God are hers. While error,
wounded, writhes in pain and dies among her worshippers."

(*The Battlefield* by William Cullen Bryant). Evil has continued to raise its head and run over quicksand while dancing on an earthquake.

Jesus, the Christ, built his spiritual prosperity on love while Joshua (Jesus) Barabbas built material prosperity on force. So all of the trials, the total proceedings constituted one of the most heinous, ridiculous and disgraceful legal farces and vagaries ever to appear in all of history.

THE VERDICT, THE CRUCIFIXION, THE CROSS

The trials were over, the verdict had been given after much persuasion of Pilate to do something to Jesus and not release him but release Barabbas. To the howling mob, Jesus was Public Enemy Number One. Three times Pilate tried to avoid giving in to their cries, "Crucify him, crucify him." Nothing else would appease them. They wanted the shedding of blood. So strong and fierce were the shouts that they won the day while Pilate in the final analysis threw his conscience into the hands of the mob.

Reason and truth do not rule a mob yelping and howling like dogs after their prey. Crucifixion called for a cross. (See Appendix 20.) There were three kinds of crosses in those days: one in the shape of a T, one in the shape of an X and one in the shape of a plus sign +. Jesus was nailed to the one the shape of the plus and it is interesting that a person who follows him, that person's life, plus the real significance of the cross, is greatly added to and made far more useful.

The Gospels do not tell where the wooden cross came from. Were crosses available nearby or had someone made this one and had it handy for immediate use? Romans would administer crucifixion on the cross but no Roman would be crucified for it was against their law. In order not to lose any time in carrying out their horrible act, Jesus was forced to bear his cross along with two criminals who had been assigned a like fate. Enroute to the hill of Golgotha, which was outside of the city wall of

Jerusalem, Jesus, having endured such strain, fell beneath the weight of his cross. A great crowd was watching and following closely and in the crowd was one from Africa, Simon from Cyrene, who was commanded to bear it for Jesus. The poet Countee Cullen has written a very provocative poem which follows.

Simon The Cyrenian Speaks

He never spoke a word to me,
    And yet He called my name,
He never gave a sign to me,
    And yet I knew and came.

At first I said, "I will not bear
    His cross upon my back;
He only seeks to place it there
    Because my skin is black."

But He was dying for a dream,
    And He was very weak,
And in His eyes there shone a gleam
    Men journey far to seek.

It was Himself my pity bought;
    I did for Christ alone
What all of Rome could not have wrought
    With bruise of lash or stone.

According to tradition the journey to Golgotha has been called the Via Dolorosa, The Way of the Cross. There were supposedly 14 "way-stations" where the cross touched the ground. These are interesting and be sure to see Appendix 21 where they are listed with brief comment. Here again much before the act some planning had been done for the Scripture says, "And Pilate wrote a title, and put it on the cross. And the writing was JESUS

OF NAZARETH THE KING OF THE JEWS." It was read by many and it was a trilingual inscription written in three languages: Greek, the language of the common people; Latin the language of Law; and Hebrew the language of Religion. This inscription by Pilate incensed the chief priest of the Jews who said to Pilate, "Write not, The King of the Jews, but that he said, I am King of the Jews" (John 19:19-21).

Pilate is to be commended for his response: "What I have written, I have written." The soldiers then proceeded to take his garments and made four parts so that each soldier would have a part and for the coat they cast lots (gambled) for it. It is an irony of the ages that at one of the most crucial moments in history people were gambling. (Still true, isn't it?) While Jesus was hanging on the cross the crowd railed on him saying, "If you be the King of the Jews, save yourself for that would help us to believe on you" (Matthew 27:42).

Jesus was hanging on the center cross, too good to live and the two on the outer crosses were too bad to live. Every person will die of something but Jesus died for something. The pain and agony on the cross was excruciating from the nails having been driven into his hands and feet and the flogging previously given him. In the midst of such suffering the Nazarene from Nazareth spoke seven different utterances:

THE SEVEN SAYINGS ON THE CROSS

1. Luke 23:34

   "Then said Jesus, Father, forgive them; for they know not what they do. And they parted his raiment, and cast lots."

2. Luke 23:43

   "And Jesus said unto him, Verily I say unto thee, Today shalt thou be with me in paradise."

3. John 19:26-27

   "When Jesus therefore saw his mother, and the disciple

standing by, whom he loved, he saith unto his mother, Woman, behold thy son! Then saith he to the disciple, Behold thy mother! And from that hour that disciple took her unto his own home."

4. Mark 15:34

"And at the ninth hour Jesus cried with a loud voice, saying, Eloi, Eloi, lama sabach-thani? which is, being interpreted, My God, My God, why hast thou forsaken me?"

5. John 19:28

"After this, Jesus knowing that all things were now accomplished, that the scripture might be fulfilled, saith, I thirst."

6. John 19:30

"When Jesus therefore had received the vinegar, he said, It is finished: and he bowed his head, and gave up the ghost."

7. Luke 23:46

"And when Jesus had cried with a loud voice, he said, Father, Into thy hands I commend my spirit: and having said thus, he gave up the ghost."

The painful, throbbing suffering on the cross had ended but the disrespectful crowd kept up the taunting, affronting mockery for a brief while until nature broke forth out of respect for the Lord of Creation in both audible and visual exclamations. There was darkness over the earth from noon until three p.m. which no man could bring to pass. This was a most revealing display of divine control and rejection of those who had shut their minds and removed integrity from the real facts. Following the darkness the veil of the temple was rent from top to bottom. No human hands did this. The holy of holies had been only for the high priest on certain occasions but now it was open to all believers in him who were now priests unto themselves. It also signaled the Day of Atonement which had been completed. That which had been concealed by the veil was now a clear pathway for all into the sanctuary of full redemption. "For Christ is not entered into the holy places made with hands, which are the figures of the true; but into heaven itself, now to appear in the presence of God for us: Nor yet that he should offer himself often, as the high priest entereth into the holy place every year with blood of others; For then must he often have suffered since the foundation of the world: but now once in the end of the world hath he appeared to put away sin by the sacrifice of himself" (Hebrews 9:24-26).

Next the earth cracked open as if a huge earth-cracker had broken it and the bodies of many of the saints who had fallen asleep came forth and entered into the holy city. This no man could do, crack open the tombs. The earth quaked and "quivered the timbers" of the city. These were the expressions of nature, in rebuke of the disrespect and closed hearts of those who would not heed Jesus' innocence.

Nature's display of unhappiness of man's consent to do away with Jesus had spoken elegantly and forthrightly. The soldiers, to make sure of his death, took a sword and pierced his side. The infamy and ignominy had erupted in full force. What else was there left to do to this sinless person too good to live? The conclusion was to take him from the cross and get him off their hands. The Jews had a law that the victims of crucifixion could not remain on the cross on their Sabbath day. At least some of their laws had to be obeyed but they stretched some of the laws as has been noted in the unjust trials. Herodotus was right: "Circumstances rule men, men do not rule circumstances." Aren't some laws to be broken for convenience and some must be rigidly obeyed? Joseph of Arimathea came and asked Pilate for the body. The request was granted. There came then another friend, Nicodemus, who was the one who had come to Jesus by night asking the way of eternal life, with about 100 pounds of myrrh and aloes and wrapped the body with burial cloth to place in a tomb which had been hewn in the rock and which belonged to Joseph. This was done and a large stone was rolled in front of the opening of the tomb. Everything seemed to be safely and securely taken care of, at least for the moment.

Not many persons hang around a burial tomb, other than to place flowers. In large cemeteries there is some stealing of flower baskets. Though much precaution had been taken in his burial there lingered much fear and anxiety among both the Romans and the Jews. As an extra-extra precaution a guard was stationed at the tomb. But the plan of God in Heaven exceeded the careful plans of the Jewish laws and the Roman government. There are always chinks in man's armor. When it was time for the divine clock to ring, the stone was rolled away. How did that happen? Who had failed at their post? Was the guard to be blamed? Had someone come and pushed the stone away? Who would want a dead body? But mystery of all mysteries a dead body was placed in the tomb but a newly resurrected body came out.

On the Sunday morning following his burial, still there with loving hearts, were Mary Magdalene and Mary, the mother of Jesus, watching and grieving. But again nature played its role at the command of God. There was another earthquake and an angel of the Lord descended from heaven and rolled away the stone and sat upon it as successful big-game hunters who have captured their prey will sit upon it as a token of victory. This account of the conquest over the sealed tomb was clear evidence that the glory belonged to God and not to man. Mankind was only a spectator in this grand drama and not a participant. The action which had transpired was out of man's reach.

Jesus' body was in the grave from late Friday afternoon until early Sunday morning. As the faithful group of women came early Sunday morning to the tomb, Mary Magdalene had run a bit ahead and when she reached the tomb she could hardly believe what she saw. An empty tomb! (Now read Mark 16:5-6).

The joy bells began to ring in the hearts of the women and his disciples, even though there was a heaping smidgen of "hanging around doubt." Occasionally the eyes blink and in the blinking perhaps something becomes a bit out of focus. But now at the dawning of the day as well as the dawning of eternal, divine truth Christ had risen. He was alive. Victory had mastered the tomb.

The good that had come out of Nazareth had now come out of death's chamber.

Things had been happening rapidly. The world was stunned. A man had come from the grave and had shaken off the grave clothes. His closest friends were excited but slow to spread the good news. Who would believe them? The Romans and Jews were also stunned. To downplay his resurrection from the tomb they sought to bribe the soldiers to falsify what they knew and had seen. The momentum was too swift to be trapped by tainted money. The witnesses had seen too much (Matthew 28:11-15). The news had gone too swiftly to push it into a nonsensical rumor.

The fact was: Christ had risen from the tomb unaided by any person or persons. Mysteries were fast emerging as facts. Christ had been seen. He had appeared to many and conversed with them.

Through the centuries the credibility has been questioned. Explanations and theories have arisen but still melt like snow in July. One theory held by some is the Swoon theory. It holds that Jesus never really died. He just fainted or became incapacitated, powerless and out of control of himself from strain and pain. Further, that when he was placed in the cool tomb he revived and recovered the use of his faculties. If that had been true, where were the guards?

A second weak explanation which "holds little water" is the account of claiming pure fraud. It holds that the disciple took him from the tomb and circulated a rumor as the guards were told to do and gladly became privy to this to have the heat taken off of them.

A third theory has been labeled "the mistake theory." This has rested on a supposition that the women went to an old deserted tomb and in their grief had lost a sense of direction. This, one of the weakest of the four theories, came out of desperation to nullify the truth. Those women were not stupid for they had been to the tomb on Saturday and Sunday and their judgment and memories were not dull.

The fourth theory, the "vision theory," is that the disciples were agitated and the women too emotional and both were in a state of hallucination. They had a vision in their minds that it had and possibly could have happened so they just changed their imagination into reality and perpetrated their conclusions. His followers were not guilty of deception. Time has taken care of that. They talked with him, ate with him and Jesus even invited Thomas to examine his hands and side.

The gospel writers appeared to be very decisive and clear about the physical appearances of Jesus among them after his personal, triumphal resurrection from the tomb. The writers have recorded eleven of these appearances; too numerous and too solid to have been "cooked up" for distribution. (See Appendix 22.)

The eleven appearances have been questioned as somewhat of a stacked deck, but there was then too much evidence to the contrary, and that evidence has not been proven false.

Years ago an eminent American jurist in the field of the Law of Evidence thought he could prove the weaknesses in the testimonies of those who claimed to have seen and fellowshipped with Jesus after the resurrection. His intentions were to write a book to share his findings and thus discredit what had been accepted. He studied the testimonies of those whom Jesus had appeared to and came to a conclusion entirely opposite from the initial position he had taken. He wrote his book but the theme was credible veracity of the biblical accounts.

The effects of the risen Lord upon the lives of his disciples changed their lives from timid, meek men into what one writer's book described their subsequent actions as *The March of Eleven Men*. They then became confident men, heads up, hearts aflame, with eagle-eyed expectancy. Their actions underscored again the truthfulness of the Bible which has been an anvil wearing out the critics hammers. They became bold, enthusiastic and totally committed. "They out lived, out loved and out died their contemporaries." Here is a quote from the book by Frank S. Mead: "Truly the Eleven Men had swept the scholarship of the most impregnable citadels of ancient learning to the floor of the cross of the Nazarene, and made it worship there. Christianity took prisoner the finest learning of Athens, Alexandria and Antioch." A "religion of slaves," forsooth! [2]

Paul, the great apostle of Christ, put unbelievable weight on the viability and validity of the cross. His fifteenth chapter of I Corinthians is a logical, polemical expression of the resurrection and the centrality in the kingdom of God as well as upon his preaching, his theology and his faith. "Now if Christ be preached that he rose from the dead, how say some among you that there is no resurrection of the dead? But if there be no resurrection of the dead, then is Christ not risen: And if Christ be not risen, then is our preaching vain, and your faith is also vain. Yea, and we are found false witnesses of God; because we have testified of God that he raised up Christ: whom he raised not up, if so be that the dead rise not. For if the dead rise not, then is not Christ raised: And if Christ be not raised, your faith is vain; ye are yet in your sins. Then they also which are fallen asleep in Christ are perished. If in this life only we have hope in Christ, we are of all men most miserable" (I Corinthians 15:12-19).

Paul made many statements in his writing about the power of the cross and its pivotal place in the doctrines of the Christian faith. To him it was simply no cross, no crown. "For the preaching of the cross is to them that perish foolishness; but unto us which are saved it is the power of God" (I Corinthians 1:18).

"But God forbid that I should glory, save in the cross of our Lord Jesus Christ, by whom the world is crucified unto me, and I unto the world" (Galatians 6:14). "And that he might reconcile both unto God in one body by the cross, having slain the enmity thereby" (Ephesians 2:16). "And, having made peace through the blood of his cross, by him to reconcile all things unto himself; by him, I say, whether they be things in earth, or things in heaven" (Colossians 1:20).

Christians today sing meaningful hymns about the cross, such as:

In The Cross of Christ I Glory
The Old Rugged Cross
The Way of the Cross Leads Home
When I Survey The Wondrous Cross
Beneath the Cross of Jesus

There is the story of the little lad who wandered so far from home in a great metropolitan city that he became frightened and greatly disturbed. A kind policeman approached the lad and inquired where he needed to go. He had, out of fear forgotten where he lived. After a few minutes of chatting with the officer he exclaimed, "Sir, there is in this city a hill with a cross on top of it. It is near my home. If you can take me there I can find my way home." Following the shadow of the cross is a good path to home.

There Is A Green Hill Far Away

There is a green hill far away,
Without a city wall,
Where the dear Lord was crucified,
Who died to save us all.

We may not know, we cannot tell
What pains He had to bear;

But we believe it was for us
He hung and suffered there.

He died that we might be forgiven,
He died to made us good,
That we might go at last to heaven,
Saved by His precious blood.

There was no other good enough
To pay the price of sin,
He only could unlock the gate
Of heaven and let us in.

Oh, dearly, dearly has He loved,
And we must love Him, too,
And trust in His redeeming blood,
And try His works to do.

—Cecil F. Alexander

THE ASCENSION

A perusal of all the recorded words that Jesus spoke in the period of forty days, from his resurrection to his ascension, revealed some of the thoughts and ideas which occupied Jesus' mind and heart. (These are fully recorded in Appendix 23.) A summary of those words was revealing and quite central to the completion of his ministry while on earth. Here are some of the words uttered:

- Rejoice
- Peace be to you
- Receive ye the Holy Spirit
- Follow me
- Go ye
- It is up to you

These commands added specifics as to the spiritual emphases and territory he wanted his disciples to cover: "But ye shall receive power, after that the Holy Ghost is come upon you: and ye shall be witnesses unto me both in Jerusalem, and in all Judea, and in Samaria, and unto the uttermost part of the earth" (Acts 1:8). No time was left for loafing on the part of his followers. The time was ripe and the journey uncertain but all could be assured of his presence. He had tacked these instructions on the door of their hearts for immediate attention.

These instructions called for much prayer, careful planning and courage to go on without him but they could fasten their faith in the leadership of the Holy Spirit. It was big business and it still is big business. It was more than just business as usual, it was unusual business. Momentum was moving and it must be kept moving. There was every indication of urgency in his words. He knew that his time with his disciples was short and he wanted to make sure that all of the signals were clear and instructions adequate.

Most of all he wanted the words, "Go, Go, Go" to keep ringing in their hearts. They were to enlist others to join the fellowship in the kingdom by coming into it through regeneration in Christ. They were to sow seed and tell all that "He is risen."

His last words were to be taken seriously. They were like a codicil to a will, not an afterthought but an over-looked thought. His resurrection had stunned the world but it had opened the eyes of doubters, and many were anxious to hear more.

For Jesus during these days the time kept getting shorter, the days busier, the items on his agenda kept getting longer, while some of his disciples grew impatient. Simon Peter grew a bit disillusioned that Jesus was not going to restore the kingdom to Israel and decided that he would take control of his life and go fishing. That was something he knew he could do. Other disciples said we will go with you. Seven of them fished all night and as luck would have it they had caught nothing. What a sad and defeated spirit possessed them as they came to shore in the early morning hours. So tired were they that when Jesus spoke to them they recognized him not. "Children, what have you caught?" he asked them. He gave them then four quick instructions:

- Cast your nets on the other side of the boat. They did and caught 153.
- Come and dine for he was cooking fish on the shore.
- Feed my sheep.
- Do you love me? If so, follow me.

For those present, and Peter especially, he asked three times if they loved him. Peter had denied his Lord three times. This was the third time he had shown himself to his disciples. And three times he told Peter to feed his sheep and tend the lambs. The Master had called them to be fishers of men and they could no longer, without him, even catch fish. With all of their knowledge of the lake, they were in need now of divine guidance. With their love for fishing, they needed to prove their love for the hungry sheep of the Great Shepherd. Jesus took nothing for granted in making sure that there was no misunderstanding about his plans, his need of them and the responsibilities incumbent upon them. The Nazarene was an expert in using words, former deeds and repetition in order to drive home his point. He wanted his followers to know that they could call on him, depend on him and that he would come to them if they would leave their personal desires and former labors and lock step with him.

He kept stressing that they would have great success in bringing men into the kingdom, provided they would carry forward their work under his direction.

His earthly life was coming to a close. He had come from heaven, descended to earth and now the time had arrived for him to ascend to his heavenly abode. His ascension was at hand. There are three meanings for the word "ascension." It means "to go up, to be taken up, and to go." He had predicted this event on several occasions.

"Let not your heart be troubled: ye believe in God, believe also in me. In my Father's house are many mansions: if it were not so, I would have told you. I go to prepare a place for you" (John 14:1-2). "But now I go my way to him that sent me; and none of you asketh me, Whither goest thou? But because I have said these things unto you, sorrow hath filled your heart. Nevertheless I tell you the truth; It is expedient for you that I go away: for if I go not away, the Comforter will not come unto you; but if I depart, I will send him unto you. And when he is come, he will reprove the world of sin, and of righteousness, and of judgment: Of sin, because they believe not on me; Of righteousness, because I go to my Father, and ye see me no more" (John 16:5-10). "After the Lord Jesus had spoken to them, he was taken up into heaven and he sat at the right hand of God. Then the disciples went out and preached everywhere, and the Lord worked with them and confirmed his word by the signs that accompanied it" (Mark 16:19-20—NIV).

Even though these passages indicated his return to his heavenly home, there was much work left for him to do for his followers while at the right hand of his Father. It would not be a pleasant thought to think what if he had gone away from his followers, leaving them to "root for themselves" The ascension was exaltation and glory for him. It meant redemption had been completed but the work as High Priest would go on. He had established his church while on earth but he would remain the life and Lord of it. He would be making intercession on behalf of his kingdom subjects. He would be their Advocate. His going away would signal the coming of the Holy Spirit. He would not forsake his promise, "Lo, I am with you always, even until the end of the world." He would continue to be ready to come again. He had completed his earthly task and was now free of its limitations. His parting gift was the gift of the Holy Spirit.

In the gospel of Luke there has been given a more vivid description of that ascension. It took place on Mt. Olivet between Jerusalem and Bethany. "And he led them out as far as to Bethany, and he lifted up his hands, and blessed them. And it came to pass, while he blessed them, he was parted from them, and carried up into heaven" (Luke 24:50-51). He was borne on a cloud, slowly and visibly before their eyes. It was in keeping with his spiritual nature that the last act he performed was blessing those who saw him depart. His entire life had been a blessing. His coming was a blessing. Could Nathaniel still ask of Philip, "Can any good thing come out of Nazareth?"

John in his gospel concluded with a remarkable statement, one that showed how much he had fallen in love with Jesus and just how much Jesus' life and deeds had been shared with him and others. "And there are also many other things which Jesus did, the which, if they should be written every one, I suppose that even the world itself, (25,000 miles in circumference) could not contain the books that should be written" (John 21:25). This is referring to the boundless richness and beauty of his teachings, his deeds and the totality of his life.

CHRIST AS REDEEMER AND SAVIOUR

Does Christ save you from your sin?
Call Him Saviour!

Does He free you from the slavery of your passions?
Call Him Redeemer!

Does He teach you as no one else has taught you?
Call Him Teacher?

—Howard S.Bliss

CHAPTER IX

HIS CHARACTER

THE MAJESTY AND STATELINESS
OF THE CHARACTER OF JESUS

The previous pages of this book have dealt with the person who came out of Nazareth at the age of thirty and spent most of the remaining three years of his life in ministry to others. That life has been and is the most active catalyst in the life of an individual in the formation of the highest spiritual character. The personal life and deeds of Jesus when studied, evaluated and applied are an inspiration to any individual.

The author now attempts to define what constituted the marvelous character of the Nazarene. Character is comprised of thoughts, actions, influences and relationships. The claims of Jesus as bread of life, water of life, way and truth are claims that must be verified. The available materials are sparse, yet we as followers of Him need to fall in love with his unparalleled, impeccable and sinless character.

Charles E. Jefferson was so impressed with the character of Jesus that he wrote a very worthwhile book entitled, *The Character of Jesus,* in which he dealt with twenty-three character traits which to him summarized the salient traits of Jesus. (See Appendix 24.) Anyone who tries to do justice to Jesus' character is faced with finiteness dealing with infinity, but the study will or at least can be very rewarding.

It is not trite to say about Jesus "never a man so spake," and it is then not trite to say "that never a man so lived." The character of Jesus, therefore, will be under the theme, "Never a man so------." It is in this manner that his character will be brought on the stage for viewing, hearing, consumption and emulation. The study in itself of such an impeccable character causes one to sit up in admiration; marveling at how such an achievement could be attained in the midst of those who tried to bring him down. He protected truth with a passion, without any trace of arrogance or pontifical verbiage. It is also in this study that hopefully a fire will be kindled within each reader. A burning heart will provide fuel for faith and put a glow on the face.

NEVER A MAN SO SPOKE

The world has produced many great speakers. Demosthenes of Ancient Greece was a famous orator and statesman and many through the centuries have graced a podium. The Western world has had Winston Churchill, Patrick Henry, Henry Grady, Abraham Lincoln and Billy Graham. They have used the spoken word with power as food for thought, solace for the soul and as an energizer for action. Words can have both positive and negative effects.

It is not easy to describe the components of a great speech as well as a great speaker. Some of the following are essential: the reputation of the speaker, the character of the speaker, content of the speech, skill in delivery, applicable relevancy and the mood and mission of the listeners.

Of all the great speakers, Jesus stands at the head of the list. Why is that so? It is because he spoke for God, he spoke with authority and he always knew more and spoke less. It has been said that a good speaker must stand up, speak up and shut up. Jesus knew these qualities. Additionally, he always spoke the truth; his speech was clean and pure, relevant and soul-searching to the hearers. "They heard him gladly" (Mark 12:37). That is with the exception of the Scribes and Pharisees who received a tongue-lashing for their hypocrisy and misplaced devotion (see Matthew 23). Not only did people hear and obey him but the wind and the waves responded to his commands.

The gospels speak of his uniqueness in speaking with people. "And they said one to another; Did not our heart burn within us, while he talked with us by the way, and while he opened to us the scriptures?" (Luke 24:32). "The officers answered, Never man spake like this man" (John 7:46). "And the people, when they knew it, followed him: and he received them, and spake unto them of the kingdom of God, and healed them that had need of healing" (Luke 9:11).

Whatever Jesus might have spoken, his life stood good for it. He was truth and spoke the truth in love. He was great in a one-on-one situation. In John 3:1-18 in which is recorded Christ's conversation with Nicodemus, there is a remarkable interview which showed the skills of the Master.

Nicodemus came to Jesus under the cover of night. He was a very inquisitive man, skilled in asking questions. He addressed Jesus in a complimentary manner "thou art a teacher come from God." He knew of the miracles Jesus had performed. Nicodemus was a Pharisee. He had to somehow protect his standing and dignity. His imperfect confession lacked genuineness. The rabbi from Nazareth had no certificate of authority. However, Jesus spoke directly to the heart of the matter: "Verily, verily, I say unto thee, Except a man be born of water and of the Spirit, he cannot enter into the kingdom of God" (John 3:3). "Born again?" asked Nicodemus. How could that be possible? Jesus left little room for Nicodemus to wander from the pivotal lesson. He told him there were two divine imperatives necessary for eternal life: "Marvel not that I said unto thee, Ye must be born again" (v. 7) and "as Moses lifted up the serpent in the wilderness, even so must the Son of man be lifted up" (v. 14). These two "musts" were hard morsels to swallow. But no one could slide into the kingdom, whether Jew or Gentile, without grace through Christ making it possible for them to begin life anew and thus share in the kingdom. The water signified a purifying factor while the spirit was an efficient principle of a new life.

Natural birth did not qualify one to be a member of a spiritual kingdom. Jesus then spoke of the wind as an illustration of the secret and mighty agent of grace working with the Holy

Spirit in regeneration. There then followed the important verse John 3:16: "For God so loved the world, that he gave his only begotten Son, that whosoever believeth in him should not perish, but have everlasting life." This went back to the work of redemption, its root source. The motive was the eternal love of God. The priceless gift was the giving of God's only Son. The blessed work of redemption would be continued forever.

This was very unusual talk. Nothing of its kind had been heard previously. The speaker was the Saviour. It was He who would make the supreme sacrifice on the cross. He looked at the Cross not as humiliation but as exaltation. It was the most tender revelation of his perfect love.

Never man so spake of his life, his love and his sacrifice as did Christ on this occasion. No man could duplicate his life. He was the original One, loving, giving and saving.

Never a Man So Lived

Jesus lived a full life even though he had little to go on materially. Things were not important to him for life was a sacred trust with stewardship obligations attached. His time on earth was the fulfillment of his Messianic mission and not an intermission from the right hand of his Father. He lived in two worlds at the same time. He was then not a vagabond or a tramp with no road map. He was in the world but not of the world.

He lived a stable life, a noble life and a tender emotional life, weeping on one occasion over the city of Jerusalem. He had a healthy body, an alert mind and a sensitive soul. His time was short here but he never strayed from a straight path. He took no detours to explore distant lands, no vacations and therefore he experienced no burnout. He was often agitated by the pesky Pharisees and Scribes. They could not "out fox him with their questions."

Jesus somehow was able to live a life of love in a world bloated with hate. There was never a negative thought about his past or one of fear and uncertainty about the future. He lived a right-side-up life in an upside down world. He had learned how to master his time and "fill the unforgiving minute with sixty seconds worth of distance run."

What are some of the qualities of living on the high side of the pathway of life? One is being in love with the job, or one's mission in life. In that way the stress is changed to being a blessing. Another is having a family, or associates, where there is mutual respect and shared responsibilities. A relationship with God is essential. These should be under-girded with a commitment of service to others and to God. Certainly Jesus experienced disappointments. The twelve disciples kept him well supplied. It took a heap of living for him to keep his legions of angels restrained so they would not interfere with the weight of his mission. Surely he was tempted to shuck it all and leave the world to enjoy its follies.

There is always danger in living. A lady who had taken her husband to the doctor, asked the doctor before leaving his office, "Doctor, is my husband in danger of dying?" "No," replied the doctor, "He is in danger of living." The danger in living is that all emphasis will be placed on making a living instead of making a life.

The public bent like reeds around Jesus, but they also sought to lasso him in order to get him to conform to their calloused culture and blurred hopes. He continued to stride across the hills and valleys of their lives changing stagnant swamps into fragrant rose gardens.

Jesus did not live a lonely life. He was not a homesick person, craving for the good old days. He lived joyfully in the midst of it all. Every cloud had a silver lining. One could come to the conclusion that Jesus was then at times somewhat reckless and out of sync. But the opposite is true. There was a clear sense of urgency about what he did. Several musts, divine imperatives, dominated his life. He was conscious of that urgency from the age of twelve when he responded to his parents who found him in the temple reasoning with the wise men.

"And he said unto them, How is it that ye sought me? wist ye not that I must be about my Father's business?" (Luke 2:49). "And he began to teach them, that the Son of man must suffer many things, and be rejected of the elders, and of the chief priests, and scribes, and be killed, and after three days rise again" (Mark 8:31). "And the gospel must first be published among all nations" (Mark 13:10). "And he said unto them, I must preach the kingdom of God to other cities also: for therefore was I sent" (Luke 4:43). "I must work the works of him that sent me, while it is day: the night cometh, when no man can work" (John 9:4). "And other sheep I have, which are not of this fold: them also I must bring, and they shall hear my voice; and there shall be one fold, and one shepherd" (John 10:16). These imperatives taught him that careless, wasted effort could never be re-cycled, recalled or reclaimed. He did not need top-billing to push him onward. With the cross and the critics looming before him in Jerusalem he marched right on into the city. "And they did not receive him, because his face was as though he would go to Jerusalem" (Luke 9:53).

So Jesus taught us how to live: with resolute purpose, with patience, with following the straight and narrow path, with urgency and with our faces pointed toward the new Jerusalem. He fulfilled the truth of a Chinese proverb: "Without the rocks, the stream would lose its song."

NEVER A MAN SO LOVED

Was not Jesus the world's greatest lover? He loved the world and all that was in it. He loved nature: the flowers, the birds, the streams and the people. The glories of nature and human nature caught his attention.

He loved even his enemies. Society has had a saying: "It is expected that there will be different opinions, disagreements but the two should disagree agreeably." That is not a bad statement but Jesus went further and instructed his followers to go deeper in such relationships. "Ye have heard that it hath been said, 'Thou shalt love thy neighbor, and hate thine enemy.' But I say unto you, Love your enemies, bless them that curse you, do good to them that hate you, and pray for them which despitefully use you, and persecute you; That ye may be the children of your Father which is in heaven: for he maketh his sun to rise on the evil and on the good, and sendeth rain on the just and on the unjust. For if ye love them which love you, what reward have ye? do not even the publicans the same? And if ye salute your brethren only, what do ye more than others? do not even the publicans so? Be ye therefore perfect, even as your Father which is in heaven is perfect" (Matthew 5:43-48).

The poor, the downcast and the sick caught his attention. He never shied away from lepers, even though leprosy was considered contagious. His love and sympathy went out to them. He responded to the hatred in life with love.

He loved children. They get on some persons nerves, but Jesus welcomed them. "Then were there brought unto him little children, that he should put his hands on them, and pray: and the disciples rebuked them. But Jesus said, Suffer little children, and forbid them not, to come unto me: for of such is the kingdom of heaven. And he laid his hands on them, and departed thence" (Matthew 19:13-15).

His love looked through a telescope while some people look through a microscope, hoping to find only what they are looking for. Jesus shared his love and that made both parties winners.

Henry Drumond, Scottish clergyman and author of the nineteenth century, wrote a book entitled, *The Greatest Thing in the World,* in which he equated the "greatest thing" to be love. The apostle Paul, one of the stalwart expounders of the Christian faith, wrote the outstanding description of love in the thirteenth chapter of First Corinthians in which he closed the chapter: "And now abideth faith, hope and love but the greatest of these is love."

John wrote while on the isle of Patmos (Revelation 1:5b-6) these beautiful words: "Unto him that loved us, and washed us from our sins in his own blood, And hath made us kings and priests unto God and his Father; to him be glory and dominion for ever and ever."

Jesus showed the quality and quantity of his love. He held nothing back. His love could not be hidden. In fact, he never tried to hide it.

Real love is the sharing of a part of one's self. It is possible to give without loving but one can't love without giving. This is how life's extras come about.

The love that Jesus showed to the world was unique, impartial and emotionally warm.

In June 2001, Fred Craddock, Professor emeritus in the School of Theology at Emory University in Atlanta, was a featured speaker at the Chautauqua in New York State. He asked this question: "God do you notice the difference between these two young ladies? One is from a privileged family, beautifully dressed, 16 years of age, and is greatly admired as she descends the circular stairway in an extremely well furnished home. The other is a 16 year-old young lady standing on the front porch of a one-room shack in a remote area with a baby clinging to her like a leech and no husband-father around. She has nothing to look forward to and nothing to hope for while the other girl had everything and much to look forward to in the days to come." The reply from God was that he did not see the difference. Is God getting old and senile? No, there is no preferential treatment with God.

> I know not where His islands lift
> Their fronded palms in air;
> I only know I cannot drift,
> Beyond his love and care.
> —Anonymous

There seems to be more joy than sadness in love but the loveliness in the character of Jesus never shone more brightly than when He wept over Jerusalem. "O Jerusalem, Jerusalem, thou that killest the prophets, and stonest them which are sent unto thee, how often would I have gathered thy children together, even as a hen gathereth her chickens under her wings, and ye would not! Behold, your house is left unto you desolate" (Matthew 23:37-38).

NEVER A MAN SO DIED

Jesus so lived, so loved and so died in order that we may love both life and death. He removed the veil between the two eternities. Or did Jesus really die or did he just come to earth from heaven and was he just lifted from earth again into heaven?

The Gospels spoke of his three days in a sealed tomb but he came forth from that tomb at the appointed time. His experience with death was a short period of time but he taught much about death so that the dread and bitterness of it was removed. He, however, died in infamy but he died with courage, love and forgiveness and to go on to prepare the place for those coming after him who have died in him through his saving grace.

Birth and death are linked together. As sure as there has been a birth there will be a corresponding death. Death has or will come to all who have been born. Death has become both a welcomed and an unwelcomed visitor. Most persons enjoy living and do not wish to die. There are those where illness and much suffering have caused some to wish to die. How could that be? The answer is: if death were denied, poor man would have lived in vain. But Jesus has made death a stepping stone to more beyond. There is now no reason to be morbid about death.

Jesus taught that the best is yet to be. He taught that there is a land that is fairer than day which by faith can be seen afar. He taught that death is a sleep with an awakening in a bright tomorrow. He taught that death came to see that our inheritance in Christ would come without any heavenly tax. He taught his followers that life is a comma not a period. Alfred Lord Tennyson caught what Christ taught when he wrote:

Crossing the Bar

> Sunset and evening star,
> And one clear call for me!
> And may there be no moaning
> of the bar,
> When I put out to sea............
>
> For tho' from out our bourne of
> time and place
> The flood may bear me far,
> I hope to see my Pilot face to face
> When I have crossed the bar.

Even though everyone has a rendezvous with death that is just heading home when the day is done. It is like the sun setting today and rising tomorrow upon some distant joyful shore.

Since life is short and death is inevitable there is no time to hate. There is only time to prepare for homecoming in Canaan's fair and happy land. So death is the beginning again that comes after parting. Death is the bedroom of the saints in Christ awaiting a summons to arise so that they can go with steady steps and sure. Baggage will not be a burden for as we came into the world bringing nothing with us we shall leave this world, regardless of our possessions, with empty hands. Only that which has been sent through love and service will be in our account. So death, then, is not departure, but arrival; not loss, but gain; not sleep but waking; not sunset but sunrise; not destruction, but expansion.

Here is a beautiful description of death.

I am standing upon the seashore. A ship at my side spreads her white sails to the morning breeze and starts for the blue ocean. She is an object of beauty and strength, and I stand and watch her until at length she hangs like a speck of white cloud just where the sea and sky come down to mingle with each other. Then someone at my side says, *There! She's gone.*

Gone where? Gone from my sight—that is all. She is just as large in mast and hull and spar as she was when she left my side, and just as able to bear her load of living freight to the place of destination. Her diminished size is in me, not in her; and just at the moment when someone at my side says,There! She's gone, there are other eyes watching her coming, and other voices ready to take up the glad shout, *There she comes!*

—Anonymous

This poem by Anna Barbauld has come to the rescue:

Life! I Know Not What Thou Art,

Life! I know not what thou art,
But know that thou and I must part;
And when, or how, or where we met
I own to me's a secret yet.

Life! we've been long together
Through pleasant and through cloudy weather:
'Tis hard to part when friends are dear—
Perhaps 'twill cost a sigh, a tear;
Then steal away; give little warning,
Choose thine own time;
Say not Good Night—but in some brighter clime
Bid me Good Morning.

NEVER A MAN SO TRUSTED

The trust which was so alive in the person of Jesus came from two sources: his great faith and the stimulation which came from an inner voice.

His trust in God was without comparison. There was no parallel in history. It was as if his trust was tethered to a pole, that being God, and he never went out of the circle of faith in God. It filled him with virile power and gave him a glorious radiance. Because of that his words ran and rippled with a glow as they permeated the Gospels.

The trust that Jesus had in God became a part of him at the age of twelve when he told his parents that he must be about his Father's business. It went on to become his consuming passion. There was an at-one-ness with God. He followed that God-consciousness throughout his life. He was motivated by a strong conviction that he must work the works of him who sent him into the world. "But Jesus answered them, My Father worketh hitherto, and I work" (John 5:17). "Then said they unto him, What shall we do, that we might work the works of God?" (John 6:28). "I must work the works of him that sent me, while it is day: the night cometh, when no man can work" (John 9:4). In the garden he prayed three times, "Not my will but thine be done." His will and that of God for his life were his major goals. Later as his days were drawing to a close he said, "Father, into thy hands I commend my spirit" (Luke 23:46). His voice was the voice of God as were his words the Father's words for his life.

The courage that Jesus showed amid the troubles he endured and the taunts and injustices of his trials were met by his faith in God. Every day he experienced God which went way beyond just an affirmation of God.

Trust in God does not lead one down a blind alley but it throws light upon life's pathway. This will result in vigorous, contagious buoyancy. Trusting in God also provided Christ with a fearlessness which caused others to tremble. Trust in God gave Jesus a solid foundation in a shaky world. It gave him a purpose and a will that "stirred up the gift of God that was within him."

On the surface it would seem that Jesus, being the Son of

God, would not be in need of further trust in God. The opposite, however, was true. He knew his Father and wanted to make the most of the trust God had placed in him. It was a reciprocal action delivered with love. He was proud of his Father and wanted his Father to be proud of him. They trusted each other supremely, confidently, and consistently.

Christ had a lot of faith and trust in man. He saw great potential in mankind. He identified himself with the human race and wanted to help lift it to a higher level. Man by being a creature of Almighty God had good stuff possibilities. Jesus, familiar with the ubiquitous tendency toward evil in every person's life, was dedicated and desirous of helping man to a higher plane by becoming man's friend.

He taught the world to pronounce the name "man" with a new reverence and a higher expectancy level. He saw the incredible worth of the human personality. He showed respect for the individual and instead of forcing his way across the threshold of a single person, but through compassion and concern, he was able to establish an at-one-ness with man. They learned to walk and talk together.

To him, man had been created in the image of God and that made it possible for him to establish a brotherhood with all men through the fatherhood of God. Man was not an orphan of the apes; he was not a tale told by an idiot, but was in apprehension like a brother.

He found a spark of divinity in man and sought to fan that spark into a bright flame. Maltbie B. Babcock's poem *Companionship* adds a new and brighter insight into this relationship.

Companionship

No distant Lord have I,
Loving afar to be
Made flesh for me, he cannot rest
Unless he rests in me.

Brother in joy and pain
    Bone of my bone was he,
Now-intimacy closer still,
    He dwells himself in me........

Ascended now to God,
    My witness there to be,
His witness here am I, because
    His Spirit dwells in me.

O glorious Son of God,
    Incarnate Deity,
I shall forever be with thee
    Because thou art with me.

NEVER A MAN SO TAUGHT

One strong aspect of Jesus' ministry and mission was that he came to teach that God was no dim abstraction, infinitely separated from the world. He came as one to ask the world to re-think about God. God was not a stern despot but rather a God of love. God did not want ritual and sacrifice nor pompous scrupulosity but that he was a God of mercy, grace, justice and humility.

Jesus was called "rabbi" several times. The words meant "teacher, master and the great one." He cautioned his disciples not to seek such a title (Matthew 23:7-8).

Jesus never wrote a book about his teachings. Where did he get his education? He had no certificate of teaching but he taught as one having authority. There was an unusual freshness about his teachings. The world was his classroom. He taught by precept, action and example. His major themes were simple, not of theological depth but more of a practical, pragmatic slant. Here are some of the meaningful principles he stressed:

- Love one another
- He who would be greatest among you let him be servant of all
- Bear ye one another's burdens
- If any compel you to go one mile, go with him two miles
- Give to him that asketh of thee
- To him that would borrow, turn not away
- If one smites thee on one cheek, turn the other cheek
- Don't cast thy pearls before swine
- God is a spirit; worship him in spirit and in truth
- Judge not that ye be not judged
- The kingdom of heaven is no longer tribal
- Pray without ceasing
- Ask and it shall be given to you
- Seek and ye shall find
- Knock and it shall be opened unto you
- And, of course, The Golden Rule

The list could go on and on. Is not such a list capable of giving one the spiritual intellectual itch? He was able to keep his thoughts and teachings from being fuzzy. There was no hint of an absent-minded professor in his make-up. One such individual told his class that a child should never be corrected or sharply directed. There should always be freedom so as not to produce inhibitions. One afternoon as he journeyed home he saw upon arrival his son putting footprints in the yet un-hardened concrete. Instantly the professor reacted. "Get out of that concrete you little so-and-so." A student perchance was coming that way and upon hearing what was transpiring he said, "O, professor never scolds a child." "That is when they are in the abstract, never when they are in the concrete," responded the professor.

Good teaching is an art. It should come from the heart as well as the mind. The writer's life was changed by the interest and love a teacher shared with him. So deeply did it penetrate his soul that even today, seventy-two years later the influence is still alive. Do not teachers teach more by what they are than by what they say? Teaching is not pouring in the information but planting seed in the mind and hearts of the students.

In biblical times it was usually the custom for pupils or learners to sit at the feet of the teacher. "Now it came to pass, as they went, that he entered into a certain village: and a certain woman named Martha received him into her house. And she had a sister called Mary, which also sat at Jesus' feet, and heard his word" (Luke 10:38-39).

In the book of Acts it is recorded that Peter in giving his defense before the rulers of the people and the elders of Israel was so forceful that the reaction of the hearers was thus reported: "Now when they saw the boldness of Peter and John, and perceived that they were unlearned and ignorant men, they marveled; and they took knowledge of them, that they had been with Jesus" (Acts 4:13). It has been said that a teacher affects eternity; he can never tell where his influence stops.

James A. Garfield, twentieth president of the United Sates, in an address at Williams College on December 28, 1871 said: "I am not willing that this discussion should close without mention of the value of a true teacher. Give me a log hut, with only one simple bench, Mark Hopkins on one end and I on the other, and you may have all the buildings, equipment and libraries."

NEVER A MAN SO
EXEMPLIFIED FORGIVENESS

Forgiveness was not a pagan virtue. It showed a weak-spirited person. Their laws called for an eye for an eye and a tooth for a tooth (Exodus 21:24). It was an act of revenge, of retaliation, a sort of vendetta. But Jesus saw things in a different light. He taught that in order to be forgiven one must forgive. "For if ye forgive men their trespasses, your heavenly Father will also forgive you; But if ye forgive not men their trespasses, neither will your Father forgive your trespasses" (Matthew 6:14-15). In other words forgiveness was predicated on forgiveness. However, forgiveness is not based on the number of times but the repentance of the offender and the grace of the offended one.

The Christian must always take the initiative in trying to bring restoration of the broken fellowship. The longer a broken fellowship remains unforgiven the harder is restoration possible. The big heart will put the offense aside.

Jesus taught specifically that forgiveness was to be sought and practiced. He lived that sort of life. When the woman taken in adultery was brought to Jesus, (John 8:3-11) Jesus put her situation in plain focus before the Scribes and Pharisees. They said the law as given by Moses said she should be stoned. Jesus replied: "He that is without sin among you, let him first cast a stone at her" (John 8:7b). The statement convicted the crowd in their own consciences and they departed the scene. Jesus then in a forgiving spirit told her to go and sin no more.

Jesus told Peter who posed the question, "Lord, how often shall my brother sin against me, and I forgive him? Up to seven times?" Jesus quickly responded: "I say not unto thee, until seven times: but, until seventy times seven" (Matthew 18:22). In other words, the sky is the limit. Jesus was urging his disciples to remove the cancerous offensive thought harbored in the heart and take action as soon as possible to set things straight.

Forgiveness was a duty, not something to toy with. That went far beyond the Old Testament where it seemed that the one asking for forgiveness was in the position of subserviency to another. Reconciliation called for immediate action. There was to be no limit to the repetitions of forgiveness. Forgiveness sought must be received or else there could be no sense of restoration.

The Talmud of Babylon put the limit of times to be forgiven at three but when forgiveness is in the spirit of love the limit becomes quite extensive.

The parable given by Jesus of the unforgiving servant in Matthew 18:21-35 spoke of a servant who begged his master to forgive the ten thousand talents owed to him. The master was moved with compassion and forgave the debt. The forgiven servant went out and found another servant who owed him a small amount, a hundred denarii, about seventeen dollars, and demanded that he pay him immediately. He could not but begged for forgiveness but was thrown into prison. The fellow servants conveyed this action to the master who upon hearing of what had happened delivered the wicked servant to the torturers until he paid.

Forgiveness should be accompanied by compassion of the heart for it to be real. There should also be deep sorrow. Just to verbalize and say "I forgive you" is not adequate.

There are two passages in the Bible which seemed to limit God's forgiveness. "Wherefore I say unto you, all manner of sin and blasphemy shall be forgiven unto men: but the blasphemy against the Holy Ghost shall not be forgiven unto men. And whosoever speaketh a word against the Son of man, it shall be forgiven him: but whosoever speaketh against the Holy Ghost, it shall not be forgiven him, neither in this world, neither in the world to come" (Matthew 12:31-32). "This is he that came by water and blood, even Jesus Christ; not by water only, but by water and blood. And it is the Spirit that beareth witness, because the Spirit is truth" (I John 5:6). These somewhat narrow the scope of forgiveness which showed that forgiveness is a serious matter.

Christ while suffering on the cross prayed, "Father, forgive them for they know not what they do" (Luke 23:34). This was forgiveness and compassion at the highest level.

The writer once had a fellow student who spit on him, refusing to take a dare from another student. For years that act rankled in his heart. He tried to think of how he could get revenge. One day on the basketball court he saw the culprit dribbling down the floor. He stuck out his foot and tripped the one who had spit on him. Did he get even? No!

NEVER A MAN
SO WELL BALANCED

They tried to trap Jesus with questions, but they could not succeed. They tried to lasso him by pushing him into hasty words or an unrighteous mood but to no avail. He never lost his mental alertness or his moral footing. He was so poised, so even-tempered, except when he drove the money changers out of the temple. He was courageous but never reckless.

Jesus was well aware of what extremism in mind, body and soul would create. He was pious but never sanctimonious. He knew that being emotionally extreme could go into hysteria and some types of religion could become superstitious, and far-out. In the midst of storms, he remained calm and poised. He kept his eyes focused on his Messianic mission and did not let his imagination run wild. He knew how to balance self-assurance with humility. He could be both liberal and narrow.

Two familiar hymns of the Christian church illustrate different character qualities in Jesus' life that clearly point to how well balanced he was on every occasion.

The hymn by Dorothy Thrupp, Saviour Like a Shepherd Lead Us, depicts Jesus as a gentle person.

> Saviour like a shepherd lead us
> Much we need thy tender care;
> In Thy pleasant pastures feed us,
> For our use thy folds prepare:
> Blessed Jesus, Blessed Jesus,
> Thou hast bought us thine we are.

The other hymn which shows the other characteristic of Jesus is the one written by Ernest Shurtleff entitled, Lead On, O King Eternal.

Lead on, O King Eternal,
The day of march has come;
Henceforth in fields of conquest
Thy tents shall be our home:
Through days of preparation
Thy grace has made us strong,
And now, O King Eternal,
We lift our battle song.

The Tender Shepherd on the one hand and the Eternal King going forth to war called for a well balanced person to be able to assume both roles.

The Scribes and the Pharisees were ever trying to trap Jesus with loaded questions. The Ten Commandments were precious to them. Moses had brought them down from the mountain and they formed the foundation for their moral structure. Each of the commandments was important and of equal weight. So the question that was asked of Jesus: "Which is the greatest of the Commandments?" (Mark 12:28) he answered: "The first of all the commandments is 'Hear, O Israel; The Lord our God is one Lord: and thou shalt love the Lord thy God with all thy heart, and with all thy soul, and with all thy mind, and with all thy strength: this is the first commandment. And the second is like, namely this, 'Thou shalt love thy neighbor as thyself.' There is none other commandment greater than these" (Mark 12:29-31).

Once again he was able to keep his balance and to throw off his adversaries. The Gospel of Mark indicated that the question just posed to Jesus put the Scribes at ease for he wrote these words "And no man after that dared ask him any question" (Mark 12:34). The use of the word "dared" indicated that those asking the question figured they had had enough and they could gain no advantage in that manner. Jesus never let his guard down. He could brush off the questions with ease. But even though the Scribes left off pounding Jesus with questions his disciples took up the slack. Peter, James, John and Andrew thought they might, in private, get a good question answered and that would put them more knowledgeable than the other disciples. Their question was one concerning the end of the age and the sign of the times. Jesus gave a lengthy answer to that question which is recorded in Mark 13:5-37. He told them that no one knew saved the Father and they should "Take ye heed, watch and pray" (Mark 13:33). "And what I say to you, I say unto all, Watch" (v. 37).

Never did Jesus' equilibrium depart from him. He was solid on his feet, clear in his thinking and sure of his answers. People could feel the throbbing of his heart, but he never became hysterical. His enemies tried the use of dilemma thinking they would catch him on one horn or the other but here they failed again. Their efforts were like trying to catch a shadow but to no avail. In order to convict him, they had to do it with a trumped-up lie.

NEVER A MAN
SO FILLED WITH THE HOLY SPIRIT

The spiritual world has been described as having been of three segments: The time when God was central, the era of Christ, and the time when the Holy Spirit was dominant, which includes the present. Jesus Christ was steeped in the Spirit and rejoiced throughout his life with his association with the Spirit. He had the Spirit of God without measure.

At the beginning of his ministry Jesus said, "The Spirit of the Lord is upon Me, because he has anointed Me" (Luke 4:18) which was in fulfillment of the prophecy of Isaiah 1:1-2. Other Scripture verses have spoken of this anointing: "And the spirit of the Lord shall rest upon him, the spirit of wisdom and understanding, the spirit of counsel and might, the spirit of knowledge and of the fear of the Lord" (Isaiah 11:2); "And John bare record, saying, I saw the Spirit descending from heaven like a dove, and it abode upon him" (John 1:32); "How God anointed Jesus of Nazareth with the Holy Ghost and with power: who went about doing good, and healing all that were oppressed of the devil; for God was with him" (Acts 10:38). The Holy Spirit took part in his birth, "And the angel answered and said unto her, The Holy Ghost shall come upon thee, and the power of the Highest shall overshadow thee: therefore also that holy thing which shall be born of thee shall be called the Son of God" (Luke 1:35); at his baptism, "And the Holy Ghost descended in a bodily shape like a dove upon him, and a voice came from heaven, which said, Thou art my beloved Son; in thee I am well pleased" (Luke 3:22); during his temptations in the wilderness, "Then was Jesus led up of the Spirit into the wilderness to be tempted of the devil" (Matthew 4:1) and during his public ministry, "And Jesus returned in the power of the Spirit into Galilee: and there went out a fame of him through all the region round about" (Luke 4:14).

Since this present age is the age of the Holy Spirit the author has chosen to designate the work of the Holy Spirit as that of a Helper, a cheer-leader, who is ever present to urge the Christian on and on. During the presence of the Holy Spirit in the life of a Christian that life can produce fruit. "But the fruit of the Spirit is love, joy, peace, long-suffering, gentleness, goodness, faith, meekness, temperance: against such there is no law" (Galatians 5:22-23).

The work of the Holy Spirit is of a great variety. It guides, comforts, empowers, teaches, awakens, infills, quickens, unites, sanctifies and will convict the world of righteousness, good and evil. It is the Spirit of discernment and it knows the mind of man and the mind of God. Charles Haddon Spurgeon, prince of English Baptist preachers of the nineteenth century said: "If we have not the Spirit which Jesus promised we cannot perform the commission which Jesus gave."

The Apostle John wrote pointedly about the Holy Spirit which has been preserved for us in chapters 14-17 of his Gospel.

In a small sense the Holy Spirit was the counterpart of the Sermon on the Mount. In the Sermon on the Mount the law of the kingdom was expounded while the Spirit is the means of the realization of the kingdom for now the kingdom has become the kingdom of the Spirit.

The work of the Holy Spirit in the life of the Christian has been described in John 14:17 and John 16:5-15. Such work of the Spirit has been done through empowering those who seek its presence. The Spirit has at times come as a dove, with quickening power. It has been called "the breath of God." Christians have sung about this Spirit with words like these: "fill me with life anew, until my heart is pure and I am wholly Thine."

Jesus spoke very clearly and strongly that no one should speak against the Spirit. Paul in his letter to the church at Ephesus cautioned the members not to grieve the Holy Spirit. "And grieve not the Holy Spirit of God, whereby ye are sealed unto the day of redemption" (Ephesians 4:30).

Jesus and the Holy Spirit were fellow workers. Each helped the other. Jesus' favorite title for the Holy Spirit was "Helper." He felt good about the coming of the Holy Spirit and its manifestation of power was in evidence on the day of Pentecost. Christians today are doubly blessed. They have Jesus as Saviour who maketh intercessions for them and they have also the Holy Spirit who does likewise.

NEVER A MAN
SO PERSONIFIED GOD

Could any man ever personify God? Yes, only the God-man, Christ Jesus, could so represent God. John in his gospel described Jesus as the express image of the Father. The likeness was obvious. There is a likeness in family members. Frequently the son looks like the father, the daughter like the mother.

The writer recalls an experience in a Baptist church in Rome, Italy some fifty-five years ago. The Italian pastor, after greeting our party, said, "You look so familiar to me. Where have we seen each other before? Well, we haven't I guess, but we are brothers and sisters in Christ and that is why you look familiar."

Jesus' disciples responded to his question as to who he was:

"Some say that thou art John the Baptist: some, Elijah; and others, Jeremiah, or one of the prophets. He saith unto them, But whom say ye that I am? And Simon Peter answered and said, Thou art the Christ, the Son of the living God. And Jesus answered and said unto him, Blessed art thou, Simon Barjona: for flesh and blood hath not revealed it unto thee, but my Father which is in heaven" (Matthew 16:14-17).

The big question is how did Peter come to this conclusion? The disciples did not begin their ministry with a doctrine about the person of Christ. It did not then come about through a process of reasoning but was a consequence of the fellowship of being in the presence of Jesus. They began to follow him, to see his miraculous healing power, to hear his wonderful teaching and to work side by side with him and all of that produced a knowing of him as God's Son. It was impossible to be in the presence of Jesus without seeing how he personified his Father, God.

Jesus was somebody special. One would stand amazed in his presence for it would be a never to be forgotten experience. There radiated from his face, his spirit and his gentleness a warm and affectionate feeling. There was also an aura about him.

Bernard of Clairvaux wrote a hymn in the twelfth century, *Jesus, the Very Thought of Thee,* that caught the true spirit of Jesus as the personification of God.

> Jesus the very thought of Thee
> With sweetness fills my breast;
> But sweeter still to see Thy face
> And in Thy presence rest.

The call comes today to every Christian to personify Christ which in turn personifies God. The opportunities abound. One cannot personify Christ just by wearing a false mask, supported by pious sounding words. Facial expressions are rooted in the heart. An evil heart cannot bring forth good facial features or well chosen words. The heart, soul and mind work together and cannot be completely isolated the one from the other.

The earliest disciples focused on his divineness not on his humanity for they saw in their leader something that man alone could not provide. When they saw Jesus, they realized that he personified their deepest thoughts about God. It was hard for them to think about Jesus without thinking about God and was just as hard for them to think about God without thinking about Jesus. One was a divine portraiture of the other.

Cleland McAfee wrote a heart warming hymn, *Near to the Heart of God*, which indicated that Christ personified his Father by being near to God's heart.

> There is a place of quiet rest,
> Near to the heart of God,
> A place where sin cannot molest,
> Near to the heart of God.
> O Jesus, blest Redeemer,
> Sent from the heart of God,
> Hold us who wait before Thee
> Near to the Heart of God.

Through Jesus divine love burned most brightly and warmly. To look at Jesus was to heighten one's consciousness of God. And so the early followers of the Nazarene set out to tell the good news which came out of Nazareth that Jesus was the Way, the Truth and the Life. He was the incarnate Son of God treading the highways of Palestine introducing himself and his Father to the world. He tried to act like God for he told his disciples that if they had seen and known him they had fellowshipped with the Father. He did not try to elevate himself in their presence but he did personify God so that men would fall more in love with God. We as Christians are to let others see Jesus in our lives. This is how we try to personify Christ to the world.

NEVER A MAN
SO LEARNED OBEDIENCE THROUGH SUFFERING

There is a saying, "No pain, no gain." Many of the things learned through pain produce a lasting gain. Children learn through pain. A parent may tell a child all day long not to touch something hot, but the child must experience the pain of touching something hot. Cut fingers come most of the time with disobedience when a child is playing with a knife having been told not to fondle a knife.

Well does this writer remember the pain that came to him in his early teens when he disobeyed his father. He was cautioned by his father to stop throwing a ball against the front of the house because he could easily break a window. He tried to assure his father that he would be careful, but father knew best. Shortly, in the absence of his father, the ball went right through a large front window. When his father came out of the field at lunch he saw the broken window. It did not take the father long to punish his errant son. The punishment was sufficient that the son became a believer in his father's admonitions.

In John's gospel (6:60f), after a teaching session of Jesus in the synagogue, many of his disciples spoke of his teaching as "a hard saying, who can understand it?" Jesus tried to explain what he had said but from that time many of his disciples went back and walked with him no more (v. 66). The weakness of those who turned back certainly grieved Jesus.

The betrayal by Judas was a painful experience for Jesus. He had been one of the twelve, close to Jesus. In the garden just prior to the betrayal Jesus had prayed three times if it was possible let the cup of suffering pass from him. So severe was he agonizing in prayer "His sweat was as it were great drops of blood falling down to the ground" (Luke 22:44).

The writer of the book of Hebrews spoke of the reward which comes to those who endure the pain and suffering in running the race of life. "Wherefore seeing we also are compassed about with so great a cloud of witnesses, let us lay aside every weight, and the sin which doth so easily beset us, and let us run with patience the race that is set before us, looking unto Jesus the author and finisher of our faith; who for the joy that was set before him endured the cross, despising the shame, and is set down at the right hand of the throne of God" (Hebrews 12:1-2). The life of Jesus was a prime example of endurance in suffering for the crown which is in reserve for those who willingly pay the price of humiliation and suffering. This was the joy that was set before him. This led to his place at the right hand of the throne of God. The feeling that comes after the pain is one that compensates for the suffering.

The great prize before Jesus who endured the cross brought joy in the endurance. No one would dispute the suffering he endured on the cross, but that cross provided grace and salvation from sin for the believer. Twice Jesus spoke of the value of enduring to the end. One of the times was when he sent his disciples out for service and the other was when he was speaking of the end of time and the end of the age (Matthew 10:22 and 24:13).

Endurance is a spiritual virtue. God made Abraham a promise which called for endurance. "For when God made promise to Abraham, because he could swear by no greater, he sware by himself, saying, Surely blessing I will bless thee, and multiplying I will multiply thee. And so, after he had patiently endured, he obtained the promise" (Hebrews 6:13-15). The following quotation presents clear statement of how endurance is at times a part of God's response to prayer.

> I asked for strength that I might achieve;
> He made me weak that I might obey.
> I asked for health that I might do greater things;
> I was given grace that I might do better things.
> I asked for riches that I might be happy;
> I was given poverty that I might be wise.

I asked for power that I might have the praise of men;
   I was given weakness that I might feel the need of God.
I asked for all things that I might enjoy life;
   I was given life that I might enjoy all things.
I received nothing that I asked for; all that I hoped for,
   My prayer was answered.

                                        —Author unknown

Ponder these words by Longfellow:

   Only those are crowned and sainted
   Who with grief have been acquainted.

NEVER A MAN
SO PROCLAIMED HUMAN VALUES

Jesus was well aware that all which glitters is not gold and the supreme values in life are not material. He was in the towns of Caesarea Philippi with his disciples and a crowd that had also gathered when he spoke of the cost of following him. "Whosoever will come after me, let him deny himself, and take up his cross, and follow me. For whosoever will save his life shall lose it; but whosoever shall lose his life for my sake and the gospel's, the same shall save it. For what shall it profit a man, if he shall gain the whole world, and lose his own soul? Or what shall a man give in exchange for his soul?" (Mark 8:34-37). This admonition pointed out what things are valuable in life and they must establish some priorities of moral and ethical implications. Those values would naturally fall under such themes as freedom, justice, equality, brotherhood of all, preciousness of the human soul and the elevation of women who long dreamed of a better world. Somewhat more specifically the list would include rejection of compromise, integrity, avoidance of covetousness, do not steal, and do not kill.

   Jesus carried other values to a higher level, those that would be of the heart. Official holiness on the part of priests, Levites and the established religion did not insure the practice of spiritual values, which called for service from the heart. There are two biblical stories which underscore Christ's conception of those values. The first is the Parable of the Good Samaritan (Luke 10:25-37) and the other is the story of the rich man and Lazarus (Luke 16:19-31).

In the familiar parable of The Good Samaritan one is introduced to racial repugnance, the laxity of the pious priests and the casualness of the Levite. As the story goes a good man was going down from Jerusalem to Jericho and fell among thieves. He was robbed and beaten. Jericho was known as the city of priests. It was then not unusual for priests to travel that way. Priests were not as likely to be robbed and beaten as much as a common citizen. The poor man lay suffering on the side of the road obviously not able to walk alone. When a certain priest came by he saw the injured man on the other side of the road but gave only a glance at him and passed on. Perhaps in a hurry. Shortly a Levite of the priestly class also came upon the scene and he crossed over, took a good look and scampered back to the other side and walked on.

A Samaritan who was not very highly regarded by the Jews came upon the scene. He was of little recognition by the Jewish priests as well as by the general public. A Samaritan was a descendant of the inter-marriage of a Jew and a person from Babylon. Thus a Samaritan was of mixed origin. The Samaritan was not expected to do much for the suffering man. But the heart of the Samaritan was bigger than that of the official religious establishment. He not only bound up the wounds but took his new found friend to an inn and promised to pay any charges for the care of the wounded man when he returned.

The other account of the sensitivity of Jesus was revealed in the story of the rich man and Lazarus. In this story there are two totally different lines of experience. On the one hand there was the sensuality and luxury of the rich man with whom pomp and circumstance got his major attention. Lazarus, the poor man, was in much pain for he had suffered many maladies causing his body to be covered with sores. His poverty prevented him from having any sort of medical attention. He placed himself near the rich man's residence hoping to attract his attention and thereby possibly receive some help. But it all didn't work that way. Both men die and both received their just reward: the rich man punishment and torment and Lazarus in peace and comfort. Quite a switch. For real spiritual values to exist there must be a sensitive heart and active immediate service.

No doubt the apostle Paul thought about the highest values which should characterize the Christian. He wrote to his dear friends in Philippi these words: "Finally, brethren, whatsoever things are true, whatsoever things are honest, whatsoever things are just, whatsoever things are pure, whatsoever things are lovely, whatsoever things are of good report; if there be any virtue, and if there be any praise, think on these things" (Philippians 4:8). He stressed that those values should be a life long challenge for this was the goal of the called of God in Christ. "Not as though I had already attained, either were already perfect: but I follow after, if that I may apprehend that for which also I am apprehended of Christ Jesus. Brethren, I count not myself to have apprehended: but this one thing I do, forgetting those things which are behind, and reaching forth unto those things which are before, I press toward the mark for the prize of the high calling of God in Christ Jesus" (Philippians 3:12-14).

NEVER A MAN
SO BEQUEATHED A NEW WAY OF LIFE

It has been often said that "All the king's horses and all the king's men can't put Humpty Dumpty together again." Jesus can, however, take the broken pieces of life and give new life, a new breath of life, to a person. He can and does make all things new. These new things are his work through the Spirit and not through a physical transformation. There is a land of beginning again (see Appendix 25) where a new start is possible.

Through the regenerative work of the Spirit man has become a new creation not just a temporary repair job. "Therefore if any man be in Christ, he is a new creature: old things are passed away; behold, all things are become new. And all things are of God, who hath reconciled us to himself by Jesus Christ, and hath given to us the ministry of reconciliation; To wit, that God was in Christ, reconciling the world unto himself, not imputing their trespasses unto them; and hath committed unto us the word of reconciliation" (II Corinthians 5:17-19). Not only can one receive a new spiritual life in Christ but Christ has made a new covenant with the new person. "Likewise also the cup after supper, saying, This cup is the new testament in my blood, which is shed for you" (Luke 22:20). But the new creation and the new covenant are not all the newness. He has made a new way of life possible. It is more than just a new ribbon on an old Easter bonnet. It is a new spirit, a new walk, one that is lived in righteousness and holiness. There is always time for this newness to begin.

One of the most memorable events in the world of football occurred on January 1, 1929 when Georgia Tech was playing California in the Rose Bowl. A Tech player took the ball down the field but was tackled hard and the ball popped loose into the hands of the California center, Roy Riegels, who started running in the right direction but became confused and whirled around and started in the wrong direction. A teammate shouted to Riegels to turn around but Riegels had to be tackled by his own teammate at his own two yard line. Through another mistake the ball scooted loose, into the end zone and Tech had the two points for an 8 to 7 victory. Riegels did not want to return to play the second half but his coach said, "Roy, the game is only half over. Go back in there." He tried to resist his coach but with another chance he played a great second half. What a coach, but what a God who not only gives another chance but a new chance with a new life.

After mistakes, boners if you please, in life, Christ gives

man another chance. The Bible gives instructions. Speak truth, don't let the sun go down on your wrath, play fair, do not become involved in false corrupt communications and most of all, do not grieve the Holy Spirit, life's spiritual coach.

The game of life is a daily walk so well defined in the rule book, the Bible. Christians have been admonished to walk circumspectly. "Then, see that ye walk circumspectly, not as fools but as wise, redeeming the time for the days are evil" (Ephesians 5:15-16).

Wherever Christians walk there is a shadow cast. That shadow is influence falling upon another. The apostle Paul gave the church at Ephesus instructions as to how they should walk. They were to walk in love, in the light, in wisdom and in unity. They were to give thanks for such a privilege. "I therefore, the prisoner of the Lord, beseech you that ye walk worthy of the vocation wherewith ye are called. With all lowliness and meekness, with long-suffering, forbearing one another in love; Endeavoring to keep the unity of the Spirit in the bond of peace. There is one body, and one Spirit, even as ye are called in one hope of your calling; One Lord, one faith, one baptism. One God and Father of all, who is above all, and through all, and in you all" (Ephesians 4:1-6).

Those who had shared in the wonderful gift of a new life in Christ were given special gifts by him. "And he gave some, apostles; and some, prophets; and some, evangelists; and some, pastors and teachers; For the perfecting of the saints, for the work of the ministry, for the edifying of the body of Christ" (Ephesians 4:11-12). A new start, a new life, a new endowment of God's grace and a new walk: all worthy gifts for a new person in Christ.

The Spirit in Christ has always been busy working in the kingdom of God to bring about righteousness and holiness. So there is in Christ not only a second chance but a second chance with a new creation in Christ. A Christian is to walk worthy of the calling in Christ, to run with patience the race that is set before him and to do it encompassed about by a great cloud of witnesses. These witnesses in the balconies of life can become a source of real strength and encouragement to cheer the runners on. Their role is vital. That race is a life-time marathon, not a 100 yard dash.

NEVER A MAN
SO CREATED SPIRITUAL DYNAMICS

Jesus loved us as we were but he loved us too much to leave us as we were. He made such a change in persons by having the spiritual dynamic which came to him by having the ability to coordinate the power of spiritual forces. Love was the generator of those spiritual forces.

A dynamic force is an explosive power. It can move rock and stone and tear quite a hole in the surface of the material world. The word "dynamic" conveys that idea. It has the capacity for unusual capability. The word comes from the Greek word "dynamis" and dynamite was invented by A. Nobel who established the Nobel Peace Prize. It is quite paradoxical that it became such an item used in war. It is a mixture of nitroglycerine and a mixture of such materials with nitrates. It is exploded by means of a fuse and a detonating cap of mercury. The word "dynamo" is from the same root and it is primarily a machine for light, heat and power.

The spiritual dynamite is love. The strongest force was generated 2,000 years ago and has not lost its power. It does not rest on the shifting sands of arbitrary hypothesis but on a solid foundation. The power has been preserved in the accumulated residual in well annotated human lives.

The power in the physical world is simpler than that in the spiritual world because in the physical world it functions according to certain scientific principles while in the spiritual world much of the power comes from the force of the human soul reacting with the power of the Holy Spirit. That love is rooted in the love of God, the love of Christ, the love of others, the love of the church and the love of the Bible which when coordinated with other spiritual elements become a spiritual dynamic, dynamite.

Michael Pupin, born in Yugoslavia, moved to the United States as a young emigrant lad, became professor of electro mechanics at Columbia University, once wrote the following: "Christ created a spiritual dynamic long before Newton had announced his dynamics of matter in motion, Maxwell his electrodynamics and Carnot his thermodynamics."

Both the Ten Commandments and the Sermon on the Mount have provided spiritual power to form a world encircling dynamo with warm love, power and a beautiful life. In the early stages of the release of such power, it shook the Roman Empire and began to explode many of the religious clichés of that day. It started a spiritual action and reaction effect. Subsequent action has called the modern world to have the courage to love amid so much hate; to seek for peace in the midst of selfish strife; and to clean up a nasty, dirty world.

It has made hope spring eternal in the human breast and when even hope seemed to be on its last leg it has seen that faith still stands. That faith clearly projects the knowledge that God is not dead and with his help the world can still be a good place in which to live. Some spiritual dynamite is still waiting to be exploded and in so doing would open vistas of fertile horizons.

The love in Christ is like the gravitational force in the physical world. It holds the universe together. Such is the power of the love of Christ. It is the current, the yeast, the magnet and the dynamite that when harnessed and put into action it has provided a spiritual force, a spiritual dynamic, that bonds and brings together the forces in the spiritual world.

Billy Graham has been the spiritual dynamic during the 20th century as he proclaimed God's redeeming love in Christ. He has challenged the world to become acquainted with Christ and to share his love. It would be impossible to try to estimate how many persons have responded to his simple, straight forward call to seek salvation in Christ. Thousands of lives have been changed and thousands of lives have found that Christ is the world's spiritual dynamo.

Martin Luther once expressed his feeling about Christ as spiritual dynamite. "In his life, Christ is an example showing us how to live; in his death, he is a sacrifice, satisfying our sins; in his resurrection, conqueror; in his ascension, a king; in his intercession, a high priest."

Power is a test of man's character as well as adversity. Is there enough spiritual power available in Christ going to waste that would put Niagara Falls to shame? Yes. I think so! Let it be coupled with prayer, love and humility and it will light up a person even in darkness and the darkness cannot put it out.

> There is power in the blood
> Wonder working power
> In the precious blood of the Lamb.
> —Lewis E. Jones

NEVER A MAN
SO CLAIMED THE HEARTS OF PEOPLE

The reason why Jesus claimed the hearts of people is that the heart of a person is the center of control. He did not want half-hearted persons. He did not want faint-hearted, hard-hearted persons but those that were tender-hearted, whole-hearted and with uprightness of heart. The author of the book of Proverbs gave the reason why: "Keep thy heart with all diligence; for out of it are the issues of life" (4:23). That is it!

The heart and the mind work closely together and must alike be committed to the sameness of purpose and desire. Physically the heart has never won a beauty contest, for it is about six inches long, four inches wide, pear-shaped more than valentine-shaped, weighing about twelve ounces. However, this organ of the body is also the seat of affection and warms the love and desires of life. Today, mechanical hearts are placed into human beings and one wonders how it would act spiritually without the soul and the mind being associated together—all within the same body.

Frequently one will hear the words "broken-hearted." That means that something has disturbed the relationship of this togetherness and detoured the warmth and peace issuing from the heart. Persons are the happiest when their hearts beat for others. That means the heart has given useful lessons to the head which may also issue forth in deeds for others and tenderness shown always across the board.

Charlotte Brontë, pen name for Mrs. A.B. Nicholls and novelist of the nineteenth century, wrote in *Evening Solace*, these profound words: "The human heart has hidden treasures, in secret kept, in silence sealed." The head and the heart should be filled at the same time or else it would be to no avail as pouring water down a rat hole. Christ was well aware of the centrality and power of the human heart which works day and night while asleep as well as when awake. A Christ-committed life, one where Christ is in possession of the heart, also works day and night. Evil is not always time conscious and must be restricted at all hours by a pure heart.

The door of the heart can only be opened from the inside with the consent of the heart and the conscience. But it is well to sound a caution here. Jeremiah the prophet alerted the people of Judah to a danger when he stated: "The heart is deceitful above all things, and desperately wicked: who can know it? I the Lord search the heart, I try the reins, even to give every man according to his ways, and according to the fruit of his doings" (17:9-10).

Evil and sin never sleep, always trying to challenge who or what is enthroned within the heart. The throne of the human heart has not room enough for Christ and sinful desires. If evil is allowed to sit upon the throne within the heart it will in time harden the heart. That in turn will harden the arteries through which the heart pumps blood which in turn will hamper and more quickly age the individual.

Christ can break the hard heart with his hammer of love and forgiveness. He can then make a new one in accordance to his plan; one more tender, clean and pure.

It is very difficult to trace the origin, movement and consummation of a thought or idea until there is fruition of the thought. The pathway is at times dangerous and uncertain. But if the heart belongs to Christ he will go with it to ward off the enemies. Great thoughts come only from a great heart and those thoughts need to be massaged, cleansed and nurtured by Christ, the water and bread of life.

Jesus claimed the hearts of mankind. He did not just automatically conquer their hearts. The claim had to be accepted and when accepted there were conditions incumbent upon the one who opened the door of the heart and invited Christ to sit upon the throne. So as athletes are described as having a heart in an action contest, and just as soldiers put their hearts into the courage and sacrifice they make, we speak freely of them having heart. Christians must take care of their hearts and not give them away for selfish gain.

The control and nourishment of the heart is a spiritual art.

> 'Tis Being and Doing and Having that make
> All the pleasures and pains of which mortals partake.
> To Be what God pleases, to Do a man's best,
> And to Have a good heart, is the way to be blest.
>   —Anonymous

Here is a thought to ponder: A person can have no better epitaph than that which is inscribed in the hearts of his family and friends!

Never A Man
So Raised Man's Nature

These comments will center on a man-to-man relationship. It will attempt to show how Jesus, the Man, effected man's nature: how he elevated it, raised it to a higher level and brought it up out of the miry clay, the horrible pit of sin. In so doing he vested the human race with dignity, nobility and made no exception so that every descendant of Adam was thenceforth to be admitted into the brotherhood with Jesus Christ. It took a mighty power to uplift the human race to that position. In fact, the Son of God sacrificed his life in the act.

The man originally created did not, I think, arrive on the scene through an evolutionary process. Like produces like. The similarity in body structure of man with the ape has caused some to consider both as being from the same original species but the monkey may disagree and may have had it right:

> Three monkeys sat in a coconut tree
> Discussing things as they're said to be
> Said one to the other, "Now listen you two
> There's a rumor that can't be true,
> That man descended from our noble race,
> The very idea is a terrible disgrace,
> No monkey ever deserted his wife,
> Starved her babies and ruined her life.......
> Yes man descended the ornery cuss,
> But brothers, he didn't descend from us!"
> —Author unknown

The monkey was probably right, for through Christ I do not refer to my brother, man, as "the ornery cuss." The author agrees with Shakespeare as he penned it in Hamlet.

> What a piece of work man is:
> How noble in reason

208

How infinite in faculty
In form and moving,
   how express and admirable
In action, how like an angel
In apprehension, how like a god.

But better still is the quotation from I Corinthians 3:16-17, "Know ye not that ye are the temple of God, and that the Spirit of God dwelleth in you? If any man defile the temple of God, him shall God destroy; for the temple of God is holy, which temple ye are."

Perhaps both the author and the reader would do well to ponder what Emily Dickinson left us:

I thought that nature was enough
Till human nature came
But that the other did absorb
As Parallax did in flame.

Actually human nature is hard to define. It is the essence of the individual. It is the endowment given to the individual through natural birth. It is the attributes, attitudes, affirmations of each person in response to life. Jesus wants to uplift, enlarge and elevate each human being to become what each one can become through full association with him. Each person has a distinctive human nature. No two respond the same. Far too many persons give way to selfishness, indifference and just pure laziness which stifle the potential which resides in his/her human nature. Christ as the master potter, the master teacher and the great physician can help an individual move up, move on and move outside of the basement of life in which many spend too much time.

Education, even though most all persons are much alike, can make all become different. Time is part of the essence and no matter how hard one may try to improve Mother Nature; Father Time is taking his toll. Human nature is very hard to control and even more difficult to improve. That is why one needs an expert. Jesus, through his endowment from his Father and through his experiences with life, stands ready to give the push. Once in a science laboratory a professor mixed the wrong elements in a test tube. The tube exploded and destroyed one of the scientist's eyes. The doctor told him he could place a glass eye in place of the destroyed one and no one could tell the difference. "That is fine," was the reply. "But doctor," added the patient, "you must put a twinkle in that glass eye." Ah, that is where Jesus excels. He can put the twinkles in the glass eyes.

Human nature can be raised, elevated and expanded, but not solely by lifting one's self by one's bootstraps. The object of all endeavors in reacting to human nature is "Whether therefore ye eat, or drink, or whatsoever ye do, do all to the glory of God" (I Corinthians 10:31). When persons so perform they are able "to come boldly unto the throne of grace, that they may obtain mercy, and find grace to help in time of need" (Hebrews 4:16).

NEVER A MAN
SO REVEALED HIS CONCEPTION OF GOD

Every person has some kind of conception of God. The basic answer is quite simple: either God is or God isn't. The assumption is that God is, was and always will be. That is His infinity, without any beginning. Jesus was a man while on earth. He was human and there is therefore room for consideration as to what he thought of God. How did the human within him think of God? He obeyed the will of God. He was submissive to God. He prayed to God. He talked to God. Did not his voice sound like the voice of his Heavenly Father?

There are many references of Jesus speaking on this recorded in the gospel of John.

John 4:34
"Jesus saith unto them, My meat is to do the will of him that sent me, and to finish his work."

210

John 5:39

> "Search the scriptures; for in them ye think ye
> have eternal life: and they are they which testify
> of me."

John 8:18-19

> "I am one that bear witness of myself, and the Father that
> sent me beareth witness of me. Then said they unto him,
> Where is thy Father? Jesus answered, Ye neither know me,
> nor my Father: if ye had known me, ye should have known
> my Father also."

John 10:37-38

> "If I do not the works of my Father, believe me not. But if I
> do, though ye believe not me, believe the works: that ye
> may know, and believe, that the Father is in me, and I in
> him."

John 12:44-45

> "Jesus cried and said, He that believeth on me, believeth not
> on me, but on him that sent me. And he that seeth me seeth
> him that sent me."

The author just this morning called his daughter's home and her husband answered the phone. He thought it was the voice of his grandson and asked to speak to his mother. Father and son do sound alike. This is quite commonplace. Mother and daughter frequently sound alike.

It is also quite commonplace that father and son will work together. "But Jesus answered them, My Father worketh hitherto, and I work" (John 5:17).

Most everyone has at one time or another recognized the son of a friend because they looked alike and to know one is to know something about the other. "Then said they unto him, Where is thy Father? Jesus answered, Ye neither know me, nor my Father: if ye had known me, ye should have known my Father also" (John 8:19).

Jesus gave the world his conception of God as perfect love. "He that loveth not knoweth not God; for God is love" (I John 4:8). That was a rather blunt, harsh statement about love which usually conveys the idea of tenderness and grace. One may wonder how God can be love when God is King, Ruler, Master and "Head-honcho in everything." Kings and rulers usually carried with them the idea of sternness, firmness and arbitrariness. Only God could fulfill the role of absolute love and only Jesus could interpret that kind of love to the world. Jesus did that in many ways. He loved everybody, which is most difficult to emulate. He loved his enemies which few can emulate. He loved the sinners but not their sins. He loved the unlovely. He loved the outcasts. He loved the unwanted. He loved the poor as well as the rich.

George Matheson's marriage plans were broken by his bride-to-be when she learned that he was losing his eye-sight. He wrote a hymn, *O Love That Wilt Not Let Me Go*, that touched the tender nerve of love.

> O Love that wilt not let me go,
> I rest my weary soul in thee;
> I give thee back the life I owe,
> That in thine ocean depths its flow
> May richer, fuller be.

Mankind is grateful that God as love never has treated anyone by breaking His vow. He even pursues mankind like the hound of heaven to pour out his love. Love is something which only God can define and only God can share it in its fullest meaning and power. Jesus, however, being a paragon of that love, has opened wider the door of understanding.

NEVER A MAN
SO REJECTED COMPROMISE

Compromise was never on Jesus' agenda. He avoided it with a passion. He never tried to maneuver, manipulate or misrepresent an action or a truth. It has been oft quoted that if Moses had wanted his people to have a permissive society he would have given 10 suggestions instead of Ten Commandments. Isn't it quite logical from the way Jesus dealt with eternal principles that he would not have compromised his phraseology? If he wanted to compromise his teachings in the Sermon on the Mount he would have given a sermonette, vignette, instead. He would have spoken in half-truths and delivered a bouquet of rhetorical flowers instead of straight-forward, straight-laced eternal truths.

He rejected such a flimsy procedure. He cut it into shreds and relegated it to a waste basket. Compromise may be a useful procedure in government but not in Christianity. A compromise is a detour around, a straddling of the fence, a bowing of the knee in submission. It is in most cases an act when two persons get what neither wants.

There are cases where a compromise can work for the benefit of each party. This is true in government as well as in business with the hope that no moral and ethical principles were set aside in order to work out the compromise. Haste at times taken with unbending rapidity, causes some to take a compromising stance, when later on to discover that there is need for revision and a give and take of both parties; a compromise so to speak. The history of our national government has recorded several actions of compromise. In fact, it is still used with care and good judgment. There was the Compromise Tariff Act of 1833 which was called by its opponents the Tariff of Abomination which called for gradation of reduction on export duties. Then at the 1787 Constitutional Convention there were three compromises. First, equality of representation by the states; second, counting of slaves at 3/5 of their actual number relating to representation and taxes; third, the granting of power to Congress to regulate commerce which seemed favorable to the north and the withholding of power to prohibit slave trading before 1808 which seemed favorable to the south. In retrospect these compromises appear to be of dubious wisdom. Seldom is there wisdom enough in any compromise to have the skill to cut the cake so everyone thinks he got the biggest piece.

Since Jesus rejected compromise it would be wise to consider why he did so and how he handled matters discreetly. The compromises he rejected referred to passing judgment on inheritance benefits and taxation for the ruling government. There were in existence laws governing these matters and he endorsed loyalty and respect of those laws. In spiritual matters it was a different story. Since he came not to destroy religious laws but to fulfill them, he had the right to interpret them and change them if necessary. Time and time again he said, "You have heard it said, but I say unto you." On the other hand, he was able to respect the old and endorse the new.

In the structure of our present society one often hears such terms as "situation ethics and moral relativism." These would permit the use of "little white lies" and "do whatever the situation called for." Christianity is not a religion of pure absolutes but it takes its stand on many situations and there is an obligation for the believer to attempt to get at the heart and soul of an issue but still have enough grace, love and wisdom to love God and neighbor as himself.

It becomes easier each time a compromise is followed for a habit to be formed. It is not always clear what would Jesus do. Therefore one is obligated to seek the great spiritual principles in the Bible and be careful that all judgments, attitudes and actions do not set aside those moral and ethical principles. It isn't easy.

A person may not know what to do in every case but most

persons know enough of what is right and what is wrong to avoid sin-traps and compromise.

Character frequently collapses when compromise is practiced. Moral and ethical rigidity can and frequently does create piousity of the Pharisaical intensity which in itself is sinful. The word "compromise" is not in the Bible. Could it have the color of a man-made shanghai, shenanigan deal? Give much prayer and thought to the occasions that appear to call for an adjustment.

"Jesus answered and said unto them, Though I bear record of myself, yet my record is true: for I know whence I came, and whither I go; but ye cannot tell whence I come, and whither I go" (John 8:14).

Here is some good advice: cut the truth straight. Shoot straight in all business dealings and in all of life go straight forward. Leave all compromises in file 13.

A BALLAD OF TREES AND THE MASTER

Into the woods my Master went,
Clean forspent, forspent,
Into the woods my Master came,
Forspent with love and shame.
But the olives they were not blind to Him,
The little gray leaves were kind to Him,
The thorn-tree had a mind to Him
When into the woods He came.

—**Sidney Lanier**

CHAPTER X

WHAT THINK YE OF CHRIST?

Jesus asked the Pharisees that question but it today has much relevancy and should likewise be answered by all, including those who are his followers. Frequently, the Pharisees had questioned Jesus trying to trap him. He had answered their questions admirably and they should have been pacified but Jesus took no chance and put a question to them. "What think ye of (the) Christ? Whose son is he?" All along their conception of him was defective. They just could not conceive of him as being the promised Messiah. Jesus had told members of the Sanhedrin that he was "the Christ, the son of God." So what response did he get on this occasion? A very brief one, "The son of David." Their minds fastened on the physical genealogy instead of that as Messiah. The Jews were expecting a Messiah at some time, but this person had been referred to by the blind man and others as "the son of David" and that was deep enough for them. Jesus, however, wanted to clarify the fact that to call him the son of David would be evasive and incorrect in this context. Matthew started his gospel by referring to him as the son of David (1:1). Jesus therefore gave them another question to ponder: "How then does David in the Spirit call him Lord, saying 'The Lord said to my Lord, sit at my right hand, till I make thine enemies thy footstool? If David then call him Lord, how is he his son?'" (Matthew 22:42-45).

The Pharisees could not see him as both transcendent, heavenly Lord, and human descendant of David. They were too steeped in Jewish tradition and could not open their hearts to behold him as both man and God, Messiah. The response they got from Jesus satisfied them for awhile but it did not convince them of his Messianic mission. It only put an end to their questioning (v. 46), awaiting a time to strike from a different vantage point. They would not and could not see that one who came out of Nazareth as being worthy of adulation or acceptance.

The question Jesus asked that day still rings in the ears and hearts of all Christians, "What think YE of Christ?" It is not a question of genealogy or of his role as Messiah, but a personal one as to how much and what does he mean in each life in today's world. Does he mean much or little? The more he means to the individual the more meaningful that person's life becomes.

Through the centuries men and women of various talents have presented Jesus in such a way as to underscore how important he has been in multiple areas.

In the area of MUSIC his influence stands at the head of the list. There is no piece of music which exceeds the work done by Handel in his production of *The Messiah*. Handel was born in Halle, Germany. He wrote the composition in 24 days, August 22 to September 14, 1741. During the writing he is quoted as saying "I did think I did see all Heaven before me, and the Great God himself."

The words are taken bodily from Isaiah, the Gospels, and Revelation and are divided into three parts.

1. The announcement of the hopes for a Saviour, then the story of his birth.
2. The suffering and crucifixion, at the close of which comes the Hallelujah Chorus.
3. The confession of faith and belief in the life everlasting.

Handel conducted *The Messiah* 34 times. This was the beginning of the widespread and enduring era of choral culture in England which was centered in Handel's work. At a presentation of The Messiah King George II was so affected by the Hallelujah Chorus that he rose to his feet. That mark of honor has been the reward of the Hallelujah Chorus to this day.

Handel produced 17 oratorios on Scriptural subjects: *Saul*,

Israel in Egypt, Samson, and *Joseph*....He wrote hymns, *Te Deum and Jubilate.*

Hundreds of the hymns of the Christian church focus on Jesus Christ. Two most noteworthy in this category are: *Amazing Grace* and *The Old Rugged Cross.*

Negro Spirituals carry the Jesus-thrust. Slaves interpretation of the stories taken from the Scripture: *Steal Away, By and By, Were You There, Go Down Moses, The Old Ark's a-Moving, O, Didn't it Rain, Where Shall I Be When the First Trumpet Sounds, The Great Getting Up Day,* and *Wasn't That a Morning.*

National hymns of a patriotic nature with a similar focus include *America, Star Spangled Banner* and *The Battle Hymn of the Republic.*

> Music: It wakes the soul, and lifts it high
> And wings it with sublime desires
> And fits it to bespeak the Deity.

DRAMA has paid its tribute to Christ especially in the long-running production of *The Passion Play* in Oberammergau in the Bavarian Alps, sixty miles from Munich, Germany.

It was during the Thirty Years War that the deadly and contagious disease known as Black Plague broke out in Germany. Before it ran its course, it struck down one in every three persons throughout Europe and left in its wake untold misery, panic, and hunger. It reached everywhere, even to sailors out at sea who had not been to port for months. Nowhere could safety or escape be found from this dreadful disease. Oberammergau suffered the same fate as the rest of Bavaria in 1632. The village's parish register lists 84 victims of the Black Death.

The Vow—At that point, the vow-to enact the Passion of Christ every 10 years was made and the plague claimed no further victims!

The Play—Thus the first Passion Play took place in 1634.

Originally it was a small performance, played on a meadow by the villagers and local peasants. Throughout the years, however, Oberammergau has produced several gifted poets who have set the Play to verse as well as lengthened it, until it achieved its present form as an artistic masterwork. To qualify as actors the performers must be native Oberammergauers, amateurs and persons of high moral and ethical principles. It is a great honor to be chosen to play the part of a saint and the highest earthly honor to be chosen to play the part of Christ. The beautiful costumes are made by the local villagers and their long hair is natural (no wigs) as they start to grow their hair and beards a year or more in advance in preparation for the Play.

A Labor of Love—For the Oberammergauers the Play is a labor of love. The hundreds of actors, children as well as adults, receive little reimbursement for their time and devotion to the exhausting performances (seven hours a day, four days a week from May to October). Although the widespread fame of *The Passion Play* and international tourism have brought thousands of people from the four corners of the earth to see the Play, the complete sincerity of the Oberammergauers has never been dimmed. Their vow is still the most important thing in their lives.

Since the first production, repeated every ten years, it has been presented at least 1900 times. Other companies have likewise produced the play, namely Eureka Springs, Arkansas and Spearfish, South Dakota and the impact has become so impressive that local church congregations have done a condensed version.

ART has come in for its share of attention and emphasis upon the life of Christ. Cynthia Pearl Maus in her magnificent book, *Christ and the Fine Arts*, has given a list of 60 artists and an accompanying picture and description of their work. Included in this list are many well-known artists:

- Burne-Jones—*The Resurrection*
- Albrecht Durer—*Praying Hands*

- Holman Hunt—*The Light of the World*
- Bartolome Murillo—*The Immaculate Conception*
- Peter Paul Rubens—*Christ on the Cross*
- Bernard Plockhorst—*Christ Blessing the Children*
- Sanzio Raphael—*The Sistine Madonna* and *The Transfiguration*

These artistic works and the interpretation of each one are most outstanding and with such excellent work done one feels that it has been difficult for the artists to put a heart beat of the Saviour on the canvas for this can come only from within the viewer.

The author has hesitated to recommend some "must" books for the serious Bible student but this by Maus is one of rare distinction. He treasures the copy given to him in 1940 on the occasion of his graduation from the Southern Baptist Theological Seminary by the Baptist Bookstore manager in Louisville, Kentucky.

Everyone knows it is difficult to know just how Jesus looked as to physical features, but there is something in the soul which seems to say that he was altogether lovely and every inch of a real man.

POETRY and LITERATURE. There appears to be something in the good man that came out of Nazareth that challenges, inspires and touches the best heart-beat of the poets.

Alfred Lord Tennyson ranks right at the top as one of the greatest poets of all times. His immortal poem, *In Memoriam A.H.H.*, is a tribute to his friend Arthur H. Hallam, who died at an early age. The 103 page poem speaks thus in the prologue:

> Strong son of God, immortal love
>> Whom we, that have not seen thy face,
> By faith, and faith alone, embrace,
>> Believing where we cannot prove.

When Tennyson was asked what he considered to be the greatest stanza of poetry he ever wrote, he did not quote from *In Memoriam* but from *Locksley Hall*:

> "Love took up the harp of life,
>   and smote on all the chords with might;
> Smote the chord of Self, that, trembling,
>   past in music out of sight."

Many other poets have written of the Christ who dominated their poetic thoughts, who tipped their caps to Jesus, are: Elizabeth and Robert Browning, James Russell Lowell, John Masefield and Sidney Lanier, etc. (See Appendix 26.)

Two other poems are beautifully expressive and worthy of note here.

L'Envoi

When earth's last picture is painted, and the tubes are
    twisted and dried,
When the oldest colors have faded, and the youngest critic
    has died,
We shall rest, and, faith, we shall need it-lie down for an
    aeon or two,
Till the Master of All Good Workmen shall set us to work
    anew!
And those that were good will be happy: they shall sit in a
    golden chair;
They shall splash at a ten-league canvas with brushes of
    comets' hair;
They shall find real saints to draw from-Magdalene, Peter,
    and Paul;
They shall work for an age at a sitting and never be tired at
    all!

And only the Master shall praise us, and only the Master
   shall blame;
And no one shall work for money, and no one shall work for
   fame;
But each for the joy of working, and each, in his separate
   star,
Shall draw the Thing as he sees It for the God of Things as
   They Are!

—Rudyard Kipling

and,

Lead Kindly Light

Lead, kindly Light! amid th' encircling gloom, Lead Thou
   me on;
The night is dark, and I am far from home, Lead Thou me
   on;
Keep Thou my feet; I do not ask to see
The distant scene; one step enough for me.

I was not ever thus, nor prayed that Thou shouldst lead me
   on;
I loved to choose and see my path; but now, Lead Thou me
   on;
I loved the garish day, and spite of fears,
Pride ruled my will; remember not past years.

So long Thy pow'r has blessed me, sure it still will lead me
   on
O'er moor and fen, o'er crag and torrent, till the night is
   gone;
And with the morn those angel faces smile
Which I have loved long since, and lost awhile!

—John H. Newman

In the area of literature, Jesus The Nazarene, has had a field day. Lloyd C. Douglas wrote two impressive works: *The Robe* and *The Magnificent Obsession* which focus sharply on Christ. Nathanel Hawthorne's *The Scarlet Letter* is among the best-known. Other works are:

- John Milton—*Paradise Lost, Paradise Regained*
- Henry Van Dyke—*The Other Wise Man*
- Victor Hugo—*Les Miserables*
- Sholem Asch—*The Nazarene*

The apostle John sensed the growing popularity of Jesus and the impact he would have on the world of writers (John 21:25). The greatest of all literature about Jesus resides in the 66 books of the Bible, especially the Gospels. The statistics on the publication popularity of the sacred Scriptures are quite appalling. The population of the world is in excess of 6 billion. There are 6,803 languages currently spoken in today's world. There are Bibles printed with some or parts thereof in 2,261 languages; 987 languages have been used in New Testament publications. According to the Society of the Gideons and the International Bible Society the number of new Bibles sold, given away or distributed per day in the United States has been estimated to be about 168,000. It has been and still is the Book of ALL Books.

One is at a loss to know how to gauge, weigh, estimate or evaluate how much good has been achieved by Christianity's impact upon scientific research, care of the poor, the elderly and the many charitable organizations that are alive and quite healthy within the total spectrum of extensive and specific scientific activities. (See Appendix 27.)

The dignity, freedom and equality of women had Christianity as its catalyst. The establishment of health care programs such as hospices and the love of unwanted children shared by orphanages and special groups are rooted in Christian principles. It is possible that slavery might have never been corrected without Christianity's influence. It has been such a moral force with benefits for the entire world.

Modern medicine and hospitals have felt the warm, friendly breeze of Christianity blowing daily upon their endeavors. Hospitals have chaplains, prayer rooms and special ministries to patients. It would be impossible to think accurately of just what the world might be like if good had not come out of Nazareth.

Out of Nazareth

Out of Nazareth came a Prophet,
A soul on fire with primeval force,
A Master of the cosmic mysteries,
A kingly Man who made His throne a cross.

A Democrat, who loved the common people,
A Rebel, sensitive to every wrong,
A Teacher of the Truth that love must triumph,
He fought the old injustice all life long.

He was a Radical of fiery faith
Because He dug down deep to divine wells,
Because the thing that tore His loving heart
Was suffering and sorrow in earth's hells.

He stood high up upon the hills of light
Where few indeed have had the strength to stand;
He dared grief, pain, death, a criminal's fate
That He might make this world a fairer land.
—Vincent G. Burns

Human rights, equality under the law and economic freedom have flourished within the Christian ethic. Judges, juries and the various court systems in America have been enhanced by Christianity's impact.

EDUCATION: Jesus was high on education. He grew in wisdom and no doubt was a good student at the synagogue. He spoke of the truth making men free: "If you continue in my word, then are ye my disciples indeed; and ye shall know the truth, and the truth shall make you free" (John 8:31-32). These words he spoke to his Jewish followers who believed in him. The Jews were seekers of wisdom. There was more; however, to becoming a follower than just familiarity with the Scripture. He cautioned the Jews with these words: "And this is the Father's will which hath sent me, that of all which he hath given me I should lose nothing, but should raise it up again at the last day. And this is the will of him that sent me, that every one which seeth the Son, and believeth on him, may have everlasting life: and I will raise him up at the last day" (John 6:39-40).

The apostle Paul was an ardent student of the law and likewise wrote of the importance of searching for knowledge of Christ. In II Timothy 2:15 these were the words of admonition to Timothy: "Study to show thyself approved unto God, a workman that needeth not to be ashamed, rightly dividing the word of truth." In this expression, he was saying that when you study be sure to cut truth straight. Avoid trying to make it say that which you hoped it would say.

Christians have also been very high on education. Today there are many programs of Bible study. The churches have Bible study on Sunday morning (called Sunday School). Most churches have for their youth in the summer Vacation Bible Schools. Bible study groups are held during the weekdays in homes, businesses and through special clubs. There are many Christian schools sponsored by individual churches which run through high school. On the level of higher education, which has been a landmark in America, 372 of the first 394 colleges established in America were church-related. The first one in America was Harvard University established in 1636 to prepare "literate ministers." That percentage and number has changed today due to the establishment by the individual states of Land

Grant Institutions. There are 72 of these in the fifty states with some states having two which participate in the states' financial resources. There are 294 Christian Colleges and Universities in the fifty states. These are partially funded by the various denominations with which they are affiliated.

Most denominations have gone one step higher in education by having seminaries and Bible schools. According to the accrediting agency of American Theological Schools, there are 244 member schools. Thirty seven of that number have been added since 1992. Christian schools are on the upswing.

Many of the Christian private colleges, universities and seminaries bear the name or names of the founders or generous donors. In the purposes and aims of these institutions one will find that the Christian influence is relevant, purposeful and dynamic. The God-Man who came out of Nazareth 2,000 years ago has caused so much good to be accomplished that his shadow of influence is not diminishing but increasing. He truly does live. He is alive. His "inasmuch" work must go on.

IN THE BLEAK MID-WINTER

What can I give him,
*   Poor as I am?*
If I were a shepherd
*   I would bring Him a lamb.*
If I were a Wise Man,
*   I would do my part,—*
Yet what can I give Him,
*   Give my heart.*
              —Christini Rosetti

CHAPTER XI

THEY SAY, WHAT DO
THEY SAY, LET THEM SAY

Philosophers, theologians, sociologists, psychologists, ministers and Christian laymen have through the centuries loudly vociferated in a thousand tongues the praise and glory that rightly belonged to the "Nazareth-person." They have had a good word for Jesus through trials and hardships. It has not always been the point of focus because there are moments when self pushes its way to the front and a reminder is desperately needed.

SAY A GOOD WORD FOR JESUS

Ian Maclaren, pseudonym of John Watson, wrote a touching story of a young theological student preparing for his first sermon in the village parish. In "His Mother's Sermon," Watson tells of the man's desire to show his scholarship. His aunt reminded him of an experience that transpired five years earlier at his mother's death. She requested that he "speak a gude word for Jesus Christ, an' John I'll hear ye that day, though ye'll no see me, and I'll be satisfied."

As the day approached, his sermon had been written with sophisticated theological terminology. Again, his aunt reminded him of his mother's words. The day before the event, he twice crushed his sermon to throw it away, but both times he smoothed it out. At last in the stillness of his room, he heard a voice saying, "Speak a gude word for Jesus Christ." He knew the sermon had to go and he cast it into the fire. After hearing the sermon that day, his aunt flung her arms around his neck and said, "Yir mither has heard every word and is satisfied for ye did it in remembrance of her. Ye did speak a gude word of Jesus Christ."

The eulogies or the accolades or the praises or whatever or however given sing a beautiful oratorio of honor and glory to his name. No person has ever had such an avalanche as Jesus Christ. He never asked for any, he never reveled in them but hopefully his heart rejoiceth to hear them. The author feels he can do no better than to share a baker's dozen with the readers. So here are thirteen from different authors of hundreds that could be called forth.

"As the print of the seal on the wax is the express image of the seal itself, so Christ is the express image—the perfect representation of God."

—St. Ambrose

"Jesus Christ and his precepts are found to hit the moral experience of mankind; to hit it in the critical points; to hit it lastingly; and when doubts are thrown upon their really hitting it, then to come out stronger than ever."

—Matthew Arnold

"If Christ is not divine, every impulse of the Christian world falls to a lower octave, and light and love and hope decline."

—Henry Ward Beecher

"Perhaps the Christian volume is the theme,
   How guiltless blood for guilty man was shed,
How He who bore in heaven the second name
   Had not on earth whereon to lay His head."

—Robert Burns

"If Shakespeare should come into this room, we would all rise; but if Jesus Christ should come in, we would all kneel."

—Charles Lamb

"I will place no value on anything I have or may possess except in relation to the Kingdom of Christ."

—David Livingstone

"If I could hear Christ praying for me in the next room, I would not fear a million enemies. Yet distance makes no difference. He is praying for me."

—Robert M. McCheyne

"After reading the doctrines of Plato, Socrates or Aristotle, we feel the specific difference between their words and Christ's is the difference between an inquiry and a revelation."

—Joseph Parker

"Jesus was the greatest religious genius that ever lived. His beauty is eternal, and his reign shall never end. Jesus is in every respect unique, and nothing can be compared with him." All history is incomprehensible without Christ."

—Joseph Ernest Renan

"I am no more of a Christian than Pilate was, or you are, gentle hearer; and yet, like Pilate, I greatly prefer Jesus of Nazareth to Amos or Caiaphas; and I am ready to admit that I see no way out of the world's misery but the way which would have been found by his will."

—George Bernard Shaw

"He wakes desires you never may forget;
    He shows you stars you never saw before;
He makes you share with Him forevermore
    The burden of the world's divine regret."

—Alfred Lord Tennyson

"After six years given to the impartial investigation of Christianity, as to its truth or falsity, I have come to the deliberate conclusion that Jesus Christ was the Messiah of the Jews, the Saviour of the world, and my personal Saviour."

—Lew Wallace

"Only once did God choose a completely sinless preacher."
—Alexander Whyte

When Karl Barth, a Swiss theologian, was asked what was the most profound theological truth he knew, he replied, "Jesus loves me, this I know . . . ."

Epilogue

Philip along with Andrew had come, with other townsmen, to Bethany to hear John the Baptist. There he had received his call to follow Christ in the words "Come follow me." Like Andrew he immediately won his friend, Nathanael. Nathanael raised the question about the petty insignificant town of Nazareth: "Can any good thing come out of that town?"

Three and one-half years passed and he now is with a group of seven disciples to whom Jesus appeared after his resurrection (John 21:2). Soon thereafter he is in Jerusalem with the disciples and Jesus gave them the Great Commission. After he had spoken to them he ascended into heaven and sat down at the right hand of God (Mark 16:19). This vanishing act is sure to have stirred the disciples' imagination and sparked much conversation.

It is easy to think that Nathanael, being of such nature, called his friend Philip aside for a good man-to-man conversation. He wanted to talk some things over. He probably invited Philip to his home. Thus began a most interesting, intimate and imaginative conversation. "Philip, our Lord has gone from us now. I guess I was wrong when I blurted out the question several years ago: 'Can any good thing come out of Nazareth?' for there is no way to estimate the good he did while on earth among us. Now, the road ahead, without him, will be very rough and life just won't be the same. He was always on top of every situation. He did say thoughtfully that he was sending the Holy Spirit to guide us into all truth and to empower us, and to help us in so many ways. But the Holy Spirit is invisible and I have not exactly known how to tap on to that Spirit. I will just have to learn. Jesus is not going to come back soon to check on how we are doing. He is, however, looking down on us."

Philip spoke up, "You are right, my friend. Jesus was a most unusual person. He gave of himself most freely. He seemed at times to live in two different worlds at the same time as God-man and as God's man. He was so intelligent and perceptive and so engrossed in what he was doing. He really knew the Old Testament which he must have learned at the synagogue. He was acquainted with and respected the Jewish traditions and the law which he sought to fulfill. I am temporarily in a daze. I can't get him off my mind and heart. I guess I never will. I remember as if it were yesterday when Jesus wanted to feed the 5,000 that he turned to me and asked 'whence are we to buy bread for this crowd.' I had no answer but with the help of a lad he fed them with food left over. He kept on showing me his greatness. I recall after the observance of the Last Supper I spoke up and addressed him as 'Lord.' I even asked him to show us the Father."

"That man from Nazareth had a way of growing on a person. The more one knew of him the more one thought of him. He melted my materialistic bent of mind and focused it on spiritual things."

"Philip, you are right. He had a way of growing on you. It was hard for us to see him as God incarnate in human flesh for he was so human and practical along with his divine qualities. His acute discernment of human nature and the human heart was outstanding. Our initial concept of him was too narrow, too small, and too askew. Will the world ever get over the way it treated him? He did not deserve such treatment. Perhaps in the centuries following he will come into his own. People will see him for what and who he is."

"Well, my friend Philip, I want to apologize to you for the hasty, critical and prejudiced remark I made when I sharply uttered such an irascible, ill-timed remark about the man who came out of Nazareth. I have regretted it a thousand times. My bigoted eyes can see better now and my warped heart is beginning to open completely to him."

And so the people in the world continue to size-up Jesus, to think of him even in minor terms. Hearing about him is not like experiencing him. He is the world's model of how to live in relationship with God. Let him be held high, let him be lifted-up, let him find a habitat in the human heart. The good that came out of Nazareth cannot be compressed into words, nor estimated by human standards. He continues to carry out his eleven word mission which he uttered in the temple at the age of twelve: "Wist ye not that I must be about my father's business." He has invited all to "Come follow me."

Keep Your Eyes on Jesus

Keep the Son in your eyes
    Keep His light shining through
Keep your eyes on Jesus
    He keeps His eyes on you.

All of the times we stumble
    All of the times we fall
Like Peter upon the ocean
    Frightened by what he saw.

And just like the world around us
    With all of the waves and the wind
We can fall captive of the storm
    By taking our eyes off of Him.

Keep the Son in your eyes
    Keep His light shining through
Keep your eyes on Jesus
    He keeps His eyes on you.

Whenever the darkness tries to steal you away
Remember, the Saviour can light up the way.

Good Came Out of Nazareth

Keep the Son in your eyes
     Keep His light shining through
Keep your eyes on Jesus
     He keeps His eyes on you.

He keeps His eyes on you
     So you keep the Son in your eyes.
        —Scott Wesley Brown

APPENDIXES 1-27

Appendix 1:Books of Old and New Testament
Appendix 2: Dates and Chronology
Appendix 3: The I AMS of Jesus
Appendix 4: The Work of the Holy Spirit
Appendix 5: Scripture References to Nazareth
Appendix 6: Like Other Boys (poem)
Appendix 7: Sermon on the Mount
Appendix 8: Six "Ye Have Heard it said but I say unto you."
Appendix 9: Nine Beatitudes
Appendix 10: Eight "do nots" from the Sermon on the Mount
Appendix 11: Eight Woes of the Scribes, Pharisees, etc.
Appendix 12: Parables of the Early and Late Ministry
Appendix 13: Jesus Parables and Old Testament Parables
Appendix 14: The Vision of Pilate
Appendix 15: Miracles of Jesus and of the Disciples
Appendix 16: Prayers of Jesus
Appendix 17: Prophets
Appendix 18: New Testament Prophecies
Appendix 19: Crucify! (poem)
Appendix 20: The Cross Was His Own (poem)
Appendix 21: The Fourteen Stations of the Via Dolorosa
Appendix 22: The 11 Appearances of Jesus
Appendix 23: Words Jesus Spoke after His Resurrection
Appendix 24: The Character of Jesus
Appendix 25: The Land of Beginning Again (poem)
Appendix 26: God's Autographs (poem)
Appendix 27: If Jesus Came Back Today (poem)

APPENDIX 1

The Books of the Old Testament Apocrypha

The First Book of Esdras
The Second Book of Esdras
The Book of Tobit
The Book of Judith
The Rest of the Chapters of the Book of Esther, which
   are found neither in the Hebrew, nor the Chaldee
The Wisdom of Solomon
The Wisdom of Jesus the Son of Sirach, or Ecclesiasticus
The Book of Baruch
The Song of the Three Holy Children
The History of Susanna
The History of the Destruction of Bel and the Dragon
The Prayer of Manasses, King of Judah
The First Book of the Maccabees
The Second Book of the Maccabees

The Books of the New Testament Apocrypha

History of James
Revelation of Peter
Travels and Teachings of the Apostles
Letter of Barnabas
Acts of Paul
Revelation of Paul
Teaching of Clement
Teaching of Ignatius
Teaching of Polycarp
Gospel according to Barnabas
Gospel according to Matthias

These books, however, are worth reading and do not lessen one's appreciation of the present canon but only enhance the one we have because of its central focus on the central figure, Christ.

APPENDIX 2

Summary of dates and the chronology of the writing of the 27 New Testament books.

The List of the Synod of Carthage (397 A.D.)

Four gospels
Acts
Letters of Paul XIII
The same to the Hebrews
Peter, two
John, three
James
Jude
Revelation of John

Summary of Dates

Death of James, son of Zebedee 44
Death of Herod Agrippa I 44
Famine under Claudius 44-48
Epistle of James, brother of Jesus . . . . before. . . .50
First missionary journey 45-49
Edict of Claudius49 50
Proconsulship of Sergius Paulus . . . . before 51
Apostolic Council 50
Second missionary journey 50-53
1 and 2 Thess. from Corinth 52/53
Proconsulship of Gallio 52/53
Third missionary journey 54-58
Paul in Ephesus 54-57
1 Cor. and Gal. from Ephesus 55-57
2 Cor. from Macedonia 57
Romans from Corinth 57/58
Arrest of Paul in Jerusalem 58
Accession of Festus . . . . not before . . 57
probably . . 60

First Roman imprisonment of Paul 61-63/4

Col., Eph., Philem. from Rome   62

Phil. from Rome   63

Release of Paul and journeys in West and East 64-67

1 Timothy and Titus from Macedonia 65-66

2 Timothy from Rome   67

Death of Paul in Rome 67/68

Synoptic Gospels, Acts, Jude and Hebrews. . . . . . .before . .67

1 and 2 Peter from Rome 64-67

Death of Peter in Rome 64-67

Death of James the Just . . . . .about . . 66

Fourth Gospel, Revelation, Epistles of John from Ephesus

. . . . before 100

Death of John 98-100

From the *International Standard Bible Encyclopedia*, "The Chronology of N.T. Church," p. 650

APPENDIX 3

The I AMS of Jesus—His Opinion of Himself

I am the Way, Truth, Life
John 14:6—"Jesus saith unto him, I am the way, the truth, and the life: no man cometh unto the Father, but by me."

I am the Vine
John 15:1—"I am the true vine, and my Father is the husbandman."

I am the Resurrection
John 11:25—"Jesus said unto her, I am the resurrection, and the life: he that believeth in me, though he were dead, yet shall he live."

I am the Good Shepherd
John 10:16—"And other sheep I have, which are not of this fold: them also I must bring, and they shall hear my voice; and there shall be one fold, and one shepherd."

I am the Bread of Life
John 6:35—"And Jesus said unto them, I am the bread of life: he that cometh to me shall never hunger; and he that believeth on me shall never thirst."

I am the water of life

I am the Light of the World
John 8:12— "Then spake Jesus again unto them, saying, I am the light of the world: he that followeth me shall not walk in darkness, but shall have the light of life."

I am the Son of Man
Matthew 16:13—"When Jesus came into the coasts of Caesarea Philippi, he asked his disciples, saying, Whom do men say that I the Son of man am?"

I am the Alpha

>Revelation 22:13—"I am Alpha and Omega, the beginning and the end, the first and the last."

I am the Omega

>Revelation 22:13—"I am Alpha and Omega, the beginning and the end, the first and the last."

I am the Master and Lord

>John 13:13—"Ye call me Master and Lord: and ye say well; for so I am."

APPENDIX 4

The Work of the Holy Spirit

Participated in creation

Genesis 1:2—"And the earth was without form, and void; and darkness was upon the face of the deep. And the Spirit of God moved upon the face of the waters."

Is a Comforter—Paraclete

John 14:17—"Even the Spirit of truth; whom the world cannot receive, because it seeth him not, neither knoweth him: but ye know him; for he dwelleth with you, and shall be in you."

Is eternal

Hebrews 9:14—"How much more shall the blood of Christ, who through the eternal Spirit offered himself without spot to God, purge your conscience from dead works to serve the living God?"

Speaks

I Corinthians 14:2—"For he that speaketh in an unknown tongue speaketh not unto men, but unto God: for no man understandeth him; howbeit in the spirit he speaketh mysteries."

Teaches

I Corinthians 2:13—"Which things also we speak, not in the words which man's wisdom teacheth, but which the Holy Ghost teacheth; comparing spiritual things with spiritual."

Reveals the future

I Corinthians 2:10—"But God hath revealed them unto us by his Spirit: for the Spirit searcheth all things, yea, the deep things of God."

Bears Witness

Hebrews 10:15, 16 —"Whereof the Holy Ghost also is a witness to us: for after that he had said before. This is the covenant that I will make with them after those days, saith the Lord, I will put my laws into their hearts, and in their minds will I write them."

Guides to the truth

John 16:13—"Howbeit when he, the Spirit of truth, is come, he will guide you into all truth: for he shall not speak of himself; but whatsoever he shall hear, that shall he speak: and he will shew you things to come."

Gives life (quickens)

John 6:63—"It is the spirit that quickeneth; the flesh profiteth nothing: the words that I speak unto you, they are spirit, and they are life."

Reproves

John 16:8—"And when he is come, he will reprove the world of sin, and of righteousness, and of judgment."

Of Promise

Ephesians 1:13—"In whom ye also trusted, after that ye heard the word of truth, the gospel of your salvation: in whom also after that ye believed ye were sealed with that Holy Spirit of promise."

Grieve not

Ephesians 4:30—"And grieve not the Holy Spirit of God, whereby ye are sealed unto the day of redemption."

Makes Intercession

Romans 8:26—"Likewise the Spirit also helpeth our infirmities: for we know not what we should pray for as we ought: but the Spirit itself maketh intercession for us with groanings which cannot be uttered."

Indwells the believer

Romans 8:13—"For if ye live after the flesh, ye shall die: but if ye through the Spirit do mortify the deeds of the body, ye shall live."

Distributes gifts

Acts 2:38—"Then Peter said unto them, Repent, and be baptized every one of you in the name of Jesus Christ for the remission of

sins, and ye shall receive the gift of the Holy Ghost."
I Corinthians 12:1, 4—"Now concerning spiritual gifts, brethren, I would not have you ignorant.".......... "Now there are diversities of gifts, but the same Spirit."

Seals the believer
II Corinthians 1:22—"Who hath also sealed us, and given the earnest of the Spirit on our hearts."

Invites the Sinner
John 16:9—"Of sin, because they believe not on me."

Can be Blasphemed
Matthew 12:31—"Wherefore I say unto you, All manner of sin and blasphemy shall be forgiven unto men: but the blasphemy against the Holy Ghost shall not be forgiven unto men."

Conceived Jesus in Mary
Luke 1:13—"But the angel said unto him, Fear not, Zacharias: for thy prayer is heard; and thy wife Elisabeth shall bear thee a son, and thou shalt call his name John."

APPENDIX 5

Scripture References to Nazareth

Nazareth

Matthew 2:23

"And he came and dwelt in a city called Nazareth: that it might be fulfilled which was spoken by the prophet, He shall be called a Nazarene."

Matthew 21:11

"And the multitude said, This is Jesus the prophet of Nazareth of Galilee."

Mark 1:24

"Saying, Let us alone; what have we to do with thee, thou Jesus of Nazareth? Art thou come to destroy us? I know thee who thou art, the Holy One of God."

Mark 10:47

"And when he heard that it was Jesus of Nazareth, he began to cry out, and say, Jesus, thou son of David, have mercy on me."

Mark 14:67

"And when she saw Peter warming himself, she looked upon him, and said, And thou also wast with Jesus of Nazareth."

Mark 16:6

"And he saith unto them, Be not affrighted: Ye seek Jesus of Nazareth, which was crucified: he is risen; he is not here; behold the place where they laid him."

Luke 4:34

"Saying, Let us alone; what have we to do with thee, thou Jesus of Nazareth? art thou come to destroy us? I know thee who thou art; the Holy One of God."

Luke 18:37

"And they told him, that Jesus of Nazareth passeth by."

Luke 24:19

"And he said unto them, what things? And they said unto him, Concerning Jesus of Nazareth, which was a prophet mighty in deed and word before God and all the people."

Luke 1:26

"And in the sixth month the angel Gabriel was sent from God unto a city of Galilee, named Nazareth."

Luke 2:51

"And he went down with them, and came to Nazareth, and was subject unto them: but his mother kept all these sayings in her heart."

Luke 4:16

"And he came to Nazareth, where he had been brought up: and, as his custom was, he went into the synagogue on the Sabbath day, and stood up for to read."

John 1:45-46

"Philip findeth Nathanael, and saith unto him, We have found him, of whom Moses in the law, and the prophets, did write, Jesus of Nazareth, the son of Joseph. And Nathanael said unto him, Can there any good thing come out of Nazareth? Philip saith unto him, Come and see."

John 18:5, 7

"They answered him, Jesus of Nazareth, Jesus saith unto them, I am he. And Judas also, which betrayed him, stood with them. . . Then asked he them again, Whom seek ye? And they said, Jesus of Nazareth."

John 19:19

"And Pilate wrote a title, and put it on the cross. And the writing was, JESUS OF NAZARETH THE KING OF THE JEWS."

Acts 2:22

"Ye men of Israel, hear these words; Jesus of Nazareth, a man approved of God among you by miracles and wonders and signs, which God did by him in the midst of you, as ye yourselves also know...."

Acts 4:10

"Be it known unto you all, and to all the people of Israel, that by the name of Jesus Christ of Nazareth, whom ye crucified, whom God raised from the dead, even by him doth this man stand here before you whole."

Acts 6:14

"For we have heard him say, that this Jesus of Nazareth shall destroy this place, and shall change the customs which Moses delivered us."

Acts 22:8

"And I answered, Who art thou, Lord? And he said unto me, I am Jesus of Nazareth, whom thou persecutest.
Then Peter said, Silver and gold have I none; but such as I have give I thee: In the name of Jesus Christ of Nazareth rise up and walk."

Acts 10:38

"How God anointed Jesus of Nazareth with the Holy Ghost and with power: who went about doing good, and healing all that were oppressed of the devil; for God was with him. I verily thought with myself, that I ought to do many things contrary to the name of Jesus of Nazareth."

Nazarene

Matthew 2:23

"And he came and dwelt in a city called Nazareth: that it might be fulfilled which was spoken by the prophets, He shall be called a Nazarene."

Acts 24:5

"For we have found this man a pestilent fellow, and a mover of sedition among all the Jews throughout the world, and a ringleader of the sect of the Nazarenes."

Nazarite:

Numbers 6:2, 13, 18-21

"Speak unto the children of Israel, and say unto them, When either man or woman shall separate themselves to vow a vow of a Nazarite, to separate themselves unto the Lord . . . And this is the law of the Nazarite, when the days of his separation are fulfilled: he shall be brought unto the door of the tabernacle of the congregation . . . And the Nazarite shall shave the head of his separation at the door of the tabernacle of the congregation, and shall take the hair of the head of his separation, and put it in the fire which is under the sacrifice of the peace offerings. And the priest shall take the sodden shoulder of the ram, and one unleavened cake out of the basket, and one unleavened wafer, and shall put them upon the hands of the Nazarite, after the hair of his separation is shaven. And the priest shall wave them for a wave offering before the Lord: this is holy for the priest, with the wave breast and heave shoulder: and after that the Nazarite may drink wine. This is the law of the Nazarite who hath vowed, and of his offering unto the Lord for his separation, beside that that his hand shall get: according to the vow which he vowed, so he must do after the law of his separation."

Judges 13:5, 7

"For, lo, thou shalt conceive, and bear a son; and no razor shall come on his head: for the child shall be a Nazarite unto God from the womb: and he shall begin to deliver Israel out of the hand of the Philistines. . . . But he said unto me, Behold, thou shalt conceive, and bear a son; and now drink no wine nor strong drink, neither eat any unclean thing: for the child shall be a Nazarite to God from the womb to the day of his death."

Judges 16:17

"That he told her all his heart, and said unto her, There hath not come a razor upon mine head; for I have been a Nazarite unto God from my mother's womb: if I be shaven, then my strength will go from me, and I shall become weak, and be like any other man."

Nazarites:

Lamentations 4:7

"Her Nazarites were purer than snow, they were whiter than milk, they were more ruddy in body than rubies, their polishing was of sapphire."

Amos 2:11-12

"And I raised up of your sons for prophets, and of your young men for Nazarites. Is it not even thus, O ye children of Israel? saith the Lord. But ye gave the Nazarites wine to drink; and commanded the prophets, saying, Prophesy not."

APPENDIX 6

Like Other Boys

He was a boy like other boys,
        And played and sported with the rest;
He had His troubles and His toys,
        And strove for mastery with the best.

He was a very boy, and had
        His little faults-like other boys;
But he was always gay and glad,
        And eager in His small employs.

With all the rest He went to school,
        But gave His lessons more concern,
And school to Him was never dull,
        He had so keen a wish to learn.

He loved all birds and beasts and flowers
        And in the hills spent happy days
Lying unseen in cunning bowers
        Where He could watch their curious ways.

He was great-hearted, tender, true,
        And brave as any boy could be,
And very gentle, for He knew
        That Love is God's own Chivalry.

He was a boy-like you-and you-
        As full of jokes, as full of fun,
But always He was bravely true,
        And did no wrong to anyone.

And one thing I am sure about-
        He never tumbled into sin,
But kept himself, within, without,
        As God had made Him, sweet and clean.
            —John Oxenham

APPENDIX 7

Sermon on the Mount

The Sermon on the Mount—Clovis G. Chappell

Poverty that Makes Rich . . . . .Matthew 5:3
Blessed Mourners . . . . .Matthew 5:4
The Meek . . . . .Matthew 5:5
A Good Appetite Matthew5:6
The Merciful .Matthew5:7
The Vision Splendid . . . . .Matthew 5:8
The Peacemakers . . . . .Matthew 5:9
The Persecuted . . . . .Matthew 5:10-12
"Salt" . . . . .Matthew 5:13
:Light" . . . . .Matthew 5:14-16
Fulfilling the Law . . . . .Matthew 5:17-48
Drastic Operations . . . . .Matthew 5:29-30
The Motive Test- . . . . .Matthew 6:1-18
A Wise Investment . . . . .Matthew 6:19-20
"Ask—Seek—Knock" . . . . .Matthew 7:7-8
The Way of Life . . . . .Matthew 7:13-14
The Two Builder . . . . .Matthew 7:24-27

Studies in the Mountain Instruction
— George Dana Boardman

Introductory .Matthew 5:1-2; 7:28-29
Christ's Doctrine of Blessedness . . . . .Matthew 5:3-12
Christ's Doctrine of the Church . . . . . .Matthew 5:13-16
Christ's Doctrine of Fulfillment . . . . . .Matthew 5:17-20
Christ's Doctrine of Reconciliation . . .Matthew 5:21-24
Christ's Doctrine of Asceticism . . . . . .Matthew 5:27-32
Christ's Doctrine of Words . . . . .Matthew 5:33-37
Christ's Doctrine of Perfection . . . . . . .Matthew 5:38-48
Christ's Doctrine of Worship . . . . .Matthew 6:1-18
Christ's Doctrine of Prayer . . . . .Matthew 6:9-13
Christ's Doctrine of Wealth . . . . .Matthew 6:19-24
Christ's Doctrine of Sonship . . . . .Matthew 6:25-34
Christ's Doctrine of Society . . . . .Matthew 7:1-12
Christ's Doctrine of Character . . . . . . .Matthew 7:13-27

APPENDIX 8

Six "Ye have heard it said, but I say unto you."
From the Sermon on the Mount—Matthew 5

1. "Ye have heard that it was said by them of old time, Thou shalt not kill; and whosoever shall kill shall be in danger of the judgment. But I say unto you, That whosoever is angry with his brother without a cause shall be in danger of the judgment: and whosoever shall say to his brother, Raca, shall be in danger of the council: but whosoever shall say, Thou fool, shall be in danger of hell fire" (verses 21-22).

2. "Ye have heard that it was said by them of old time, Thou shalt not commit adultery. But I say unto you, That whosoever looketh on a woman to lust after her hath committed adultery with her already in his heart" (verses 27-28).

3. "It hath been said, Whosoever shall put away his wife, let him give her a writing of divorcement. But I say unto you, That whosoever shall put away his wife, saving for the cause of fornication, causeth her to commit adultery: and whosoever shall marry her that is divorced committeth adultery" (verses 31-32).

4. "Again, ye have heard that it hath been said by them of old time, Thou shalt not forswear thyself, but shalt perform unto the Lord thine oaths. But I say unto you, Swear not at all; neither by heaven; for it is God's throne" (verses 33-34).

5. "Ye have heard that it hath been said, An eye for an eye, and a tooth for a tooth. But I say unto you, That ye resist not evil: but whosoever shall smite thee on thy right cheek, turn to him the other also" (verses 38-39).

6. "Ye have heard that it hath been said, Thou shalt love thy neighbour, and hate thine enemy. But I say unto you, Love your enemies, bless them that curse you, do good to them that hate you, and pray for them which despitefully use you, and persecute you" (verses 43-44).

APPENDIX 9

Nine Beatitudes
Blessed has been translated "Happy."

Matthew 5:3-11

1. v. 3—"Blessed are the poor in spirit: for theirs is the kingdom of heaven."

2. v. 4—"Blessed are they that mourn: for they shall be comforted."

3. v. 5—"Blessed are the poor in spirit; for theirs is the kingdom of heaven."

4. v. 6—"Blessed are they which do hunger and thirst after righteousness: for they shall be filled."

5. v. 7—"Blessed are the merciful: for they shall obtain mercy."

6. v. 8—"Blessed are the pure in heart: for they shall see God."

7. v. 9—"Blessed are the peacemakers: for they shall be called the children of God."

8. v. 10—"Blessed are they which are persecuted for righteousness' sake: for theirs is the kingdom of heaven."

9. v. 11—"Blessed are ye, when men shall revile you, and persecute you, and shall say all manner of evil against you falsely, for my sake."

APPENDIX 10

Eight ."do nots." from the Sermon on the Mount

These are Christ's ethical teachings, superior to that of Scribes (both Old Testament and Oral Law) from Matthew 6:1, 5, 16, 19, 24, 25; Matthew 7:1, 6.

1. Matthew 6:1—"Take heed that ye do not your alms before men, to be seen of them: otherwise ye have no reward of your Father which is in heaven."

2. v. 5—"And when thou prayest, thou shalt not be as the hypocrites are: for they love to pray standing in the syna gogues and in the corners of the streets, that they may be seen of men. Verily I say unto you, They have their reward."

3. v. 16—"Moreover when ye fast, be not, as the hypocrites, of a sad countenance: for they disfigure their faces, that they may appear unto men to fast. Verily I say unto you, They have their reward."

4. v. 19—"Lay not up for yourselves treasures upon earth, where moth and rust doth corrupt, and where thieves break through and steal."

5. v. 24—"No man can serve two masters: for either he will hate the one and love the other; or else he will hold to the one, and despise the other. Ye cannot serve God and mammon."

6. v. 25—"Therefore I say unto you, Take no thought for your life, what ye shall eat, or what ye shall drink; nor yet for your body, what ye shall put on. Is not the life more than meat, and the body than raiment?"

7. Matthew 7:1—"Judge not, that ye be not judged."

8. v. 6—"Give not that which is holy unto the dogs, neither cast ye your pearls before swine, lest they trample them under their feet, and turn again and rend you."

APPENDIX 11

Eight Woes of the Scribes, Pharisees, etc.

Matthew 23:13-16; 23, 25, 27, 29

1. v. 13—"But woe unto you, scribes and Pharisees, hypocrites! for ye shut up the kingdom of heaven against men: for ye neither go in yourselves, neither suffer ye them that are entering to go in."

2. v. 14—"Woe unto you, scribes and Pharisees, hypocrites! for ye devour widows' houses, and for a pretence make long prayer: therefore ye shall receive the greater damnation."

3. v. 15—"Woe unto you, scribes and Pharisees, hypocrites! for ye compass sea and land to make one proselyte, and when he is made, ye make him twofold more the child of hell than yourselves."

4. v. 16—"Woe unto you, ye blind guides, which say, Whosoever shall swear by the temple, it is nothing; but whosoever shall swear by the gold of the temple, he is a debtor!"

5. v. 23—"Woe unto you, scribes and Pharisees, hypocrites! for ye pay tithe of mint and anise and cumin, and have omitted the weightier matters of the law, judgment, mercy, and faith: these ought ye to have done, and not to leave the other undone."

6. v. 25—"Woe unto you, scribes and Pharisees, hypocrites! for ye make clean the outside of the cup and of the platter, but within they are full of extortion and excess."

7. v. 27—"Woe unto you, scribes and Pharisees, hypocrites! for ye are like unto whited sepulchres, which indeed appear beautiful outward, but are within full of dead men's bones, and of all uncleanness."

8. v. 29—"Woe unto you, scribes and Pharisees, hypocrites! because ye build the tombs of the prophets, and garnish the sepulchers of the righteous."

Luke 6:24-26—Luke adds these four "woes."

1. v. 24—"But woe unto you that are rich! for ye have received your consolation."
2, 3. v. 25—"Woe unto you that are full! for ye shall hunger. Woe unto you that laugh now! for ye shall mourn and weep."
4. v. 26—"Woe unto you, when all men shall speak well of you! for so did their fathers to the false prophets."

APPENDIX 12

I. Parables of the Early Ministry

THE GOOD NEWS OF THE KINGDOM OF GOD

I. The Conflict of New and Old
(a) The Parable of the Children of the Bridechamber
(b) The Parable of the New Patch and the Old Garment
(c) The Parable of New Wine and Old Wineskins
(d) The Parable of Treasures New and Old

II. Similitudes of the Kingdom (I)
(a) The Parable of Spontaneous Growth
(b) The Parable of the Mustard Seed
(c) The Parable of the Leaven

III. Similitudes of the Kingdom (II)
(a) The Parable of the Hidden Treasure
(b) The Parable of the Pearl of Great Price
(c) The Parable of the Dragnet

IV. The Responsibility of Hearing
The Parable of the Soils

V. Earnestness to Translate Hearing into Doing
(a) The Parable of the Children at Play
(b) The Parable of the Wise and Foolish Builders

VI. The Kingdom and the Perplexing Presence of Evil
The Parable of the Tares

II. Parables of the Later Ministry

THE CHILDREN OF THE KINGDOM OF GOD

A. The Conditions of Discipleship

VII. The Conditions of Discipleship
(a) The Parable of the Empty House
(b) The Parable of the Uncompleted Tower
(c) The Parable of the King's Rash Warfare

B. The Marks of Discipleship

VIII. Humility
(a) The Parable of the Chief Seats
(b) The Parable of the Pharisee and the Publican

IX. Forgiven and Forgiving
(a) The Parable of the Two Debtors
(b) The Parable of the Unmerciful Servant

X. Privilege and Duty
(a) The Parable of the Barren Figtree
(b) The Parable of the Bondservant

XI. Resourcefulness and Foresight
The Parable of the Unjust Steward

XII. Life-And "Much Goods."
The Parable of the Rich Fool

XIII. The Springs of Sympathy
The Parable of the Rich Man and the Beggar

XIV. True Neighborliness
The Parable of the Good Samaritan

XXIII. Opportunity, Fidelity, and Reward
    (a) The Parable of the Talents
    (b) The Parable of the Pounds

XXIV. The Judgment of the Kingdom
    The Parable of the Last Judgment

From George A. Buttrick, *The Parables of Jesus.* Harper & Brothers Publishers, New York and London, 1928, pp. xi-xii.

APPENDIX 13

Jesus' Parables and Old Testament Parables

Jesus' Parables	Scripture
Wise and foolish builders	Matthew 7:24-27
Children of the bridechamber	Matthew 9:15;
	Luke 5:34-35
New cloth and old garment	Matthew 9:13;
	Luke 5:36
New wine and new bottles	Matthew 9:17
Unclean spirit	Matthew 12:43
Sower	Matthew 13:3-9,
	Matthew 18-23
	Luke 8:5-15
The tares	Matthew 13:24-43
Mustard seed	Matthew 13:31-32;
	Luke 13:19
Leaven	Matthew 13:33
Hidden treasure	Matthew 13:44
Pearl of great price	Matthew 13:45-46
Net cast into the sea	Matthew 13:47-50
Meats defiling not	Matthew 15:10-15
Unmerciful servant	Matthew 18:23-35
Hired laborers	Matthew 20:1-16
The two sons	Matthew 21:28-32
The wicked husbandmen	Matthew 21:33-45
Marriage of the king's son	Matthew 22:2-14
The fig tree	Matthew 24:32-34
Man of the house watching	Matthew 24:43
Faithful and evil servants	Matthew 24:45-51
The ten virgins	Matthew 25:1-13
The talents	Matthew 25:14-30
Kingdom divided against itself	Mark 3:24
House divided against itself	Mark 3:25
Strong man armed	Mark 3:27; Luke 11:21
Seed growing secretly	Mark 4:26-29

The lighted candle . . . . .Mark 4:21;
                                Luke 11:33-36
Man taking a far journey . . . . .Mark 13:34-37
Blind leading the blind . . . . .Luke 6:39
The beam and the mote . . . . .Luke 6:41-42
The tree and its fruit . . . . .Luke 6:43-45
Creditor and debtors . . . . .Luke 7:41-47
The good Samaritan . . . . .Luke 10:30-37
The friend at midnight . . . . .Luke 11:5-9
The rich fool . . . . .Luke 12:16-21
The cloud and the wind . . . . .Luke 12:54-57
The barren fig tree . . . . .Luke 13:6-9
Chief seats at the feast . . . . .Luke 14:7-11
Builder of a tower . . . . .Luke 14:28-30, 33
The king going to war . . . . .Luke 14:31-33
The savor of salt . . . . .Luke 14:34-35
The lost sheep .Luke 15:3-7
The lost piece of silver . . . . .Luke 15:8-10
The prodigal son . . . . .Luke 15:11-32
The unjust steward . . . . .Luke 16:1-8
The rich man and Lazarus . . . . .Luke 16:19-31
Unprofitable servant . . . . .Luke 17:7
Importunate widow . . . . .Luke 18:1-8
The Pharisee and the Publican . . . . . . .Luke 18:9-14
The pounds . . . . .Luke 19:12-27
The Bread of Life . . . . .John 6:47
The Good Shepherd . . . . .John 10:1-6
The Vine and the branches . . . . .John 15:1-5

Old Testament Parables

Parables   **Scripture**

The Trees Choosing a King—
Jotham to the Shechemites . . . . .Judges 9:5-15
The Ewe Lamb—Nathan to David . . . .II Samuel 12:1-4
The Two Brethren—
by the widow of Tekoah. . . . . .II Samuel 14:1-11

APPENDIX 14

The Vision of Pilate

And so we see Pilate standing in dubious and deliberative mood, now scornfully temporizing with the multitude, and now patronizing Jesus, befriending Him with a sort of lofty condescension which was touched with regret, looking Him, as he vainly thought, through and through, though never failing to read the mind and motives of His accusers. But even when most convinced of the innocence of Jesus, he is perfectly sure of His mere manhood, though it be of a type rare in the genus fanatic. So he believes himself to have power, though he thinks Jesus has none. But let us imagine that, in the very moment when he boasted his power to crucify or to release, a lucid vision had come to him, and that he had beheld the centuries before him unroll their wondrous secret. In less than eighty years he sees in every city of the Roman world societies of men and women meeting in the name of this Jesus and singing praises to Him as to God; while so powerful has His Name grown in some provinces that the very temples are deserted, and the most famous governor of the day writes to ask the Emperor what policy he is to pursue. Then he sees Rome, astonished and angry at the might of the Name, lose her proud tolerance, become vindictive, brutal, even turning persecutor, and making the profession of the Name a crime punishable with death. But all the resources of the Empire are powerless against the Name; the legions that had carried the Roman Eagles into the inaccessible regions lying round the civilized world, forcing the tide of barbarism back before them, here availed nothing. And he beholds in less than three hundred years the symbol of the Cross on which he was about to crucify this Jesus, float victoriously from the capitol; while the Emperor sits, not amid patricians in the Roman Senate, but in a council of Christian pastors, all without pride of birth, all without names the Senate would have honoured, many maimed, some even eyeless, disfigured by the tortures Rome had inflicted in her vain attempt to extinguish the infamous thing. In another hundred years he sees the very empire herself fallen, while in her seat sits one whose only claim to rule is that he represents the Crucified; and because he does so, he builds up a kingdom beside which Rome at her vastest was but as a hand-breadth, and the city that had been proudly called eternal was in duration only as the child of a day. And if Pilate had waked from his dream as suddenly as he had fallen into it, and looked at Jesus sitting before him mocked and buffeted, helpless in the face of the howling mob, deserted of man, manifestly forsaken of His God, what could he have said but this? "What foolish things dreams are!"[1]

From Andrew M. Fairbairn, *The Philosophy of the Christian Religion.* The Macmillian Co., New York, 1928, pp. 320-321.

APPENDIX 15

Miracles of Jesus

1. Turning water into wine—John 2:1-11
2. Feeding of five thousand—Matthew 14:15-21
3. Stilling the storm—Mark 4:35-41
4. Walking on the sea—John 6:16-21
5. Providing tax money in fish's mouth—Matthew 17:24-27
6. Feeding of four thousand—Mark 8:1-9
7. Withering of fig tree—Matthew 21:17-22
8. First catch of fish—Luke 5:1-11
9. Second catch of fish—John 21:1-14
10. Healing of nobleman's son at Cana—John 4:46-54
11. Restoring sight of blind man at Bethsaida—Mark 8:22-26
12. Restoring sight of man born blind—John 9:1-41
13. Raising of Lazarus—John 11:1-45
14. Curing of demon-possessed man (men)—Matthew 8:28-34
15. Raising of Jairus' daughter—Mark 5:22-24, 35-43
16. Healing of invalid at Bethesda—John 5:1-18
17. Curing of woman with twelve-year bleeding—Luke 8:43-48
18. Restoring of paralytic at Capernaum—Matthew 9:1-8
19. Curing of leper near Gennesaret—Mark 1:40-45
20. Healing of Peter's mother-in-law—Matthew 8:14-17
21. Restoring of withered hand—Mark 3:1-6
22. Healing of child with demon—Luke 9:37-43
23. Restoring of blind and dumb demoniac—Luke 11:14
24. Giving sight to two blind men—Matthew 9:27-31
25. Healing of dumb demoniac—Matthew 9:32-34
26. Healing of deaf-mute—Mark 7:31-17
27. Restoring sight to blind Bartimaeus—Matthew 20:29-34
28. Healing Syrophoenician girl—Mark 7:24-30
29. Healing centurion's servant—Luke 7:1-10
30. Restoring demon-possessed man in synagogue
    —Mark 1:23-27
31. Raising son of widow of Nain—Luke 7:11-16
32. Restoring of woman crippled for eighteen years—
    Luke 13:10-17

33. Healing of man with dropsy—Luke 14:1-6
34. Healing of ten men with leprosy—Luke 17:11-19
35. Restoring of Malchus's ear—John 18:10-11

From Wayne H. House. *Charts of the New Testament.* Zondervan, Grand Rapids, MI, 1981, pp. 112-115.

****

Miracles of the Disciples of Jesus

1. Lame man at Temple gate healed—Acts 3:1-11
2. Death of Ananias—Acts 5:5-11
3. Death of Sapphira—Acts 5:5-11
4. Many sick healed—Acts 5:12-16
5. Apostles delivered from prison—Acts 5:19
6. Miracles of Stephen—Acts 6:8
7. Miracles of Philip—Acts 8:6
8. Saul's blindness—Acts 9:3-9
9. Ananias recovers Saul—Acts 9:17
10. Peter heals Aeneas—Acts 9:33-35
11. Dorcas restored to life—Acts 9:36-40
12. Peter delivered from prison—Acts 12:6-11
13. Elymas blinded—Acts 13:11
14. Cripple healed at Lystra—Acts 14:8-10
15. Damsel with spirit of divination—Acts 16:16-19
16. Miracles by Paul—Acts 19:11
17. Eutychus raised—Acts 20:8-10
18. Viper's bite harmless—Acts 28:3-6
19. Publius' father healed—Acts 28:8-9

From William C. Martin, *The Layman's Bible Eyclopedia.* The Southwestern Co., Nashville, TN, p. 974.

****

The Gospel and Miracles

Listed below are 15 pertinent questions for consideration.

1. What is a miracle?
2. Who and what determines who gets the miracle?
3. Aren't we all to some extent walking miracles?
4. What role does religious faith have in miracles?
5. What do you think about commercial TV faith healing?
6. Is there a medicinal role in healing?
7. How do you interpret John 14:12? Is it applicable to miracles?
8. What place do the unconscious, imaging and visualization have in healing?
9. Was the doctor correct who said: "I treat my patients, God heals them"?
10. Name some miracles other than healing.
11. Would you agree with C.S. Lewis that the greatest of all miracles is when God descended in Christ to reascend into glory having completed His mission?
12. Have you ever experienced what you call a God-wrought miracle?
13. Do you feel that science is a roadblock to spiritual or physical miracles?
14. Is there any class, apart from miracles that are especially providential? Are not all events equally providential?
15. Did Jesus ever find it necessary to redo one of His miracles? Did Jesus take credit for His miracles, or did He mostly attribute them to faith? Is this true of TV healers?

APPENDIX 16

Prayers of Jesus

1. Model Prayer (The Lord's Prayer)—Matthew 6:9-13, Luke 11:2-4
2. Jesus' Great Prayer—John 17
3. Jesus' prayers in Gethsemane—Matthew 26:36-46; Mark 14:32-42; Luke 22:17-19
4. Jesus praying by Himself—Luke 9:18
5. Jesus' thanksgiving to the Father—Matthew 11:25-26; Luke 10:21
6. Blessing at feeding of 5,000—Matthew 14:19; Mark 6:41; Luke 9:16; John 6:11
7. Jesus' prayer on the mountain—Matthew 14:23; Mark 6:46
8. Jesus prays in the desert—Mark 1:35; Luke 5:16
9. Blessing at feeding of 4,000—Matthew 15:36; Mark 8:6
10. Blessing of Lord's Supper—Matthew 26:26-27; Mark 14:22-23; Luke 22:17-19
11. Prayer on the cross—Matthew 27:46; Mark 15:34; Luke 23:46
12. Jesus prays for a deaf and dumb man—Mark 7:34
13. Jesus' prayer at baptism—Luke 3:21
14. Jesus' prayer before choosing apostles—Luke 6:12-13
15. Jesus' prayer on Mount of Transfiguration—Luke 9:28-29
16. Jesus' prayer for Peter's faith—Luke 22:31-32
17. Jesus' prayer at Lazarus's tomb—John 11:41-42
18. Jesus' prayer answered by the Father—John 12:27-28
19. Jesus prayed for children—Luke 18:15; Mark 10:16; Matthew 19:13
20. Jesus' prayer for the Comforter to come—John 14:16
21. Blessing of food on Emmaus journey—Luke 24:30
22. Blessed them, and ascended to heaven—Luke 24:50

APPENDIX 17

Prophets

Elijah—The Invincible
Elisha—The Ploughman-Prophet
Amos—The Heroic Herdsman
Hosea—The Man of the Shattered Romance
Isaiah—Prince, Patriot, Prophet
Micah—The Herald of the Morn
Jeremiah, The Man Who Failed
Zephaniah—The Zealous
Nahum—The Critic of Nineveh
Jonah—The Vacillating
Obadiah—The Antagonist of Edom
Habakkuk—The optimist
Ezekiel—The exiled Mystic
Daniel—The Daring
Haggai—The Master-Builder
Zechariah—The Enthusiast
Joel—The Prophet of Consolation
Malachi—The Puritan

From J. W. G. Ward, *Portraits of the Prophets.*

****

Isaiah—The Preacher Who Stirred Up Trouble
Amos—The Preacher Who Never Went to School
Hosea—The Preacher Whose Heart Was Broken
Micah—The Preacher Who Pitied the Poor
Zephaniah—The Preacher Who Loved the Word
Nahum—The Preacher Who Laughed at Foes
Habakkuk—The Preacher Who Doubted God
Jeremiah—The Preacher Who Buried His Clothes
Ezekiel—The Preacher Who Talked About Me
Haggai—The Preacher Who Said It With Bricks
Zechariah—The Preacher Who Discovered the Devil
Malachi—The Preacher Who Fought for Homes

From Bernard C. Clausen, *Pen-Portraits of the Prophets.*

Obadiah—"Servant of Jehovah"
Joel—"Jehovah is God"
Jonah—"Dove"
Amos—"Burden-bearer"
Hosea—"Salvation"
Micah—"Who Is Like Jehovah"
Zephaniah—"Jehovah Hides"
Nahum—"Consolation"
Habakkuk—"Embrace"
Haggai—"Festival"
Zechariah—"Whom Jehovah Remembers"
Malachi—"Mr. Messenger"

From Homer Hailey, *A Commentary on The Minor Prophets.*

****

Amos—(750- B.C.)
Hosea—(745-734 B.C.)
Micah—(c. 701 B.C.)
Zephaniah—(628-626 B.C.)
Nahum—(614-612 B.C.)
Habakkuk—(605-600 B.C.)
Haggai—(520 B.C.)
Zechariah I-VIII—(520-519 B.C.)
Malachi—(460 B.C.)
Obadiah—(400-350 B.C.)
Joel—(c. 350 B.C.)
Jonah—(c. 300 B.C.)

From Raymond Calkins, *The Modern Message of the Minor Prophets.*

****

Four Major Prophets writing in Old Testament

Isaiah
Jeremiah
Ezekiel
Daniel

"Minor Prophets" owed to St. Augustine. We call them "minor" but they have taught us major lessons.

APPENDIX 18

New Testament Prophecies

Prophecy	Scripture
"I will make you fishers of men."	Matthew 4:19; Mark 1:17
"The time will come when the bridegroom will be taken from them; then they will fast."	Matthew 9:15; Mark 2:20; Luke 5:35
Suffering from religious leaders	Matthew 17:12
Death and resurrection	Matthew 16:21; 17:22-23; 20:18-19; Mark 8:31; 9:31; 10:32-34; Luke 9:22, 44; 18:31-33
"Some who are standing here will not taste death before they see….."	Matthew 16:28; Mark 9:1; Luke 9:27
"Go to the lake and throw out your line."	Matthew 17:27
"You will indeed drink from my cup."	Matthew 20:23; Mark 10:39
"The Son of Man [came]….to give his life as a ransom for many."	Matthew 20:28; Mark 10:45
"Go to the village ahead of you, and at once you will find a donkey,…. with her colt."	Matthew 21:2-3; Mark 11:2-3; Luke 19:30-31
"May you never bear fruit again!"	Matthew 21:18-19; Mark 11:12-14

"The kingdom of God will be taken...."	Matthew 21:43-44
"Not one stone here will be left on another...."	Matthew 24:2; Mark 13:2; Luke 21:6
"One of you will betray me."	Matthew 26:21, 23; Mark 14:18, 20; Luke 22:21, John 13:21, 26
"After I have risen I will go ahead of you into Galilee."	Matthew 26:32; Mark 14:28
"This very night, before the rooster crows, you will disown me."	Matthew 26:34; Mark 14:30; Luke 22:34; John 13:38
"The demon has left your daughter."	Mark 7:29; cf. Matthew 15:28
"She poured perfume on my body beforehand to prepare for my burial."	Matthew 26:12; Mark 14:8; John12:7
"Wherever the gospel is preached... what she has done will also be told."	Matthew 26:13; Mark 14:9
"Go into the city, and a man.... will meet you."	Mark 14:13-15; Luke 22:10-12
Zechariah foretells ministry of John the Baptist	Luke 1:67-79
"Don't be afraid; just believe, and she will be healed."	Luke 8:50
"Do not be afraid, little flock, for your Father has been pleased to give you the kingdom."	Luke 12:32
"The days will come upon you when your enemies will build....and encircle you."	Luke 19:43-44

"What is written about me is reaching its fulfillment."	Luke 22:37
"Today you will be with me in paradise."	Luke 23:43
"Repentance and forgiveness of sins will be preached in his name to all nations."	Luke 24:47
"I am going to send you what my Father has promised."	Luke 24:49
"Destroy this temple, and I will raise it again in three days."	John 2:19-22
"So the Son of Man must be lifted up."	John 3:14
"I lay down my life for the sheep..... I have authority to lay it down and authority to take it up again."	John 10:15-18
Caiaphas: ."It is better for you that one man die for the people."	John 11:49-50
"The Father....will give you another Counselor."	John 14:16, 23; 16:7
"I am returning to my Father."	John 20:17
"When you are old....someone else will....lead you where you do not want to go."	John 21:18

From Wayne H. House, *Charts of the New Testament.* Zondervan, Grand Rapids, MI, 1981, pp. 33-36.

APPENDIX 19

Crucify!

Christ is walking through the streets,
Looking in each face He meets,
      Tenderly;
Not alone in church He stands,
Where suppliants kneel with folded hands;
Not alone in closet where,
He lifts the weight of human care;
But in the busy walks of life,
Amid the tumult and the strife,
Walks He with His bleeding feet,
Walks He where the people meet;
But they scorn Him, pass Him by,
And in their hearts they madly cry,
      "Crucify!"

Christ is walking through the shops;
By each workman meekly stops,
      Tenderly.
He would lift the heavy load.
He would clear the thorny road,
Smooth the wrinkles from each brow,
Wounds would heal and none allow.
Walks He with His bleeding feet,
Walks He where the people meet;
But they scorn Him, pass Him by,
And in their hearts they madly cry,
      "Crucify!"

Christ is walking through the slums;
With His cross and thorns He comes,
      Painfully.
Kneeling in each den of shame,
Seeing things too vile to name,
Yet with heart filled full of love,
Bids each sinner look above.

Good Came Out of Nazareth

Walks He with His bleeding feet;
Walks He where the people meet;
But they scorn Him, pass Him by,
And in their hearts they madly cry,
    "Crucify!"

Christ is walking everywhere,
With his face, deep scarred with care,
    Patiently;
But the people lift their eyes
Upward yonder toward the skies,
Knowing not that near them stands
Christ, the Lord, with pierced hands,
Beckoning them toward His breast,
Where alone they may find rest.
Walks He with His bleeding feet,
Walks He where the people meet;
But they scorn Him, pass Him by,
And in their hearts they madly cry,
    "Crucify!"

—William Reed Dunbar

APPENDIX 20

The Cross Was His Own

They borrowed a bed to lay His head
    When Christ the Lord came down;
They borrowed the ass in the mountain pass
    For Him to ride to town;
But the crown that He wore and the cross that He bore
    Were His own-
      The cross was His own.

He borrowed the bread when the crowd He fed
    On the grassy mountain-side,
He borrowed the dish of broken fish
    With which He satisfied.
But the crown that He wore and the cross that He bore
    Were His own-
      The cross was His own.

He borrowed a ship in which to sit
    To teach the multitude;
He borrowed a nest in which to rest-
    He had never a home so rude;
But the crown that He wore and the cross that He bore
    Were His own-
      The cross was His own.

He borrowed a room on His way to the tomb
    The Passover Lamb to eat;
They borrowed a cave for Him a grave,
    They borrowed a winding-sheet.
But the crown that He wore and the cross that He bore
    Were His own-
      The cross was His own.

        —Author Unknown

APPENDIX 21

The Fourteen Stations of the
Via Dolorosa in the Old City of Jerusalem

First Station:

Jesus is condemned to crucifixion. Pontius Pilate, under pressure from the High Priests and the crowd, passes the death sentence while trying to dissociate himself from this judgment by washing his hands.

Second Station:

Jesus bears the cross. Following flagellation, Jesus is crowned with thorns and clothed in purple as a mark of derision by the soldiers who along with crown mocked the so-called "king of the Jews." Jesus departs for the place of execution outside the city gates.

Third Station:

Jesus falls for the first time. Jesus said to his disciples: "My life, no one shall take it from me, I who shall give it."

Fourth Station:

Jesus meets his mother. The prophecy Simeon made to Mary when Jesus presented himself at the temple is fulfilled: "thy son will be a sign of contradiction, and thee, a sword will pierce thy heart."

Fifth Station:

Jesus is helped by Simon of Cryene. Simon is required to carry the cross at the side of Jesus; a gesture symbolizing the Christian conviction, "Thy brother is Christ."

Sixth Station:

Veronica wipes Jesus' face. The cloth Veronica used held the sweat of blood which covered Jesus' face.

Seventh Station:

Jesus falls for the second time.

Eighth Station:

Jesus consoles the women of Jerusalem. "Do not cry for me, cry rather for yourselves and your children," said Jesus.

Ninth Station:

Jesus falls for the third time.

Tenth Station:

Jesus is deprived of his clothes. Jesus speaks to his father through the words of the psalmist—"You wanted neither sacrifice nor obligation, you gave me one body, you did not agree on either holocaust or sacrifice, so I said, 'Here I am I come...' in order that thy will be done O Lord."

Eleventh Station:

Jesus is put on the cross. Jesus words resound: "And I, raised from the earth, will draw all men to me." In these words he indicated the manner of his death.

Twelfth Station:

Jesus dies. The last testimony of Jesus who had said "the father and I are one" gave forth his terrible cry: "My God, my God, why hast thou forsaken me?" Then "Jesus cried with a loud voice, and gave up his ghost."

Thirteenth Station:

Jesus, descended from the cross, is placed in his mother's arms.

Fourteenth Station:

Jesus is placed in the tomb. With Passover starting that day, Joseph of Arimethea offered his tomb, where Jesus was placed. The stone was rolled on top.

APPENDIX 22

The 11 Appearances of Jesus

1. The appearance of Jesus to Mary Magdalene and the message to the disciples.
   > Jerusalem. The first day of the week (Sunday)
   > Mark 16:9-11 and John 20:11-18

2. The appearance of Jesus to the other women.
   > Jerusalem. Sunday the first day of the week
   > Matthew 28:9-10

3. The appearance to two disciples (Cleopas and Another) on the way to Emmaus.
   > Sunday afternoon
   > Mark 16:12-13 and Luke 24:13-32

4. The report of the two disciples and the news of the appearance to Simon Peter.
   > Jerusalem. Sunday evening
   > Luke 24:33-35 and I Cor. 15:5

5. The appearance to the astonished disciples (Thomas absent) with a commission and their failure to convince Thomas.
   > Jerusalem. Sunday evening
   > Mark 16:14; Luke 24:36-43 and John 20:19-25

6. The appearance to the disciples the next Sunday night and the convincing of Thomas.
   > Jerusalem
   > John 20:26-31 and I. Cor. 15:5

7. The appearance to seven disciples beside the Sea of Galilee. The miraculous draught of fishes.
   > John 21

8. The appearance to above five hundred on an appointed mountain in Galilee, and a commission given.
   > Mark 16:15-18; Matthew 28:16-20 and I. Cor. 15:6

9. The appearance to James the brother of Jesus.
   > I. Cor. 15:7

10. The appearance to the disciples with another commission.
    > Jerusalem

Luke 24:44-49 and Acts 1:3-8
11. The last appearance and the ascension.
    On Olivet between Jerusalem and Bethany
    Mark 16:19-20; Luke 24:50-53 and Acts 1:9-12

From A. T. Robertson, *A Harmony of the Gospels for Students of the Life of Christ.* pp. 242-262.

APPENDIX 23

Words Jesus Spoke After His Resurrection
These words were spoken over a forty day period.

To Mary Magdalene and to the disciples.

John 20:15-17

"Woman, why are you weeping? Whom are you seeking?"
"Mary!"
"Do not cling to Me, for I have not yet ascended to My Father; but go to My brethren and say to them, 'I am ascending to My Father and your Father, and to My God and your God.'"

To the other women.

Matthew 28:9-10

"Rejoice!"
"Do not be afraid. Go and tell My brethren to go to Galilee, and there they will see Me."

To two disciples (Cleopas and Another) on the way to Emmaus.

Luke 24:17, 19, 25-26

"What kind of conversation is this that you have with one another as you walk and are sad?"
"What things?"
"O foolish ones, and slow of heart to believe in all that the prophets have spoken!"
"Ought not the Christ to have suffered these things and to enter into His glory?"

To the astonished disciples (Thomas absent) with a commission and their failure to convince Thomas.

Luke 24:36, 38-39, 41

"Peace to you."

"Why are you troubled? And why do doubts arise in your hearts?"

"Behold My hands and My feet, that it is I Myself. Handle Me and see, for a spirit does not have flesh and bones as you see I have."

"Have you any food here?"

John 20:19, 21-23

"Peace be with you."

"Peace to you! As the Father has sent Me, I also send you."

"Receive the Holy Spirit."

"If you forgive the sins of any, they are forgiven them; if you retain the sins of any, they are retained."

To the disciples and Thomas.

John 20:26-27, 29

"Peace to you!"

"Reach your finger here, and look at My hands; and reach your hand here, and put it into My side. Do not be unbelieving, but believing."

"Thomas, because you have seen Me, you have believed. Blessed are those who have not seen and yet have believed."

To seven disciples beside the Sea of Galilee. The miraculous draught of fishes.

John 21:5, 6, 10, 12, 15-19, 22-23

"Children, have you any food?"

"Cast the net on the right side of the boat, and you will find some."

"Bring some of the fish which you have just caught."

"Come and eat breakfast."

"Simon, son of Jonah, do you love Me more than these?" "Feed My lambs."

"Simon, son of Jonah, do you love Me?" "Tend My sheep."

"Simon, son of Jonah, do you love Me?" "Do you love Me?" "Feed My sheep."

"Most assuredly, I say to you, when you were younger, you gird-
ed yourself and walked where you wished; but when you are old,
you will stretch out your hands, and another will gird you and
carry you where you do not wish."

"Follow Me."

"If I will that he remain till I come, what is that to you? You follow Me."

"If I will that he remain till I come, what is that to you?"

To about five hundred on an appointed mountain in Galilee, and a commission given.

Mark 16:15-18

"Go into all the world and preach the gospel to every creature."

"He who believes and is baptized will be saved; but he who does
not believe will be condemned."

"And these signs will follow those who believe: In My name
they will cast out demons; they will speak with new tongues;"

"They will take up serpents; and if they drink anything deadly, it
will by no means hurt them; they will lay hands on the sick, and
they will recover."

Matthew 28:18-20

"All authority has been given to Me in heaven and on earth."

"Go therefore and make disciples of all the nations, baptizing
them in the name of the Father and of the Son and of the Holy
Spirit."

"Teaching them to observe all things that I have commanded you;
and lo, I am with you always, even to the end of the age."

To the disciples with another commission.

Luke 24:44, 46-49

"These are the words which I spoke to you while I was still with
you, that all things must be fulfilled which were written in the
Law of Moses and the Prophets and the Psalms concerning Me."

"Thus it is written, and thus it was necessary for the Christ to suffer and to rise from the dead the third day,"

"And that repentance and remission of sins should be preached in His name to all nations, beginning at Jerusalem."

"And you are witnesses of these things."

"Behold, I send the Promise of My Father upon you; but tarry in the city of Jerusalem until you are endued with power from on high."

Acts 1:4, 5, 7-8

"Which . . . you have heard from Me;"

"For John truly baptized with water, but you shall be baptized with the Holy Spirit not many days from now."

"It is not for you to know times or seasons which the Father has put in His own authority."

"But you shall receive power when the Holy Spirit has come upon you; and you shall be witnesses to Me in Jerusalem, and in all Judea and Samaria, and to the end of the earth."

APPENDIX 24

The Character of Jesus

The Strength of Jesus
"And they were all amazed."—Mark 1:27

The Sincerity of Jesus
"Ye shall not be as the hypocrites."—Matthew 6:5

The Reasonableness of Jesus
"In the beginning was the logos."—John 1:1

The Poise of Jesus
"No man after that durst ask him any question."—Mark 12:34

The Originality of Jesus
"I make all things new."—Revelation 21:5

The Narrowness of Jesus
"Narrow is the way."—Matthew 7:14

The Breadth of Jesus
"Preach the Gospel to the whole creation."—Mark 16:15

Jesus' Trust in God
"He trusted on God."—Matthew 27:43

The Brotherliness of Jesus
"First be reconciled to thy brother."—Matthew 5:24

The Optimism of Jesus
"Be of good cheer."—John 16:33

The Chivalry of Jesus
"And touched him."—Matthew 8:3

The Firmness of Jesus
"Get thee behind me, Satan."—Matthew 16:23

The Generosity of Jesus
"It is more blessed to give than to receive."—Acts 20:35

The Candor of Jesus
"If it were not so I would have told you."—John 14:2

The Enthusiasm of Jesus
"I came to cast fire upon the earth."—Luke 12:49

The Gladness of Jesus
"Rejoice, and be exceeding glad."—Matthew 5:12

The Humility of Jesus
"I am meek and lowly in heart."—Matthew 11:29

The Patience of Jesus
"A bruised reed shall he not break."—Matthew 12:20

The Courage of Jesus
"Fear not."—Luke 5:10

The Indignation of Jesus
"And when he had looked round about on them with anger."Mark 3:5

The Reverence of Jesus
"Hallowed by thy name."—Matthew 6:9

The Holiness of Jesus
"Which of you convicteth me of sin?."—John 8:46

The Greatness of Jesus
"His name shall be called Wonderful."—Isaiah 9:6

Taken from Charles E. Jefferson, *The Character of Jesus.*

APPENDIX 25

The Land of Beginning Again

I wish that there were some wonderful place
      Called the Land of Beginning Again,
Where all our mistakes and all our heartaches
And all of our poor, selfish grief
Could be dropped, like a shabby old coat, at the door,
      And never be put on again.

I wish we could come on it all unaware,
      Like the hunter who finds a lost trail;
And I wish that the one whom our blindness had done
The greatest injustice of all
Could be at the gates, like an old friend that waits
      For the comrade he's gladdest to hail.

We would find all the things we intended to do
      But forgot, and remembered too late,
Little praises unspoken, little promises broken,
And all of the thousand and one
Little duties neglected that might have perfected
      The day for one less fortunate.

It wouldn't be possible not to be kind
      In the Land of Beginning Again;
And the ones we misjudged and the ones whom we grudged
Their moments of victory here,
Would find in the grasp of our loving handclasp
      More than penitent lips could explain.

For what had been hardest we'd know had been best,
      And what had seemed lost would be gain;
For there isn't a sting that will not take wing
When we've faced it and laughed it away;
And I think that the laughter is most what we're after
      In the Land of Beginning Again!

Good Came Out of Nazareth

So I wish that there were some wonderful place
    Called the Land of Beginning Again,
Where all our mistakes and all our heartaches
And all of our poor selfish grief,
Could be dropped, like a shabby old coat, at the door,
    And never be put on again.

             —Louisa Fletcher Tarkington

APPENDIX 26

God's Autographs

I stood upon a hill one night
And saw the great Creator write
His autograph across the sky
In lightning strokes, and there was I
A witness to this great event
And signature magnificent!

I stood one morning by a stream
When night was fading to a dream,
The fields were fair as fields may be
At spring, in golden mystery
Of dandelion-then God came on
And wrote His signature in Dawn

One afternoon long years ago.
Where glacial tides had ebb and flow,
I found a cliff God's hand had smote;
I scanned its breast, whereon God wrote
With some great glacier for a pen
His signature for time and men.

One night I stood and watched the stars;
The Milky Way and ranging Mars,
Where God in letters tipped with fire
The tale of every tall desire
Had writ in rhyme and signed His name
A stellar signature of flame.

Creation's dawn was deep in night
When suddenly, "Let there be light!"
Awakened grass, and flower, and tree,
The starry skies, the earth, and sea;
Then to complete Creation's span
In His own image, God made man,
And signed His name, with stroke most sure-
Man is God's greatest signature!
                              —William L. Stidger

APPENDIX 27

If Jesus Came Back Today

If Jesus came back today
What would the people say?
Would they cheer Him and Strew the way
With garlands of myrtle and bay
As they did on that distant day
When He came to Jerusalem?
What would America say
If Jesus came back today?

I think without shadow of doubt
When He'd traveled and spoken about
In church and school and street
And clubs where the rich men meet,
His quiet, fearless smile
At our godless greed and guile
Would raise our wrath and bile.

When we heard those firm lips speak
In accents serene and meek:
"I have come to protect the weak
From the plunderer and the knave,
I have come to free the slave,
To lift the poor from the slime
Of need and disease and crime,
To break the grip of gold
On my brothers, young and old;
To throw the prisons wide
And put the rich sinners inside
With those who have made the law
By the rule of fang and claw ...."

We would take Him and ride Him out
Like a renegade on a rail,
Or throw Him in the county jail
As a dangerous, radical Red

Good Came Out of Nazareth

Who was probably off His head.
"Away with this common lout!"
With derisive laughter and shout
We would mock His daring dream.
"Love?" we would fairly scream,
"Why, what does the madman mean?
This talk is O.K. with rubes,
Or idealistic boobs,
But we are men of knowledge
Who have graduated from college.
Look at the things we own:
Look at our books and inventions,
Our schools, our clubs, our conventions.
We have more goods and gold
Than our mansions and homes can hold.
We have all we can eat and drink,
To the poor we freely give.
Does this fanatic think
He can teach us how to live?"

O doesn't it shame the dead
And break your heart as mine
That He who broke the bread
And offered His life's new wine
To serve the Cause divine,
That He who suffered and bled
That the hungry might be fed,
That the workman might be free,
That the blinded eyes might see,
That the captive might lose his chains
And the rich his ill-gotten gains...
To think while we mouth His name
(Does it not bring a blush of shame?)
We so callously scorn His star
And go hoarding and whoring afar
Where the follies and fleshpots are?

Good Came Out of Nazareth

We fashion great churches and creeds,
But the heart of the people still bleeds
And the poor still rot in their needs.
We display with pride His cross
In the midst of our pagan life
While we hug to our hearts the dross
Of our selfishness and strife.
What sacrifice have we made
To live the love He prayed?
What willing blood have we shed
To do the deeds He said?
To be popular and well-fed
We forsake the way He led
And follow a ghost instead!

—Vincent G. Burns

END NOTES

Chapter I

[1] Mullins, E.Y. *The Christian Religion In Its Doctrinal Expression*. Published by the Sunday School Board of the Southern Baptist Convention, Nashville, TN 1917, p. 137.

[2] Dowling, Levi. *The Aquarian Gospel of Jesus Christ*. Adventures Unlimited Publishers, Kemptonb, IL, 1996, p. 51.

Chapter II

[1] Sampey, John R. *Syllabus For Old Testament Study*. Harper & Brothers Publishers, New York, 1922.

[2] *ibid,* p. 291

[3] Fosdick, Harry Emerson. *Living Under Tension*. Harper & Brothers Publishers, New York, 1941, p. 224.

Chapter III

[1] Goodspeed, Edgar J. *A Life of Jesus*. Harper & Brothers Publishers, 1950, p. 38.

[2] Erskine, John. *The Human Life of Jesus*. William Morrow and Co., New York, 1945, pp. 176-186.

[3] Edersheim, Alfred. *The Life and Times of Jesus the Messiah*. W. B. Erdman Publishing Co., Grand Rapids, MI, 1936, pp. 248-250.

Chapter IV

[1] Bruce, A. B. *The Training of the Twelve*. Harper and Brothers Publishers, New York, 1871, p. 36.

[2] Fox, John. *Book of Martyrs*. John C. Winston Co., Phialdelphia, 1926, pp. 2-5.

Chapter VI

[1] Buttrick, George A. *The Parables of Jesus.* Harper & Brothers Publishers, New York, 1926, pp. xi-xii.

[2] Hazelton, Roger. *Renewing the Mind.* The MacMillan Company, New York, 1949, pp. 75-76.

[3] Studdert-Kennedy, G. A. *The Best of Studdert-Kennedy.* Harper & Brothers Publishers, New York, 1927, p. 149.

[4] Brunner, Emil. *Our Faith.* SCM Press LTD, London, 1936, p. 83.

Chapter VII

[1] Stevenson, Dwight E. *The False Prophet.* Abingdon Press, Nashville, 1965, p. 13.

[2] Miles, Margaret R. *Seeing and Believing.* Beacon Press, Boston, 1966, p. 103.

[3] Lahaye, Tim and Jenkins, Jerry. *Left Behind.* Tyndale House Publishers, Wheaton, IL, 1995, back cover.

[4] Trueblood, Elton. *The Incendiary Fellowship.* Harper & Row, New York, 1967, p. 105.

Chapter VIII

[1] Hester, H. I. *The Heart of the New Testament.* Broadman Press, Nashville, TN, 1950, p. 208.

[2] Mead, Frank S. *The March of Eleven Men.* Grosset-Dunlap, Inc., New York, 1931, p. 37.